Reckoning with the Imagination

Reckoning with the Imagination

Wittgenstein and the Aesthetics of Literary Experience

Charles Altieri

Cornell University Press
Ithaca and London

Copyright © 2015 by Cornell University

All rights reserved. Except for brief quotations in a review, this book, or parts thereof, must not be reproduced in any form without permission in writing from the publisher. For information, address Cornell University Press, Sage House, 512 East State Street, Ithaca, New York 14850.

First published 2015 by Cornell University Press
First printing, Cornell Paperbacks, 2015

Printed in the United States of America

Library of Congress Cataloging-in-Publication Data

Altieri, Charles, 1942– author.
  Reckoning with the imagination : Wittgenstein and the aesthetics of literary experience / Charles Altieri.
      pages cm
  Includes bibliographical references and index.
  ISBN 978-0-8014-5374-8 (cloth : alk. paper)
  ISBN 978-0-8014-5670-1 (pbk. : alk. paper)
  1. Wittgenstein, Ludwig 1889–1951—Aesthetics. 2. Criticism.
3. Literature—History and criticism—Theory, etc. I. Title.

B3376.W564A695 2015
111'.85—dc23
                                                                        2014035620

Cornell University Press strives to use environmentally responsible suppliers and materials to the fullest extent possible in the publishing of its books. Such materials include vegetable-based, low-VOC inks and acid-free papers that are recycled, totally chlorine-free, or partly composed of nonwood fibers. For further information, visit our website at www.cornellpress.cornell.edu.

Cloth printing   10 9 8 7 6 5 4 3 2 1
Paperback printing   10 9 8 7 6 5 4 3 2 1

Contents

Preface	vii
List of Abbreviations	xi
1. Why Wittgenstein Matters for Literary Theory	1
2. The Work Texts Do: Toward a Phenomenology of Imagining Imaginatively	37
3. Where Doubt Has No Purchase: The Roles of Display	63
4. The Concept of Expression in the Arts	91
5. Expression and Exemplification	130
6. What Literary Theory Can Learn from Wittgenstein's Silence about Ethics	159
7. Appreciating Appreciation	194

Notes	215
Bibliography	249
Permissions	257
Index	259

Preface

I wish this book were as good as the one I kept fantasizing I was writing. It involves two worthy projects. First, I try to restate many of the arguments by Kant, by Schiller, and by Hegel—on imagination, on aesthetic judgment, on purposiveness, and on the relation between subject and substance—in terms that can have some contemporary philosophical currency. These concepts represent the greatest achievements of philosophical aesthetics in the sense that they offer the richest characterizations of the differences between art and other discourses, and they make recognizing these differences fundamental to understanding what the arts can contribute to our appreciation of what we can experience. So it seems to me worth testing how they can regain currency. This testing is especially important for literary theory because it is the arts-related discipline that has probably strayed furthest from these idealist concerns for the nature of aesthetic experience.

Second, I base most of my efforts at reformulating these concepts on a reading of Wittgenstein that I hope has a chance to explain to literary critics why he can be of much greater interest for them than is currently the case.

So far I have failed to inspire most of my students, graduate and undergraduate, with much passion for Wittgenstein's texts. Now I have taken the occasion to explain as systematically as I can why Wittgenstein's thinking can be vital for literary study—both in the development of specific themes and in elaborating a general understanding of the nature of literary experience as centered on theories of expression. My Wittgenstein understands better than any other philosopher how to frame the limitations of our discourses about knowledge without resorting to any kind of skepticism. And he does so by stressing the intricacy of our communications as well as the importance of our recognizing our own powers to assent to and deploy that intricacy. Finally I try to make Wittgenstein's fundamentally religious sensibility matter in a secular world by stressing how we can deploy the critique of ethics this sensibility affords.

Wittgenstein also famously established the trope of discontent that I employed to open this preface. So I cannot even express dissatisfaction with satisfying conviction. But in this case my reasons are quite a bit stronger and more accurate than Wittgenstein's. I have the nagging feeling that I have not found the best ways of linking the speculative to the practical or been sufficiently convincing on what is possible, and impossible, to claim for the social significance of aesthetic experience. At best my arguments seem plausible but not compelling. Yet I am convinced I can do no better. At my age I have learned to be content that this book, like so much else, is not worse than it is. And I feel the work is possibly good enough to have its arguments provoke others to develop better ways to establish and illustrate what can be done by returning to idealist aesthetics and by adapting Wittgenstein's thinking for literary theory.

Publishing this book also gives me one more opportunity to express my gratitude for having been able to teach and to write in the environment UC Berkeley produces. How many people can say that some of their happiest moments have been in conducting oral exams? For these moments, and for much else, I want to single out for gratitude my colleagues Dan Blanton, Eric Falci, Tony Cascardi, Robert Kaufman, and Lyn Hejinian. Were I to follow Lyn's lead and write "My Life at Berkeley," I would also single out for gratitude my collegial relations with our illustrious group of poets—Lyn, Bob Hass, Cecil Giscombe, and Geoffrey O'Brien. They have all been gracious and helpful in discussing aspects of this book, as has Steve Goldsmith. I also want to thank some of our young faculty such as David Marno,

Namwalli Serpell, Emily Thornbury, and Catharine Flynn for treating me as if I were not an ancient relic and for the department staff for treating me as if I were. I have been remiss in previous prefaces for not expressing gratitude for a series of chairpersons in our department who have guided its spirit and preserved sufficient peace to get work like this done—Katharine O'Brien O'Keefe, Sam Otter, Ian Duncan, Cathy Gallagher, Jeff Knapp, Anne Middleton, and the most generous and caring of all, Janet Adelman, whom we still miss a great deal.

I feel that this book in particular has been conceived largely in solitude, in part so that I could concentrate on the excitements of thinking with and thinking against a variety of great minds—in literature as well as in philosophy. So I have been especially dependent on an extraordinary group of graduate students who have read all or parts of this book—Edward Alexander, Jeff Blevins, Jane Gregory, Christopher Miller, and Matt Langione. They are simply astonishing people for their intelligence and goodwill and enormous energy. Nicholas Gooding in the philosophy department also made heroic efforts to help make this book respectable.

Beyond Berkeley I want to thank audiences at Norwich and Hartfordshire in England, the University of Tennessee, UC Irvine, and the University of Chicago for engaging me in conversation about materials from what would be this book. I feel even more gratitude for those who set up these talks—David Nowell Smith, Danièle Moyal-Sharrock, Allen Dunn, Virginia Jackson, and Richard Strier. Strier and his colleagues were especially gracious over two days of conversation about my work.

Several editors helped shape what became chapters in this book. I am grateful to Allen Dunn for soliciting and editing work on Alice Crary, "The Poverty of Moral Theory in Literary Discourse: A Plea for Recognizing the Multiplicity of Value Frameworks," *Soundings* 94 (2011): 35–54; to Richard Eldridge for soliciting and for editing "Style," in Richard Eldridge, ed., *The Oxford Handbook of Philosophy and Literature* (New York: Oxford University Press, 2009), 420–41; to Richard Eldridge and Bernard Rhie for their demanding readings of my "Cavell and Wittgenstein on Morality: The Limits of Acknowledgement," in their edition of *Stanley Cavell and Literary Studies: Consequences of Skepticism* (New York: Continuum, 2011), 62–77; to Garry Hagberg and Walter Jost for including my "Exemplification and Expression" in *A Companion to the Philosophy of Literature* (Oxford: Wiley-Blackwell, 2010), 491–506; and to Sascha Bru for collaborating with me in

"Trakl's Tone: Mood and the Distinctive Speech Act of the Demonstrative," in Sascha Bru, Wolfgang Heumer, and Daniel Steuer, eds., *Wittgenstein Reading* (Berlin: Walter de Gruyter, 2013), 355–72. In addition, Jeffrey di Leo and Ronan McDonald solicited essays that enabled me to work out what would become my discussions of appreciation and of valuation. These collections have yet to be published.

Many, many other people deserve to be thanked for various kinds of support and more generally for taking me sufficiently seriously to convince myself that what I had to say on these topics could matter. Here I will just mention the terrific staff at Cornell University Press, especially Peter Potter for his support and helpful suggestions.

I want to dedicate this book to my youngest collaborator, my new granddaughter, Emilia Altieri, and to my oldest academic friend, Marjorie Perloff, who in the past several years has lived a truly heroic life that I am most pleased to acknowledge—for her achievement and for its giving me hope that aging even more will not be as awful as I usually imagine it.

Abbreviations

ACP	John Ashbery, *Collected Poems, 1956–1987*
AHU	P. M. S. Hacker, "The Autonomy of Humanistic Understanding"
ALF	Michael Clune, *American Literature and the Free Market, 1945–2000*
BB	Wittgenstein, *The Blue and Brown Books*
BMJ	Alice Crary, *Beyond Moral Judgment*
CJ	Immanuel Kant, *Critique of the Power of Judgment*
CN	Dodie Bellamy, *Cunt Norton*
COO	Richard Moran, "Cavell on Outsiders and Others"
CR	Stanley Cavell, *The Claim of Reason*
CV	Ludwig Wittgenstein, *Culture and Value*
DF	Heather Dubrow, foreword to *New Formalisms and Literary Theory*
EE	Jenefer Robinson, "Expression and Expressiveness in Art"
EI	David H. Finkelstein, *Expression and the Inner*

ET	Samuel Scheffler, *Equality and Tradition: Questions of Value in Moral and Political Theory*
FI	Paul de Man, "Form and Intent in the American New Criticism"
FKV	Max Scheler, *On Feeling, Knowing, and Valuing*
H	Charles Taylor, *Hegel*
LA	Nelson Goodman, *Languages of Art*
MVP	Aaron Ridley, *Music, Value, and the Passions*
NVT	David Wiggins, *Needs, Values, Truth: Essays in the Philosophy of Value*
OAE	Friedrich Schiller, *On the Aesthetic Education of Man*
OC	Ludwig Wittgenstein, *On Certainty*
PA	Richard Wollheim, *Painting as an Art*
PI	Ludwig Wittgenstein, *Philosophical Investigations*
PPF	Ludwig Wittgenstein, *Philosophy of Psychology—A Fragment*
PS	G. W. F. Hegel, *Phenomenology of Spirit*
PV	Wolfgang Köhler, *The Place of Value in a World of Facts*
R	Max Scheler, *Ressentiment*
RC	Robert Creeley, *The Collected Poems of Robert Creeley, 1945–1975*
RNC	Miranda Hickman and John D. McIntyre, eds., *Rereading the New Criticism*
SE	Tyrus Miller, *Singular Examples: Artistic Politics and the Neo-Avant-Garde*
SI	Derek Attridge, *The Singularity of Literature*
SR	Stephen Best and Sharon Marcus, "Surface Reading: An Introduction"
TLP	Wittgenstein, *Tractatus Logico-Philosophicus*
TPT	Andrew Gibson, *Toward a Postmodern Theory of Narrative*
WB	William Butler Yeats, *The Variorum Edition of the Poems of W. B. Yeats*
Z	Ludwig Wittgenstein, *Zettel*

Reckoning with the Imagination

Chapter 1

Why Wittgenstein Matters for Literary Theory

> The reality of things is the work of the things; the appearance of things is the work of Man, and a nature which delights in appearance no longer takes pleasure in what it receives but in what it does.
>
> —Friedrich Schiller, *On the Aesthetic Education of Man*

Among the several theoretical efforts to restore our attention to the virtues of close reading in the past few years, Heather Dubrow's foreword to the volume *New Formalisms and Literary Theory* stands out for its historical scope, its intellectual generosity, and its impassioned plea for uniting the interests of critics and writers through a shared interest in literary craft.[1] For Dubrow, as for many of the other New Formalists and those disillusioned with the promises of the now old New Historicism, one of the principal skills the profession should endorse and transmit is close reading, shorn of the ideological roles the New Critics were perceived to have imposed on it.

But this enterprise faces what I consider a large and troubling problem. How do we treat the distinctly literary as also worthy of attention beyond the domain of professional literary study? How can we have a professional skill that we cultivate without depending on other disciplines and still show that this skill has important ramifications well beyond the world of its practitioners? How can we treat literature as both a distinctive cultural enterprise and one that is arguably central to the quality of social life for everyone, or at least potentially central for enough people that this would make a substantial difference in the quality of collective life?

The opponents of aesthetic orientations during the past three decades were motivated largely by the fact that they could not give satisfying answers to such questions. It proved impossible for them to correlate their social consciences with their aesthetic sensibility, so many of them chose to pursue what could better satisfy those consciences. They tried to align literary studies with the disciplinary focus of various social sciences in the hope of developing clear agendas for the social information provided by imaginative tests. Then they could preserve some of the discipline's traditional emphases on close reading but focus those skills on practical rather than aesthetic concerns by asking how the skills of close readers and the canons of literary critics could illuminate fundamental social questions about political orientations, economic interests, and psychological tendencies to blind the self to what one was actually performing or producing.[2]

I believe some of us reviewing this history have to challenge those emphases. But I doubt Dubrow's defense of the literary can afford a sufficiently powerful challenge. In the effort to bring literary studies closer to the worlds writers inhabit, Dubrow suggests that we replace an "emphasis on the aesthetic with an adoption of the writers' emphasis on craft or *techne*" (*DF* xvi–xvii). One understands why she proposes this because it promises a telling response to critics who suspect that philosophical aesthetics has concentrated only on beauty rather than on any kind of power artists make available. Yet this seems to me exactly the wrong move. This turn to craft forecloses the possibility of recovering how aesthetics might be a discourse ultimately about the power of discrete objects to make differences in the sensibilities of those who engage them. And the emphasis on craft seems to me necessarily to preach to the converted because attention to craft only makes sense to those who already take pleasure in close reading. Our pressing need is to address the social uses possible for those pleasures.

This book is devoted to developing a very different response to the basic concerns I share with Dubrow. I argue that attention to the particular craft composing literary texts makes it possible to provide fresh perspectives on larger questions about values that necessarily engage literary texts in the social world—but as particular events rather than as sources of evidence for sustaining general explanatory accounts of social phenomena. In order to show how specific experiences of made objects can modify sensibilities and cultivate habits of judgment that go beyond the particulars, I believe we have to return to the Kantian heritage that Dubrow tries to evade—precisely because Kant and his heirs through Schiller were less concerned with beauty as a state than with judgments about beauty as capable of cultivating distinctive forms of power crucial for social life.[3]

This Kantian tradition in the early nineteenth century affords the richest discourse our culture has produced about the aesthetic and its relation to powers that extend beyond the aesthetic. For Kant and his direct heirs it even seemed possible for aesthetic theory to have significant force in shaping several domains of philosophy.[4] Think of how Kant's concept of imagination challenges the sufficiency of the understanding, how his concept of beauty as a symbol of the moral good provides alternative routes to the universality necessary to moral reason, and how Hegel deploys an essentially aesthetic idea of expression to challenge the Enlightenment's sharp distinction between subject and object.

For these reasons it would be a pity to throw these lines of thinking away because they have been aestheticized or remain trapped within idealist discourses. Instead I hope to restore many of the core concepts of the revolution in aesthetics created by German idealist arguments about expression in art, especially its claims for the importance of imagination.[5] But we cannot just repeat the concepts emphasized in that discourse. We also have to make these respectable within the languages that have at least some contemporary philosophical currency.

"Restore" is the challenging term here because we probably have to adapt these core concepts in terms of practices and values that are continuous with what seems acceptable to at least some plausible twenty-first-century philosophical perspective. Then the reformulation of those discourses may get a hearing. Therefore Wittgenstein plays the central role in this book. His later writings in particular make it possible to develop a very different framework for reconsidering how idealist claims about art might still make claims on us—especially in literary criticism, which tends to cultivate an uneasy relationship with contemporary philosophical aesthetics.

The Wittgenstein who emerges as relevant to these tasks in literary theory may even be of some interest to those primarily interested in philosophy. For I have to concentrate on his complex and rarely explicit thinking about subjectivity, primarily in relation to "aspect-seeing." In addition, I want to concentrate on the fact that, contra the claims of many philosophers dealing with his work, Wittgenstein had good reasons for not talking much about ethics: he preferred to think about questions of values in terms of religious concerns, which are, according to Hegel (the second hero of this book), much closer to art than to the ethics that can never reconcile forms of desire with systems for evaluating those desires.

This different framework for dealing with idealist aesthetics enables me to replace the fantasy of a grand theory of literature with an effort to characterize specific concepts and values that can be basic to our reading practices—but because of the interests they serve rather than because they are adequate to some essential properties that make something a work of literature. I cannot specify in conceptual terms which kinds of texts these concerns about reading will serve best and which will be relatively ill served: working out the limits of these concerns is a question resolvable only on a case-by-case basis. Nonetheless, I have certain bodies of literature in mind. Obviously I shape my discourse to accord with writing in the expressivist nexus of values elaborated in this idealist tradition because those ideals shaped most ambitious European literature at least from romanticism through modernism. But it would also be silly to not recognize that these philosophers were also talking about bodies of canonical European and some Asian materials not written in accord with expressivist principles. So I want to appreciate what they saw in their critical reading by speculating on how work such as classical Greek drama and Dante and Shakespeare at least might display and often model for their own cultures, and for ours, values similar to what the idealist philosophers found compelling in these authors.

The Four Basic Principles of Expressivist Views of Art

Let me first describe how antiempiricist thinkers from Kant to Schiller taught us to view art and how they produced quests such as Coleridge's to contrast the esemplastic (form-establishing) imagination with the indulgences of mere fancy. These thinkers produced four major principles for understanding how we experience works of art. Those principles differ fundamentally from views that treated literary texts primarily as rhetorical structures intended to instruct and delight or as realist efforts to produce the sensations and interests we find in the actual world.

1. *The experience of art is intensely sensual.* This principle has many features, but they all come down to an emphatic insistence that one's experience of art is the product of imaginative intuition uniting intellectual passion with something like the vital force of nature. This sensuousness in turn has the capacity to produce a harmony of the senses desperately needed if we are to retain an adequate sense of human powers under threat from both Enlightenment rationality and the isolating effects of living increasingly in a marketplace mentality. This is Friedrich Schiller:

> Every phenomenon whatsoever may be thought of in four different connections. A thing may relate directly to our sensuous condition . . . ; that is its physical character. Or it can relate to our reason, and furnish us with knowledge; that is its logical character. Or it can relate to our will, and be regarded as an object of choice for a rational being; that is its moral character. Or, finally, it can relate to the totality of our various powers, without being a specific object for any single one of them; that is its aesthetic character. (*On the Aesthetic Education of Man*, trans. Reginald Snell [New York: Frederic Ungar, 1954], 99, Letter 20; cited hereafter as *OAE*)

Embedded in this idealization of the sensuous is the corollary idea that the work of art resists being subsumed under concepts and adapted to rationalist or empiricist modes of thinking. I am thinking here of the elaborate patterning of interrelated characters in Shakespearean drama as well as the ways in which Jane Austen and George Eliot elaborate within the realistic textures of their fiction similar intricate relations among characters capable of considerable breadth of feeling that cannot be fixed by conceptual analysis. Here Kant provides the richest formulation of what in art resists the conceptual, although Wittgenstein substantially modifies our sense of how this resistance takes place: "Just as in the case of an idea of reason the imagination, with its intuitions, never attains to the given concept, so in the case of an aesthetic idea the understanding by means of its concepts never attains to the complete inner intuition of the imagination which it combines with a given representation."[6] For Wittgenstein, many practices, not just in art, resist being subsumed under practices of knowing. His later work takes as one of its fundamental tasks the drawing of conceptual boundaries that limit the tyranny that "scientific protocols for knowing" have exercised over philosophy at least since Descartes.[7]

Wittgenstein shifts the focus from how claims about knowledge can be formulated to an appreciation for how we as human beings learn to respond to cues and participate in a wide variety of social practices where concerns for knowledge are at best marginally significant. He calls attention to how the variety of practices themselves constitutes the fields of significance for our actions. Intelligibility in many domains is a matter of participation made possible by our learning languages in social settings. Intelligibility is not grounded in observation that sees through appearance but in the recognitions and attunements these practices make possible. Wittgenstein then can redo classical idealist themes such as expression and display and participation in ways that concentrate on learned behaviors woven into shared modes of social life.[8] The skills we need to engage art objects are basically the same skills we need to negotiate the many interpretive situations we encounter in our daily lives.[9] Indeed, we spend much of our lives adjusting our actions to fit these situations, and we find in the grammars that shape our actions significant resources for understanding all sorts of displays—from how people express feelings to their earnest efforts to make changes in their local worlds. Wittgenstein goes so far as to claim that "What is new (spontaneous, 'specific') is always a language game."[10] So, however much literary works have their own formal coherence, that coherence also has a functional role. We can imagine fundamentally aesthetic attitudes toward art that nonetheless do not require essentially formalist responses.[11] Rather, the work gives shape to a specific mode of utterance that has significant affinities with our expectations for making sense (even if the utterance resists the authority of those expectations, as is the case with much avant-garde writing).

Art, then, does not typically construct a formal cocoon, protected from the messiness of life. Instead, literary art invites ways of talking about concreteness that emphasize meaningfulness rather than the materiality of the medium. This art cannot avoid participating in struggles to align and to resist the forms of behavior that we come to understand through speech acts. We can treat the works as displays of states of mind or of attention that invite modes of responsiveness to how they compose situations and deploy language.[12] Particularity is entirely compatible with intelligibility, so long as we recognize that intelligibility does not depend only on propositions. We test our capacities for responsiveness to such statements constantly in our everyday practices.

2. *"The beautiful must not be judged in accordance with concepts"* (CJ, 219) *because the work of art is not a description or a chain of arguments but a making in accord with an intuition.* This stress on making is crucial because it allows theory to treat how the artwork resists concepts as affording a distinctive relation to subjectivity. In shaping the set of internal relations that constitute the piece of art, the subject works on its own expressive drives to turn them into objects for consciousness. The language of "object" would then suffice were the artists to seek concepts. But the artists give body to intuitions, so the made object takes on a power to act virtually as a subject. The objectification itself embodies a mode of active existence, as if the object were the dynamic substance that affords the feeling of being situated as a subject in the first place. For now two remarks by Schiller will have to suffice: "Beauty is therefore certainly an object for us, since reflection is the condition under which we have a sensation of it; but it is at the same time a state of our personality, since feeling is the condition under which we have a conception of it" (*OAE,* 122). Then he caps this statement with brilliant synthesis. The object as perceived form becomes correlated with what we must do to bring it within consciousness as something other than a concept: "It is then certainly form, because we contemplate it, but it is at the same time life because we feel it. In a word it is at once our state and our act" (ibid.).

We have to turn to Hegel for the richest descriptions of how feeling is the condition under which we have a conception of the state of what the construction of an aesthetic object entails. He offers an elaborate characterization of how self-consciousness fuses with substance. The goal of self-consciousness is to produce acts of comprehending the intricacy of where the self is positioned at any given moment. But that comprehension requires self-consciousness always to be addressing another aspect of self, the sensuous substantial dimension, which takes the form of the sociohistorical forces that seem objective and alien. Hegel's formula is that subject and substance are sides of an equation that the work tries to keep in balance: I=I, which is always varying and dynamic.[13] If we treat "I" in relation only to objects, we get a one-sided and non-dialectical sense of a single active power in a world of passive things. If we treat the "I" as itself an object, we become only substance driven by alien forces. Only the equation captures how "state" and "act" continue to exchange roles within concrete structures of understanding.

This is not mystification, as I show more elaborately in my chapter on the concept of expression. Wittgenstein shows that we cannot explain "now I see it as a duck" by copying the Jastrow duck-rabbit image. If we are to contextualize this remark at all, the agent has to offer a model of what one sees in that moment. The model provides information about the state of the subject as well as what the subject is seeing. The art object similarly is not simply an avowal of feeling but a taking of responsibility, by which the subject also provides an accounting of how its particular perspective makes a difference in its mode of self-awareness.

3. *We are not done with the maker.* Kant is careful to provide a precise picture of how readers and viewers can identify, and perhaps identify with, how an authorial presence emerges in our aesthetic experiences. When I regard any manufactured item, I may be surprised at its originality or uniqueness, but it is immediately possible for me to understand the concept that drove the making. In art, according to Kant I recognize the presence of the maker everywhere but cannot bring it under a concept because I experience a texture of invention and care for particulars that seems continually free to modify its own processes.

In effect an audience adapts to the making by concentrating on what he calls the "purposiveness without purpose," creating an immense gap between what art does and what the understanding can pursue: "Purposiveness can thus exist without an end, in so far as we do not place the causes of this form in a will, but can still make the explanation of its possibility conceivable to ourselves only by deriving it from a will" (*CJ,* section 10, 105).[14] Purposiveness is different from purpose because the latter does specify how a will establishes a form. With purposiveness, on the other hand, we attribute a willfulness without being able to specify the concept under which that will produces the objects in question. Moral reasoning for Kant is driven by purpose: we know what concepts legislate our activities. But with aesthetic experience—of nature and of art—we recognize that there is significant evidence of design yet cannot validly presume we have a concept capable of explaining how the relations are structured.

We cannot get far in applying Kant's term without encountering both a transcendental subject who attributes purposiveness and a transcendental dimension of experience, a "supersensible" realm by which nature and art both have the capacities to generate spiritual significance. But if we can be content just to equate "spiritual" with the capacity to embody an indefinable agency in the construction of meaningfulness, we will see why the concept of purposiveness is so useful for aesthetics, especially for demystifying the concept of expression while at the same time elaborating the work that concept can do.

I take "purposiveness" to refer simply to our need to attribute self-consciousness to authorial actions in order to establish their significance for the force of the art object even though we cannot have a definite concept of the agent's reasons. We might say that the work itself defines those reasons, but not in a way that can lead to the control of specific concepts the maker might hold. For the reasons are a series of felt rightnesses, without any need for an overall schema.

We can then elaborate how we recognize purposiveness by bringing to bear the very different vocabulary of Richard Wollheim.[15] Wollheim is wary of practices for *interpreting* works of art because they so readily approximate explanations. Instead he develops the idea of critical work as the effort to "see in" to its internal dynamics—both on the level of the artist's choices and on the level of how these choices elicit a possible appreciation of the imagined world composed by these choices.

The ideal of "seeing in" can handle both functions because it focuses attention equally on the situation and the work done in animating and interpreting that situation. Wollheim beautifully finesses questions about how art can represent or imitate life by focusing criticism on trying to identify provisionally with the activity of the artist as embedded in the work. And that focus is concrete: "seeing in" is literally an attempt at identification without any imperative to find explanations for what one sees. Seeing in orients us to how the image comes alive by virtue of appreciating what the painter accomplishes in rendering the "now" and the "this" of a specific activity. So the purposiveness and the object simply fuse: we see into the world presented by seeing into the manner of presentation and attempting to attune to what it makes possible.[16]

It is high time I used a concrete example in order to illustrate the various claims I have been making. What happens if we make an effort to see into how Shakespeare constructs Claudius's opening speech in Hamlet? Pay particular attention to the syntax because it is a form of purposiveness that seems objectively a fundamental condition shaping how any trained reader would have to approach this text:

> Though, yet of Hamlet our dear brother's death
> The memory be green, and that it us befitted
> To bear our hearts in grief, and our whole kingdom
> To be contracted in one brow of woe,
> Yet so far hath discretion fought with nature
> That we with wisest sorrow think on him
> Together with remembrance of ourselves
> Therefore our sometime sister, now our Queen
> Th' imperial jointress to this warlike state,
> Have we, as 'twere with a defeated joy,
> With an auspicious and a dropping eye,
> With mirth in funeral, and with dirge in marriage,
> In equal scale weighing delight and dole
> Taken to wife. Nor have we herein barred
> Your better wisdoms . . .[17]

Beware anyone who introduces a speech with a double qualifier. (And beware any critic who comments on the content of such passages without attending to the syntactic manner of the presentation.) If we see into the possible effect of this brilliant control of syntax, this control of paradox, this capacity to see every side of an issue, this delight in balance and antithesis, and this capacity to speak metaphorically so that he can identify with the entire society's "one brow of woe," we also realize a profound aspect of Hamlet's problem. Hamlet may need the idea of his father's ghost simply to have some alternative to the power of Claudius's intelligence. This speech establishes a capacity to control a room and leave no space for other people. They are all spoken for and so need not, or perhaps cannot, enter public space. No wonder Hamlet has to rely on puns as an effort to get free of the practical world Claudius so effectively dominates.[18] In effect, seeing in allows us to build character dialectically: the more fully we recognize what Shakespeare is doing purposively with language, the more actively and cunningly we can participate in the dramatic tension between Claudius and Hamlet.

I have one more point to make about purposiveness as illustrated by this passage from *Hamlet,* one that entails attempting to secularize another transcendental feature of Kant's argument. To read for purposiveness is to read for the two levels of action that I have been stressing—how the author presents making and how the making presents characters and worlds. So Kant establishes a useful framework for talking about how we can locate intentions in works of art. And by implication he suggests that, if one cannot establish intention, one has no consistent purchase on the texture of relations that purposiveness establishes.

From this Kantian perspective it seems plausible to expect that any other audience member who cares about the work of the work will agree with us. (At least there is something fixed to agree on.) We find ourselves judging in such a way that we mime the universals of moral judgment. But we do not have the clear and distinct ideas available from moral reason, so we have to rely on expectations deriving from a feeling of universal agreement among persons rather than a confidence in the content of moral judgment. Kant characterizes this state with his characteristically precise ambition to find the transcendental dimension of the experience:

> Now I say that the beautiful is the symbol of the morally good; and also only in this respect (that of a relation that is natural to everyone, and that is also expected of everyone else as a duty) does it please with a claim to the assent of everyone else, in which the mind is at the same time aware of a certain ennoblement and elevation above the mere receptivity for a pleasure from sensible perceptions, and also esteems the value of others in accordance with a similar maxim of their power of judgment. (*CJ*, section 59, 227)

Critics have of course labeled this idealization transcendental nonsense. But suppose we deal only with the state of the subject here rather than worry about the validity of any universal claim. Then the universality of the claim matters far less than the mere fact of its generosity. It is important that some psychological states are consumed by our involvements in immediate pleasures while others take the attitude that what we see, others could and should also recognize. Then we see ourselves occupying positions where agreement is possible on states that can matter for how we understand our own experiences. And what we mean by "our own experiences" comes to partake of the possibility that we can share even this level of intimacy.

4. *This talk of how aesthetic judgment modifies our capacities as subjects is only one of several ways in which idealist and romantic aesthetics used art to define distinctive powers of subjects to construct values and live in accord with them.* Wittgenstein provides very little guidance in elaborating this point, so I have to go my own way. Let us begin again with Schiller, this time talking

about the powers aesthetic experience realizes in the reader or viewer. Here Schiller frequently rises to quite lovely rhetorical heights, such as in the claim that "to grant freedom by means of freedom is the fundamental law" of aesthetic life (*OAE*, 137, Letter 27). But the richer the rhetoric, the more problematic it is for the contemporary theorist to appropriate the claims in language better oriented toward practical implications, so I choose a relatively restrained passage:

> Soon he [man] is not content that things should please him, he wants to give pleasure himself, at first indeed through what belongs to him, but finally through what he is. . . . Besides the service which it [what the artist produces] renders, it must reflect the genial intellect which conceived it, the loving hand which executed it, the serene and free spirit which chose and established it. (ibid.)

What concrete kinds of activity could inspire such a rhetoric? What characterizations of reading can possibly justify any talk about the realization of aspects of the self?[19] I can give a partial answer to my questions by emphasizing two aspects of self-consciousness that art solicits—the feelings of developing valuations that occur as we try to identify with the making of the text, and the second-order feelings of appreciation that occur when we reflect on what the text has enabled and "reflects." Both modes of self-consciousness depend on shifting from epistemic and instrumental analyses by critics to a complex network of readerly orientations involving attunement, participation, appreciation, and valuing as modes of reflexive judgment appropriate to an investment in how expressive behaviors engage their worlds.[20]

My basic interest in these configurations is how they offer an opportunity to make considerations about value far more central than they usually are in the characterization of reading practices. But it is important to differentiate valuing as a way of aligning with what texts do from Leavisite modes of evaluation, given their ever-present alignment with the securing of cultural capital. When we read responsively, I doubt that we formulate comprehensive value judgments or even bring to bear in fresh ways the values that we have already formed. Instead we enact what I call a constant process of valuation. We try to participate in how texts engage our affective lives. We come to treasure what we see as achievements in the text—in maintaining our interests, in cleverly manipulating the actions, in directing our interests to fresh perceptions or sensitive formulations of attitudes.

Consider what is involved in a careful reading of, or careful seeing into, the speech by Claudius that I quoted earlier. There is increasingly heightened attention as we recognize that the rendering of a character produces a distinctive and engaging person. In the case of Claudius it seems to me that no previous literary invention has just this degree of confident control over his emotions. Furthermore, it matters that this sense of originality is constructed almost entirely out of syntactic choices and speech rhythms. For the smallest building blocks of language become charged with the same sense of rightness and an originality we cannot but wish to emerge even more fully. So it is difficult not to delight in Claudius's self-delight as he warms to his characterization of his marriage. Even more striking is the recognition that Hamlet's plight has been brilliantly characterized before he even gets to speak.

These recognitions produce direct valuing. Such valuing is an aspect of every engaged reading, although it is rarely commented on because the values are not raised to the conceptual order, where we use them to interpret and direct actions. Instead, most readers are content with the modifications of sensibility that a given passage elicits. But we need not rest with how sensibility is modified. Although it is true that such valuing is possible only because we suspend our commitments to the values that shape our actions, our valuing affords another way of modifying behavior. Even without eliciting concepts, the experience of reading produces for us a range of possible examples that we can use in sorting future experiences. How Emma ultimately gushes in elaborate breathless sentences when she understands that Knightley has proposed to her affords an unforgettable image of what excitement can be. And my example of Claudius's first speech has the power to modify anyone's awareness of what it means to feel like Hamlet in that situation.

There will be much more to say about the role of examples as modes of remembering and putting to practical use how we get involved in the worlds our reading produces. But for now I want only to add another question. What happens when we reflect on our processes of valuing and consider this also the realization of significant values? This reflection puts us in a position where we can fully appreciate why appreciation has a long and beleaguered conceptual history in our discourses about aesthetic experience and, indeed, about aesthetic education. Appreciation consists in the second-order affirmation of how and why texts satisfy through these processes of microvaluation. Appreciation is simply the recognition of processes that give significant pleasure, especially in situations where we feel our own powers of responsiveness expanding, so that we are also impelled toward gratitude.

Finally, I believe there is a political dimension to appreciation that almost justifies Schiller's claims about granting freedom by means of freedom. This political dimension does not result in the shaping of political agendas or loyalties to specific struggling and resisting groups of people. Some acts of careful reading can produce such loyalties. But the practice of close reading involves appreciating a Claudius as much as we do Morrison's Sula or Breton's Nadja. So the politics of appreciation consists simply, but powerfully, in the way reading produces a practical and experiential alternative to the resentments that are so prevalent in countries that have trouble justifying how they distribute wealth and power.

One cannot resent what establishes appreciation because while the former state fosters sensibilities lamenting what they do not have, the latter thrives on gratitude for what one has been able to experience—for the content of the experience and for the awareness of the powers one has to exercise in order fully to enjoy that experience.[21] Perhaps the only people who can appreciate and resent at the same time are rival authors. Conversely, it may be our most ambitious authors who most fully understand the opposition between resentment and appreciation. It is no accident that a play containing all the forces of resentment released by Caliban ends with the possibility of finding forgiveness and freedom in the applause of the audience. Similarly, Dante's entire *Commedia* defines finding "another way" that does not allow the self to be trapped within a world defined by the she-wolf of envy. First, there must be an understanding of justice, then the exploration of how far appreciation of the order of the world can take the psyche.

Clearly, appreciation cannot be one's only entry into the political world. The powers that be would appreciate this far too much. But I suspect no art will provide the needed stimuli for effective political change: these changes will come only from persistent efforts to make us aware of the price we pay for the governments we have. Political change involves convincing huge masses of people to modify their habits and be willing to sacrifice some of their interests for a collective good. The experience of responding to writing devoted to primarily aesthetic goals has been limited to a small percentage of populations, and it is necessarily in our culture aimed toward the complexity and distinctiveness of experience rather than exhortation to particular kinds of behavior.

Why This Return to Idealist Aesthetics Is Urgently Needed Now

It is obvious that I aspire to be a wholly Italian Adorno—challenging his brilliant insistence on the power of negativity in relation to both production and consumption of works of art. I cannot deny the pleasures of the negative as necessary work for the intelligence. But in my view the negative can be at best only half the story. There seem to me to be important positive social roles that literature can play in virtually any relatively advanced culture that has developed elaborate educational structures and given its participants significant leisure time. Yet the positive claims will be haunted by the fear that in the quest to be a wholly Italian Adorno I will become instead a somewhat Italian version of George Eliot's Casaubon, caught in fantasies of intellectual achievements that whose time has in fact utterly passed.

So I have to work hard to exhibit why the task I propose is both timely and important. When I first drafted this book, I thought I had to have an elaborate critique of the various kinds of context-based readings that have displaced concerns for aesthetic values in most "sophisticated" literary criticism. One would be hard pressed to find in elite programs of literary study even two younger critics concentrating on aesthetic values or even the importance of the plural, contemplative sympathies traditionally characteristic of aesthetic attitudes. But even though the situation remains dire, other critics have produced powerful negative analyses of the prevailing academic modes of literary study. So I believe it is necessary here to give only the basic arguments of those critiques, with which I heartily concur. What is more, these authors have had the patience and the analytic intelligence to read far more of what they criticize than I could. So after summarizing those critiques I can engage with a somewhat different problem that promises to illuminate how we can still claim a significant role for aesthetic values in our reading practices.

For me, all the ladders start with the heroic efforts to clean the Augean stables by two critics—Derek Attridge, who best diagnosed the problem, and Michael Clune, who offers the best understanding of the historical factors, making it seem necessary to break with all traditions of close reading in order to bring out the work's engagement in social issues. Attridge is very good at showing how both suspicious and reconstructive cultural and political criticism serve primarily cognitive, pragmatic, and political ends.[22] In effect this criticism is primarily "instrumental" because it is not devoted to specifying how works are distinctive but rather to aligning them with other disciplines so that they can be said to reveal various cultural forces and interests. So rather than explication, the goal is explanation: the texts matter because they provide what critics can claim to be knowledge in accord with disciplinary standards for a wide variety of perspectives—from sociology to neuroscience. But for Attridge it is also important to ask what price we pay for changing the critical perspective and ignoring how most writers probably intend their work to be read—for their individual concrete and sensuous renderings of experiences in which the audience is asked to participate.

Attridge argues that the cost of putting oneself in a position to make such knowledge claims is banishing any sense of unique and important roles for concerns about aesthetic values.[23] Such practices ignore the kind of vocabulary criticism has traditionally developed—concerned with values such as sensitivity, sharpness and energy of attention, intricacy of self-consciousness, richness and variety of imaginative palette, and the capacity to control and activate complex worlds evoking sympathy, empathy, and justified anger. So on the personal level there can be no talk of powers cultivated by specific texts. And on the cultural level such criticism simply ignores or sets aside any institutional role for the training that prepares us to articulate how individual works become powerful "singular" events making significant and distinctive demands on our capacities for responsiveness. Instrumental criticism shows how texts can be useful for other intellectual frameworks. But it does not help at all in specifying how participating in the imaginative forces established by the text might be a culturally significant act.

Clune's critique is more historical, rooting instrumental criticism in the example set by New Historicism: "A polemical commitment to the continuity of the literary and the social furnished these critics with a characteristic plot: literature tries to distinguish itself with respect to other social and cultural formations and fails."[24] New Historicism was largely responsible for the displacement of aesthetic values because it "showed the process by which literature's attempt to break free from a social system was contained and redeployed by that system" (*ALF*, 7). For the power deployed by a society can be remarkably flexible and remarkably general. So even though a writer can oppose a particular form of power, the critic can show how that opposition itself is governed by the culture and deployed in ways that subordinate individual motives to collective forces.

Because he is more concerned with our social situation than Attridge, Clune allows us to shift our focus from attacking critical practices to trying to understand the situation in which critics would be willing to pay the price for rejecting aesthetic concerns. Perhaps New Historicism's sense of the limitations of literature's promise of freedom from social determinants is itself symptomatic of a crisis of faith in the humanities. If so, then it should not be surprising that contemporary literary critics hold so lightly the traditional resources and interests of literary criticism to a large extent responsible still for the skills exhibited in their intricate readings. If social systems wield the power to shape signification, it is difficult not to ask "if there is nothing special about literature, why should we study it?" (*ALF*, 8). There is increasingly little point to asking what most authors seem to be trying to do when they compose literary works. Thus increasingly little attention is also given to those particular features of literary experience that resist conceptual understanding.

Some of the turn from aesthetic concerns has to be market driven. There are too many critics and too few "original" or "innovative" ways of reading literature. So anything promising will take hold quickly. Hence the rapid emergence of diverse modes of instrumental criticism—from various versions of historicism, to "suspicious reading," to practical ethical and political judgments, to concerns for how literature affects our views of the environment, to what neurology or evolutionary approaches can contribute to literary study.

But the symptomatic features come in when we ask why this kind of criticism is considered promising. I think it fits a cultural bias that universities ought to be places devoted to the production of knowledge, not to the cultivation of sensibilities. This bias in turn cuts two ways. It becomes difficult to practice the cultivation of sensibilities without considerable unease. Not surprisingly, this discomfort has been considerably intensified by having these modes of cultivation both threatened by and subsumed into what close reading became under deconstruction. Deconstructive readings kept insisting that literary language undid any positive claim—to knowledge or to the empowerment of sensibility. One had to come to enjoy endless demonstrations of texts offering capacities to revel in the free play of the signifier.

Ultimately there was a crisis of faith in the power or the social significance of aesthetic values. Literary critics increasingly pursued what they could feel were positive forms of knowledge that might rival a skepticism that seemed at the heart of deconstruction. Any kind of knowledge looked pretty good, and, in contrast, any kind of reveling in textual details had the smell of decadence about it. Yet I think cultural criticism in fact bought into deconstruction's binary opposition between knowledge and some kind of indeterminacy or singularity.

Treating literary objects as texts rather than "works" could free critics from obligations to attribute purposiveness to distinct literary objects. Individual texts seem like collages in their weaving together of fragments of social ideology, often in tension with one another: the hope that there can be a single identity for a work seems merely chimerical. These "texts" call for being treated as bundles of rhetorical elements that literary objects share with their culture and that revealed contradictory interests at the core of social life. The units of the texts become themselves something close to social operators as bits of ideology or as signs of shared interests even in situations where texts manifestly differ in their claims on the world.

More important, once these textual elements become so malleable, it is much easier to devote criticism to political ends—both as means of exposing how ideology functions and as evidence of interests that elicit specific critiques of dominant practices and goals. Here I sympathize with much of the politics involved, yet I think that such overt commitments tend to minimize our sense of the potential powers in imaginative labor. Such critical work has no language for ends and structures developed by particular authors and no sense of desires that we might treat as internal to the texts.[25] Consequently, it has to deal primarily with collective agency, with the text's relations to specific social conditions.

Literature turns out to reflect social ills rather than challenge us to engage imaginatively in understanding how authors intentionally engage possible political consequences of their work.[26] And the fact that most of these critiques of the society have considerable justification tends to make us more interested in saving our own souls by being on the right side than in elaborating the full imaginative lives that are potential in the objects we study. So most ambitious critics have aligned with these primarily discursive models of analysis necessary in other disciplines, even though literary criticism has traditionally been the custodian of other, more immanent modes of explication that do not merely define the right side of an issue but challenge subjects to reimagine how they configure relations between individual and collective goals. Correspondingly, I hope that awareness of the sources of our sense of crisis may suffice for critics to try out the possibilities of developing new versions of the robust sense of imagination testified to by Kant, Hegel, and Schiller.

Some Problems Inherent in the Arguments for Surface Reading

I have to make one more foray into contemporary literary criticism because Stephen Best and Sharon Marcus have developed a quite interesting case for surface reading that promises renewed attention to the activity of literary texts without invoking any kind of formalism or focus primarily on craft. Here I can focus only on Best's and Marcus's original statement, "Surface Reading: An Introduction," that served as the opening salvo in the issue of *Representations* they edited in order to provide an alternative to what they claimed, rightly, to the oppressive dominance of "symptomatic reading" in ambitious literary criticism. And I cannot do justice to the power of their argument because I want to get quickly to my worries that the concept of surface reading provides a dangerously thin basis on which to ground aesthetic values. Along with its timely critique of current tendencies to indulge in a variety of "symptomatic readings" committed to interpreting deep levels of texts repressed by authors for various reasons, the essay offers a passionate defense of attending to the manifest details of texts and so aligns itself with principles of close reading.[27] But the question remains whether we can develop an adequate model of aesthetic experience bound to the figure of reading what is on the surface.

The following claim drives both the essay's critique of equating depth reading with ferreting out symptoms and the positive hope that we can return to reading for pleasure and for engagement in how the surface is deployed: "We take surface to mean what is evident, perceptible, apprehensible in texts, what is neither hidden nor hiding; what, in the geometrical sense, has length and breadth but not thickness, and therefore covers no depth.

A surface is what insists on being looked at rather than what we must train ourselves to see through" (*SR,* 9).

On the basis of these values the essay states its hopes that such a position can sponsor "many types of reading, some quite old, some fairly new" (ibid.). But its capacity for sponsorship is hampered by the oppositions produced by its basic metaphoric structure: surface must preclude depth, not just depth as the inquiry into what is hidden but also depth as something that is constructed because of how the play of surfaces develops.

However, a powerful practice of close reading need not, and probably should not, depend on the opposition between seeing what is on the surface and the desire to see through the surface. Wollheim's figure of "seeing in" provides a substantial alternative to the opposition between surface and depth. As we see into a text, various dramas emerge in the presentation of the action and in our appreciation of what the author is doing with those actions. So surface and depth start to merge. Why limit ourselves to talk about surfaces, even metaphorical and ethical talk about surfaces, when we can talk simply about the poet's gestures and their modes of significance for an active imagination?

Best and Marcus recognize this need to vary how surface is imagined, so they develop a brilliant list of six possible modes of reading that attention to surfaces can inspire or align with.[28] But this does not suffice to counter the most important limitation of their argument. The metaphor of surface and depth locks Marcus and Best into treating texts as objects, albeit both material and textual objects. I argue instead that only a language of authorial actions responsible for composing worlds that we see into is adequate to describe how literary imaginations create. And only that perspective will afford sufficient contexts for us to appreciate why we have such a complicated and multitextured vocabulary for responding to works of art. We need attitudes sponsored by the principle of seeing in if we are to show how surfaces can be manipulated to sustain intricate levels of suggestive implications about inner lives, if we are to dwell on imaginative qualities such as sympathy and precise attention to detail, if we are to engage levels of affective intensity, and if are to project a range of judgments reflecting sustained encounters with how authors deploy their skills. Such concerns indicate the impossible and unnecessary burden Best and Marcus put on the figure of "surface."

Plot Summary: The Shape of This Book's Overall Argument

I want an overall statement of what I take to be the coherence of my argument. But the condensed form an introduction requires may be better read after completing the rest of the book. (There is good reason that Hegel is one my heroes.) I say this as a barely disguised plea that if readers are frustrated by this density, they try the more patient discourse of the body of the book before giving up on it.

My first extended effort at a fresh theoretical perspective in this book will not derive from Wittgenstein. I believe our primary need is to resurrect the importance of the imagination in our practices of making and of seeing, but not with the idealizing and idealistic trappings we saw in Kant and in Schiller. So I begin by exploring what we might be able to say if we base our claims for imagination on a phenomenological approach bound to the details of secular experience: what can we see ourselves doing as we imagine? Because there are various kinds of imagining, I propose a further condition on our phenomenology that brings phenomenology close to Wittgenstein's concern for grammar. We have to ask, What are the distinctive traits of the kind of imagining that earns predicates such as "imaginatively" or "with imagination"?

To answer these questions we have to link conditions of proprioceptive feeling with a sense of appropriate uses of a vocabulary that cultures have developed around imaginative activity. This phenomenological enterprise may be able to define specific secular powers for authors and for readers that make intelligible and workable claims for basic differences between imagining and perceiving. And we may find in this grammar a better framework for valuing what the arts create than any approach grounded in one particular imaginative activity, such as expression or mimesis.

I try to exhibit the qualities stressed by this view of imaginative activity by closely reading two poems—John Ashbery's "Instruction Manual," which explicitly establishes a model for a postromantic view of imagination, and William Butler Yeats's "Leda and the Swan," which was written under a romantic disposition but proves amenable to reading and valuing in terms surprisingly similar to what it takes to engage Ashbery's imagination. For example, both poets stress creative activity as free in the sense that the author has to establish distinctive and not predictable sets of relations that constitute the conditions by which the activity takes on coherence. And because imaginative constructs do not have the obligations of accuracy that accounts of perception involve, we have to treat what details are given as providing sufficient evidence for identifying and identifying with the kind of action involved.

Analogously, because self-evidence is at stake, we have to treat the work as expressive and so imagine the goals of reading as attuning ourselves to the needs, desires, projections, and tonal intricacies that take place within the particular process of the activity in question. Acts of imagination simply require vocabularies that are different from anything our discourses of knowledge can provide, especially if we focus on evaluative terms built into our language for assessing imaginative work.

Here we also a find a vocabulary of "attunement" especially useful because it provides a way of talking about efforts at recognition and sympathy that does not presuppose the need to stabilize perception in order to make knowledge claims possible. Orchestras tune up or players attune to each other. And attunement can be a matter of sympathetic vibration with precious little intentionality, yet with high degrees of appreciation of what such vibration involves.[29]

This effort to generalize about the implications of a phenomenology of the imagination can be only as useful as the vocabularies it sponsors. So I have to offer a second chapter fully elaborating how we can connect a history of discourses about the concrete sensuousness of imaginative production to Wittgenstein's extensive analysis of why knowledge claims play a relatively small part in our practical lives. Wittgenstein's thinking on this point makes it clear how imagination is frequently active because we are always judging how best to respond to what we take as concrete activities within established language games. Hence awareness of these modes of activity may make it possible for critics who stress aesthetic orientations to claim a different but potentially more powerful model of worldliness than that claimed by instrumental orientations.[30] The separation of literary texts from the domain of knowledge becomes not a mark of weakness but of potential interpretive power for our practical lives.

Wittgenstein's concrete argument here tries to limit ambitious empiricist claims by narrowing what we can say we know to what we can recognize as overcoming doubts. If we are worried about the time or people's plans or various factual matters, we have stable ways of pursuing the facts of the matter. But if we express pain or state expectations or negotiate in making plans, the situation is quite different. Here we are playing roles and adjusting to roles others play within practices. Knowledge is much less important than powers to recognize the games being played and abilities to adapt to those practices by playing the appropriate parts. And many of these parts involve what Wittgenstein treats as display rather than as description.

Display is the clearest domain where imagination plays significant roles. Two large families of concrete actions become central. The first derives from the simple fact that our most elemental forms of life cannot be described but have to be displayed for self-consciousness. In Wittgenstein's *Tractatus*, logic is the element most pronouncedly not subject to description because it is presupposed by any propositions purportedly about this topic. Danièle Moyal-Sharrock has demonstrated how Wittgenstein's *On Certainty* returns to this sense of an irreducible ground of intelligibility that has be displayed and not reasoned to because it is itself the basis for all reasoning. But this later work does not attribute this grounding function to logic. Rather, what has to be displayed are the various grammatical structures that make our basic social practices coherent and workable.[31]

One might elaborate Moyal-Sharrock's observations in several ways. An agent could simply examine our conditions for making sense of a command such as "Slab." We manage to know whether the speaker is uttering a request or indicating the nature of an object simply by virtue of what one grasps as the nature of the situation eliciting the utterance. Or one might point out how often literary works are devoted simply to aligning our attention in accord with what underlies our abilities both to make sense and to care about the sense that gets made. This, I think, is the basic sociological and ontological role of realist fiction. And, we can point out, with Richard Eldridge, how Wittgenstein's own *Philosophical Investigations* is less concerned with developing logical arguments than with offering perspicuous remarks that themselves become exemplary modes of aligning with the fundamental grammatical features shaping our typical social practices. Thinking becomes more a process of pathfinding than it does the forging of general arguments.

The second family of actions crucial to what display offers is most clearly represented by what commentators on Wittgenstein call "avowals." Avowals are first-person-singular assertions that indicate the state of an agent at a given time. "He is in pain" is typically a description that can be right or wrong and can be open to greater specification as we examine the patient. "I am in pain" can be treated as a first-person version inviting the same description. But to Wittgenstein that would be to ignore what the first person is actually doing and to ignore the structural parallels to other kinds of avowals such as "I expect him to come." "I am in pain" is not only a request for a diagnosis but also a display by the person of an appeal for sympathy or at least a recognition that this person does not have his or her full capacities for action. Avowals need not point to some inner life in order to give us direct access to a specific state of being and so bring attention to the agent rather than to facts in the world.

Avowals are only one kind of sense-bearing display that is semantically charged yet resistant to description. We could compose a continuum of ways we make persons intelligible by focusing on features of their actions that resist description and so make an appeal to our capacities to adjust to what is being displayed. At one pole there is sheer self-expression making the person's feelings visible. At the other pole the person does not focus on the content of feelings but on the capacity to make the person's point of view recognized or felt. Wittgenstein was so interested in aspect seeing largely because of how it displays the power of point of view without manifestly expressing the affective content informing that point of view. The dawning of an aspect need bring no change to the physical world but is central to what the agent can present about his or her own orientation to the world.[32] Analogously, exclamations change nothing about the world except our sense of what an individual is making of it and can make of it.

I have already indicated why Wittgenstein on display matters so much to me. His thinking enables me to argue that attention to display and avowal can free us from the various versions of historicism that sell the imagination short because they reduce the aesthetic to little more than escapist fantasy—at the poles of creation and of consumption.[33] To take texts as aesthetic is for these critics to divorce them from the actual world in which they were composed and served particular purposes. They imagine participating in the aesthetic as buying into consumerist reification, which has to deny the critical force the work can establish when it is seen in a historical perspective. And when critics reject the effort to establish how an act of imagination adapts to its particular sense of problems and possibilities, we get only endless critical allegories vaguely linking texts to form patterns of interest and evasion of which the authors were unaware.

I have to admit that certain kinds of knowledge are indispensable to literary criticism—knowledge mainly about authors and social context. But instrumental efforts to put such knowledge to work seem to me painfully reductive. So I am trying to establish a basis for a different model of how imagination engages audiences by engaging basic social practices, complex temporalities, and intricate dispositional shifts in focus. I think most acts of literary imagination care much less about the referential power of their utterances than they do their capacity to engage an audience in the specific lives that the text can make compelling. And their historical relevance involves how authorial acts engage specific worlds.

Participation, then, is the positioning of ourselves as readers to flesh out how works project and develop a variety of existential implications that we treat as having the power to produce compelling presence. By participating in the life the text affords we try to see into what it is doing and in effect "realize" (Cézanne's term) where the meaningful qualities of the work can lead us.[34] The provisional identifications made possible by participation in the work produce encounters where we are likely to need something more intimate and capable of involving the will than can be produced by any stance seeking knowledge.

The core of my book is the fourth chapter, which attempts to show how Wittgenstein provides an account of expressive behavior capable of capturing most of what is useful for the arts in Hegel's work on that concept but without any of the ontological entailments that accompany Hegel's arguments. Expressions differ from avowals in two important respects. Avowals present states of the self; expressions dramatize them by making manifest and coming to possess certain important properties that the self can be presented as undergoing. An expression analogous to the avowal "I am in pain" might consist of making visible what the pain is and even why the agent feels the need to offer that picture of the self. And expressions try to present models that reflect on how the self is positioned in the expression of pain.

I rely here on Wittgenstein's idea, steeped in the romantic tradition, that making a model for something is sharply distinct from making a copy of that thing. Wittgenstein establishes this crucial distinction in a comment on how we can recognize what aspect an agent sees when confronted with cases of aspect seeing such as Jastrow's duck-rabbit or the figure of a Necker cube, which could be black on white or white on black: "If I know the schematic cube has various aspects, and I want to find out what someone else sees, I can get him to make a model of what he sees, in addition to a copy, or to show such a model; even though he has no idea of my purpose in demanding two accounts" (*PPF,* 135). For Wittgenstein, making a model is not an explanation but a clarification of the contexts by which agents make sense of their own actions. So the concept of model points to a kind of display that is crucial for discourse about the arts because the arts are practices of making, not just avowing or reporting on states of being. Agents elaborate avowals by incorporating them into dramatic models and by situating them in relation to broader contexts. Such models offer self-characterizations making visible and articulate the nature of a subject's intervention in the world.

Think of how often poems present speakers in the process of understanding the very emotions that generate what they are doing. Wordsworth's entire *Prelude* offers an example of this self-situating. And Keats's "Ode to a Nightingale" offers a more impersonal version of the mind trying to model its own involvement in a situation. I use examples from romanticism here in part because in retrospect we can see these works less as examples of a particular body of historical beliefs than as exercises in practical psychology in which we can still participate. Producing a copy of what one sees only reproduces what is available to the eye; the model reveals how one complements the eye by developing how the "I" modifies the available aspects that produce meaningfulness for what is seen.

The movement from the simplest perspectival features of avowal to the making of models can be elaborated concretely if we begin with a statement by Wittgenstein that I will use a great deal because of its elegant simplicity: "If I let my gaze wander round a room and suddenly it lights on an object of striking red colour, and I say 'Red!'—I haven't thereby given a description" (*PPF,* 71). "Red" followed by a period would give a description: it would employ the language game by which we identify and characterize colors. The situation is very different when "red" is followed by an exclamation point.[35] Now the speaker is characterizing an event or a moment of seeing an aspect of a scene that comes as a surprise.[36] So at stake is not a description of the world but one kind of expression that calls attention to the agent's momentary version of a world. In fact, we can say that the point of the exclamation is to announce to an auditor something that might be shared if the auditor can occupy the perspective from which the aspect dawned. Therefore, the auditor's task in responding to the exclamation is to attune herself to seeing the color in a way that makes sense of the agent's surprise.

By my logic, the writing in *Philosophical Investigations* is an exemplary case of expression. This is not because it is personal or therapeutic but because it involves a model for objectifying Wittgenstein's thinking that cannot be processed as argument. His refusal to submit to epistemic concerns is well known: "If my remarks do bear a stamp which marks them as mine, then I do not wish to lay any further claim to them as my property."[37] But I think this passage is rarely contextualized properly. For the appropriate context we need to bring to bear Wittgenstein's concern in *Philosophical Investigations* (531–35) for quite particular modes of expression that cannot be content with any kind of discursive explanation. He begins by distinguishing between sentences where the thought is "common to different sentences" and where "something is expressed only by these words in these positions. (Understanding a poem.)" (ibid., 531). Then he worries about how in the second case one can "explain the expression" and so communicate what one understands" (ibid., 533):

> Ask yourself: How does one lead someone to understand a poem or a theme? The answer to this tells us how one explains the sense here. Hearing a word as having this meaning. How curious that there should be such a thing! Phrased like this, emphasized like this, heard in this way, this sentence is the beginning of a transition to these sentences, pictures, actions.... What happens when we learn to feel the ending of a church mode as an ending? (ibid., 533–35)

Wittgenstein's "this" invokes where we can find the distinctive worldliness of the arts: it indicates attitudes seeking attunement to "sentences, pictures, actions," and it suggests the presence of a general framework by which such attunements can be considered sensitive, complex, telling, and exemplary. Similarly, Wittgenstein's remarks on Tolstoy in *Culture and Value* are not concerned with character at all but with the imposing and problematic presence of the author's insistent values. Wittgenstein is less concerned with explaining either the characters or the novelist than in directly engaging the sensibility that works through constructing the characters.

I worry that I am being pious. So I have to ask what kind of evidence we can produce of the powers I am claiming that we develop in our seeing in to works of art. This question will lead to the final three chapters in this book. First I try to handle this question purely on a level of our powers to make sense of the world; then I address the more difficult question of why these powers might matter for social life even though they must show themselves as consequential individual by individual. In responding to this question I will have to return to how I proposed to interpret the concern of idealist aesthetics for what powers art confers. The reward for bearing with such repetition is that I can finally be quite brief in summarizing the concluding two chapters.

My fifth chapter concentrates on how Wittgenstein treats the concept of exemplification because I believe this topic addresses the fundamental way that art proves useful in a purely practical sense. Fundamentally, exemplification in imaginative writing is how the qualities made manifest by "seeing in" produce fresh capacities for "seeing as."[38] When we have read a text so as to activate our sense of our powers of comprehension and sympathy, we are able to use selected images or senses of the entire project as examples that provide instruments for sorting our worlds in different ways. Finding a red that can bring exclamation is no small matter because it can modify our entire sense of how colors relate to each other and come alive because of those relations. More generally, John Gibson helps us imagine the flexibility of exemplification by developing a concept of semantic ascent and semantic descent for what literary texts make visible in their constructive activity.[39] We can focus on small features of texts in relation to worldly situations, or we can imagine using the fullness of semantic ascent to think about how the overall work might function as a mode of awareness. Think of how responding fully to the last cantos of Dante's *Paradiso* can modify our understandings of both Christianity and of reading. Here participation becomes a fully dynamic concept dramatizing how union with God has to take place at the limits of understanding. More striking yet is how Dante's text exemplifies the way readers themselves can encounter those limitations as conditions of opening themselves to what can be paradisical about understanding.

This creation of readerly expansiveness involves much more than an increased repertoire for appreciating certain modes of activity. Engaging in texts that energize the imagination also makes possible a range of experiences of valuing that modify our senses of who we are and our possible places in the natural and social world—as my use of the example of Casaubon makes perhaps too visible. So I offer two closing chapters on valuing—the first attentive to valuing as a specific aspect of slow reading[40] and the final one on the concept of appreciation, which tries to account for the reader's self-reflexive engagement in such valuing. Both chapters set the kinds of values literary experience emphasizes against various languages borrowed from ethics, which now seem the only unembarrassed way to claim values for our attentions to literary experience.

If one wants to elaborate roles evaluation can play in literary experience, one must first clear the ground by pointing out how the versions of ethics that address literary texts are severely problematic. Critics applying traditional modes of ethical evaluation tend to trust to the power to generalize from complex literary events and so put determinate judgment in the place of the intricate modes of reflection, which can be displayed and invite attunement. And those poststructuralist models focused on the singularity that requires ethical responsiveness tend to generalize this singularity into a quite general demand to be responsive to the otherness of the other. In fact, literary texts are typically neither purely other nor instances that invite categorical judgments: they are particular events that invite various modes of care and efforts at evaluating their force as particulars.

The discussion of this valuing poses substantial problems because values are very complex entities. Values fuse personal commitments with social expectations, and they emerge and get tested over long processes. I do not know what my values are, although I think I know what my commitments are at any given time. The commitments are features that one can say motivate specific actions or constrain them. Commitments depend on the values but by no means exhaust them or even adequately represent the deep structures by which they fold into one another.

I also know what is involved in valuing specific situations, real and imagined, because I immediately compare their specific qualities to other possible versions of the situation, and because I reflect on what seems to elicit the degree of caring that I can bring to the situation. Valuing seems both an outgrowth of and a reward for moving from habitual levels of perception to a sense that greater degrees of concentration and participation are called for. We might even come to feel that we have developed somewhat new powers of attention and sympathy to what had previously not been of such interest to us. Or we might develop somewhat new attitudes in relation to our reading, attitudes that range from modes of care to modes of ironic distance from typical ways of caring.

In short, a concern for valuing is what makes close reading into slow reading. And it ultimately shows why instrumental reading is so reductive because it locates value only in application rather than in participation. When we seek to apply a text, we are usually talking about it rather than becoming involved in the specific conditions established by the play of forces that constitute the work. I want to argue then that the experience of valuing the text serves as the fullest mode of the experiencing it makes possible.

When he talks about his own reading of literary texts, Wittgenstein concentrates on entirely personal powers to make identifications that absorb his self-consciousness in the lives of other people. (Or, in the case of Shakespeare, he is fascinated by worrying about why he cannot identify with the author even as he feels the power of his characters.) So I want to use his perspective on the personal to isolate how reading expands and intensifies self-consciousness while in effect giving that self-consciousness the capacity to engage itself in how other people deploy those same powers. Yet, we also see in Wittgenstein's wariness about claiming ethical values in relation to individual persons how our comfort in talking about ethics as a generalized mode of assessment leads to an immense narrowing of the kinds of values of and concerns about powers distinctive to individual agents.

In order to fight off the authority of "ethics" I think we need to develop an overall model of actually attributing values that is generated by the specific modes of attunement and participation called for by particular texts. Then we have to find a language for reflecting on how we go about valuing these texts. For this level of analysis I will try to revive the concept of appreciation. Appreciation in our responses to art is simply the acknowledgment that our pleasures in reading implicate us in asking what possible difference in the world the experience of that object might make. Appreciation is the result of reflecting on how valuing has guided and rewarded our attention. And it is a source of awareness of the self as having capacities that are blocked by the modes of resentment so common in a world where abilities and rewards seem so often incongruously matched. Appreciation puts us in a position to be ashamed at the degree to which resentment governs our own lives, and it promises a world of investments in which we are free to enjoy aspects of the world on their own terms.

Finally, appreciation serves as a reminder of how the values explored in reading are irreducibly personal. Yet that realization proves inseparable from the further realization that a sense of personal powers can often be painfully incomplete without efforts to share what proves moving and what can be appreciated for the ways it extends beyond the self. This is a much more limited claim than the fantasies of effective critique or revolutionary sympathy, which motivate a large segment of professional literary criticism. But the push against resentment is also something realizable, renewable, and teachable, so I think it justifies a life spent in those practices.

Appendix to Chapter 1

THE QUESTION OF ATTRIBUTING INTENTIONALITY TO LITERARY TEXTS

Let me be more careful in this additional comment about what is at stake in an effort to establish aesthetic intentionality. Twentieth century literary criticism for the most part labored to deny the importance of intentionality. For example, T. S. Eliot inveighed against any version of intentionality in order to supplement a work's objective structure of words and their implications. The New Critics developed Eliot's wariness into a full theory of the "intentional fallacy" because they felt positing meanings from outside the text violated the integrity of a work of art, as if readers used that concept to justify leaping to the "personality" of the author rather than attending to how the work defined its own purposes. Two influential recent positions then shift from the danger of misconstruing intention to the argument that intentions are at best fictive structures providing an unwarranted unity for the writing. Deconstructive thinking concentrates on problems inherent in postulating any kind of deep identity, given the ways that seeking such unities itself produces endless differences that deny any enabling unity. And a quite recent series of ethical arguments insists that seeking authorial intentions denies the possibility of something such as mutual creation between author and audience that provides an exemplary politics.

Let us begin by addressing the tendency in formalist criticism to argue that we do not need to hypothesize about intentions because simply accounting for the form and the manner of the writing suffices to give a shape to aesthetic experience. I think this mode of attention provides no human language for the shaping and so intensifies the danger that a language of objects will suffice for how literary experience is transmitted. This is a boon for those theorists who want to stress the materiality of the art object and its power to challenge our reliance on standard human predicates for our acts of valuing. But I think the richer language of challenge comes when we can see ourselves responding to the activity of making something that posits a pointed provocation actively threatening our complacencies. This resistance to rooting intentionality in the impersonal working of an object avoids the risk that without human predicates there will be too many possible structures and no way to counter claims about indeterminacy. The second position, deconstruction, handles that question of producing something such as practical coherence for the work by questioning the validity of that desire. Perhaps our felt need for coherence is merely a projection produced by our linguistic habits. Perhaps the freedom from the practical we give literary texts makes them a perfect testing ground for how we might resist those habits and recognize how they make us complicit in patterns of repression. Perhaps there is no text we can call an authentic one. It may be the very nature of text to be dependent on construals. And it may be the very nature of construals that they be steeped in imaginary features that establish discrete perspectives rather than cooperate in forging agreement about something as abstract as the unity or the purpose of an individual text.

One might think this deconstructive position is a dead end for criticism because it has difficulty sponsoring any kind of coherent conversation as the price we pay for recognizing our capacity for proliferating differences. Indeed I think it is. But the critique of identity thinking has generated a quite powerful third movement to locate meaningfulness in neither author nor text nor reader but in the conversations spawned by treating all three as active participants in the formation of meaning. Even if each construal is steeped in imaginary projections, we do not have to stop with individual readers. We can treat texts as if their social role is to inspire conversations among these discrete interpretations. Then such conversations become models for political organization: hierarchy is replaced by interaction and the rigidity of stable structures of meaning by the flexibility of people hearing and responding to the needs and insights of various readers.[41]

These various critiques of intentionality indicate that a great deal is at stake, conceptually at least, in how we decide what kinds of shapes we can attribute to literary experience. I say "shapes" advisedly because I want to hold open the possibility that it is not quite meanings that readings typically construct for literary works. The concept of construing a shape allows us to imagine that we do not try to fix a meaning but to characterize a set of actions folded in on one another. If we cannot structure our interpretive discourses around what the author is trying to do in the making, we are necessarily trapped in abstractions such as "meaning," which breed counterabstractions such as "free play" and "conversation." And if the only role of authors is to foster either free play or conversation, there is not much of an incentive to labor over the precise articulation of feelings or intricate structural layering establishing possible significance for the actions rendered. This is why I propose as an alternative to the figure of co-creation the ideal of the reader as the person following the leader in dancing a tango. That participatory position requires every bit of the dancer's concentration and creativity to fulfill what is potential in the music and in the situation.

However attractive the politics, the ideal of fostering conversation without any talk of recognition reduces the value of what authors achieve to sheer contingencies of response. And it has to ignore the important argument offered by Walter Michaels and Stephen Knapp several years ago—that it is very difficult to characterize any verbal act without attributing a specific intention to mean.[42] Without intention there is too much possibility and too little focus. The text remains just a thing rather than a "work" inviting a specific mode of imaginative activity. And the denial of intention makes the role of the critic primarily the recording of impressions rather than efforts to teach and to persuade about how the work achieves what it does. The best that proponents of reader-construal can do is to see art contributing to a freedom that any conversation might produce without any clear sense that this freedom is directed or rewarded by recognition of what authorship can involve. We end up celebrating how literature undoes Western identity-thinking.

Positing a concrete mode of intentionality that can resist these impulses toward freeing the reader is a difficult task, especially for someone who aligns with Wittgenstein's critiques of attributing objectness to inner psychological phenomena.[43] One has to paint an attractive picture for an alternative set of readerly practices. So let us try to imagine how there might be an aesthetic ground for positing a form of intentionality that does not necessarily explain the artist's decisions by projecting into the author's psyche, but tries instead to find a purposiveness within the text. Intentions have to be displayed—not explained. And the theory of intention has to explain why we must be satisfied with display.

There are times when we cannot characterize our experience of a text without attributing to the author a desire to open up what he or she sees as an inner psychological being—notably in Wordsworth and in Whitman and, more ironically, in Fielding and in Sterne. But I think the most prudent path is to imagine that the relevant intentionality is established simply when the author signs a work or lets it be published or perhaps even just includes it in a letter, as Emily Dickinson did. For that signature in effect indicates that there has been a carefulness in making decisions that stage responsibility toward what the audience might expect of a work of art. Such responsibility does not entail subordinating the work entirely to the assumptions of the audience at a given time in a given culture. Rather it simply entails signaling how the work might be modifying those assumptions.

We might call the signature the establishing of an aesthetic intentionality: the relevant intention becomes the signs determining how the work produces conditions for a distinctive experience. Not all aesthetic intentions will involve the same considerations because understandings of what is a literary work will change. But almost all works can be read for how an author will be responsive to the very general assumptions a culture holds about what makes an activity belong to the domain of literary imaginings. In ambitious writing since the Renaissance in the West the author's signature indicates taking responsibility for the fact that an object reflects a series of decisions elaborating a distinctive act of mind and specifying how affective values might be embodied in the modes of attention and responsiveness the work pursues. There need not be any claim that in postulating an intention one also justifies something such as an explanation or a unified account of the text. For often the intention is not to mean but to display a relation of significant force fields within which tensions need not be reconciled or actions submitted to rational form.

It is a striking fact that the major classical texts in Western culture, such as *The Aeneid* and *The Divine Comedy,* manage to be intensely personal while making it clear that it is the work itself that establishes how it is to be read. And that fact establishes the model for their most ambitious heirs: Joyce could take all sorts of freedoms with epic form because he could trust that the logic of his reworking was visible simply in how he rendered the actions of his narrative. In fact, Joyce's *Finnegans Wake* is perhaps our best example of a text that is intensely purposive and controlled yet resistant to any abstract statement of its meaning. Conversely, Pound could finally judge that he had failed to make his *Cantos* cohere because the effort at organizing his incredibly diverse materials was everywhere visible.

Chapter 2

THE WORK TEXTS DO

Toward a Phenomenology of Imagining Imaginatively

> The concept of an aspect is related to the concept of imagination. In other words, the concept "Now I see it as . . ." is related to "Now I am imagining that . . ." Doesn't it take imagination to hear something as a variation on a particular theme? And yet one does perceive something in so hearing it.
>
> —WITTGENSTEIN, *Philosophy of Psychology—A Fragment*

When is the last time that you read contemporary criticism that was explicitly concerned with the activity of the imagination? Such occasions seem increasingly rare: imagination now is very rarely invoked, like the family member whose past seems an embarrassment for an eager new generation of social climbers. I contend that this disappearance of imagination from critical discourse presents a substantial problem for literary studies. With no mode of production specific to what many literary texts claimed to embody, and with no sense of the kinds of power for which they usually strive, one comes to see immediately the negative side of contemporary criticism's turn to moral and political critical orientations. But my purposes here are not primarily to elaborate problems in contemporary attitudes. We have already considered the costs of what Attridge calls criticism's turn to the instrumental roles of using literature to establish objects of knowledge. For Attridge, literary critics increasingly ignore the values produced by attention to the singularity of the texts in order to pursue how other disciplines such as sociology and economic history might stage relations between texts and their historical contexts or, one might add now, stage relations between texts and the neurophysiology responsible for us making them present in the first place.

Instead, my job here is to develop one reason for this change in a way that may help lead us back to fascination with how particular authors pursue values that depend on the working of imagination. Devoting oneself to studying these values will probably never have the appeal of being able to test new generalizations or feeling that one is constructing knowledge on which others can build. But this loss of social purpose can be compensated for by a much richer sense of what specific literary experiences can offer individual agents. And the turn to imagination is simply more accurate to the distinctive powers literary texts both engage and develop. It is rarely for purposes of knowledge that one rereads texts or lets oneself dwell on how they handle details and shape structures. Without a powerful account of the productive forces these texts cultivate and shape as significant singular objects, we cannot see them as contributing anything distinctive to social life. They become mere instances of general conditions elaborated by the critic.

What Happened to the Role of Imagination in Contemporary Criticism?

Romantic poetry sought to resist the primarily discursive social focus of its predecessors by what Coleridge theorized as the "esemplastic imagination." This version of imagination could explain how poetry and fiction might invoke versions of Nietzsche's "slow reading" because that model of reading can make present the work of subjective energies in the process of establishing emotional significance for the phenomena engaged by the texts. Tracking the generative force of these subjective energies just is the means by which we come to encounter the text's power.

By this focus on the expressive subject, a poem such as "Tintern Abbey" could criticize the passions of the poet's youth yet dialectically find those passions the source for an expansive sense of how the imagination could view the symbolic force of this fusion of nature and mind. In addition, poetry could honor this sense of expanded spirit at home in nature by claiming for itself a distinctive mode of truth—not truth to the facts of nature but truth to what the spirit's enthusiasms might establish because of the specific modes of engagement with the world that get exemplified in the work. These ways of focusing consciousness provide public articulations of what can be involved in our reflections on our experiences.[1]

These romantic experiments in isolating imagination as a productive force do not have to be taken as efforts to shore up a waning body of Christian beliefs. But the enthusiastic speculation on what enthusiasm might involve did not fare well in the twentieth-century critical discourse, confronted by intense demands to justify what they could contribute to a secular world shaped by the discoveries of science. A scientific culture demanded ways of turning such experiences into objects of study rather than indulgences in sympathetic participation. So the dominant force in American literary criticism in the middle of the twentieth century—the writing and teaching of the New Criticism—endeavored to reject most of romantic poetry while trying to save its celebration of the imagination by transforming it into terms more appropriate for a restrained, secular set of discursive practices. The primary figure in this story has to be I. A. Richards because of how thoroughly his book on Coleridge became prelude to his utter psychologizing of reading as the activation of both positive and negative impulses in the mind. Gone entirely is Coleridge's model of expressive encounter fusing the mind with the forces driving nature.

The Christian New Critics hated Richards's versions of psychology, as they hated all scientism. But in order to combat the increasing importance of "empirical truth" in their society they had to put the claims for their beloved imagination into terms more compatible with science than even those Richards had used, complaining all the while about the increasing domination of Enlightenment values. They had to insist that the imagination was a vehicle for developing what they called "nondiscursive truths," which were capable of establishing objective ways of reflecting on experience that were undeniably as real as what empiricism could show yet indemonstrable by any resource science could invoke. And, in the same spirit, they transformed Coleridge's notion of organicism: what had been evidence in the text of how the mind could fuse with nature became merely a formal condition characterizing the density and fusion of internal relations within the literary text. The New Critics purchased a kind of truth for imagination by gutting romantic views of expressive agency and turning all assertion into paradox and dramatic irony. They thought they could expunge manifest signs of subjectivity while projecting the need to treat texts very much as persons.

The most amusing, and perhaps the saddest, aspect of my narrative involves Paul de Man's largely successful effort to resuscitate romantic poetry by showing how that poetry had brilliantly challenged every value that the New Critics would deploy to save the concept of a distinctive literary imagination:

> The lesson to be derived from the evolution of American formalist criticism is twofold. It reaffirms first of all the necessary presence of a totalizing principle as the guiding impulse of the critical process. In the New Criticism, this principle consisted of a purely empirical notion of the integrity of literary form, yet the mere presence of such a principle could lead to the disclosure of distinctive structures of literary language (such as ambiguity and irony) although these structures contradict the very premises on which the New Criticism was founded.[2]

Ambiguity and irony contradict an empirical notion of literary form because these are states that cannot be the properties of objects: such states have to be interpreted as deriving from intentions.

So de Man can also argue that the New Critics could not sustain their claim for the autonomy of the art object. That claim depends on a notion of the "intentional fallacy" that had to treat literary form itself as a property of objects rather than a property derived from intentions: "The difference between the stone and the chair distinguishes a natural object from an intentional object. The intentional object requires a reference to a specific act as constitutive of its being" (*FI*, 24). The New Critics banished the role of the maker but insisted on all the powers of what could only be made rather than found: "Second, the rejection of the principle of intentionality, dismissed as fallacious, prevented the integration of these discoveries within a truly coherent theory of literary form. The ambivalence of American formalism is such that it was bound to lead to a state of paralysis" (ibid., 32).

This critique seems to me exactly right. We do not find active formal principles in an object; we construct them as the activity of a subject (ibid., 25). But then de Man has his own dilemma. How can we characterize this attributed presence of a composing intelligence? With his next book, *Allegories of Reading,* he developed an elaborate theoretical position defining this composing intelligence as simultaneously admitting the fictionality of what is imagined and trying to posit a quasi-objective illusory substance for that difference from actual natural objects. From Sartre he learned to treat intentionality as an ontological issue rather than as a psychological one. That is, intentionality cannot be subsumed into active being. Instead it is always trying to evade the fact of the subject's difference, or nonbeing in the world of objects.

Imagination then becomes the vehicle by which intentionality produces essentially rhetorical constructs oriented toward constituting substance for an insubstantial self. The building of fictional spaces derives from efforts at naturalizing a freedom that is fundamentally negative, as in Sartre's philosophy. And romanticism becomes the often self-aware attempt to put a naturalized theology to this endless rhetorical task of establishing substance for human subjectivity. But de Man just assumes on philosophical grounds that the theology is a rhetorical prop, however brilliantly applied. He does not consider the possibility that the brilliant applications are so striking because they actually find in our relations to nature something worth celebrating about ourselves.

We might quarrel about the details that are given short shrift in my account of the fate of imagination over two centuries. But I do not think we can quarrel about the results—that criticism has abandoned the concept and that the lack of a model for literary production has left ambitious critics no choice but to turn to other disciplines for grounding their work on what literary imaginations have produced. I am not sure any talk now about imagination will have much impact on this situation. But as modes of reading proliferate without any serious concern for imagination, it is worth testing whether a persuasive case can be made for its capacities to develop much thought without any determining concept.

The first step is to see that de Man could collapse imagination into intentionality because he treated consciousness as an ontological issue rather than a psychological one. Imagination had one central inescapable task of concealing and partially acknowledging the illusory basis by which we construct a meaning-bearing human world different from the world we find in the objects that confront us. But the entire idea of an ontology of intentionality seems to me problematic. In an age of neuroscience it is hard not to think that de Man, like Sartre, offers at best an oversimplified sense of nature as objects rather than as consisting also of relations and forces, among which there are the functions of mental life. So he necessarily also has an oversimplified sense of intention as only a principle compensating for this lack of objectivity by producing constant illusion and self-evasive fictions.

The way out of de Man's morass is first just to examine the variety of functions imagination performs rather than to derive these functions from what they might seem to have to perform within a given philosophical schema. Then we can shift our focus from an ontology of imagination to a psychological focus on ways of imagining, where multiple functions might be visible that matter for our recognizing what human powers we can exercise in secular worlds.

Therefore I will elaborate a phenomenological approach to imagination that I hope will provide an entirely secular yet highly suggestive model capable of both eliciting and justifying many of the powers attributed to it by my holy trinity of Kant, Hegel, and Schiller. Such a model will also enable us to make claims for the social significance of literary experience because of the self-reflexive modes the active imagination can afford social life. In my view this active imagination invites participation in sensibilities at work in trying to clarify the nature and possible consequences of our affective investments in various aspects of experience. And in a society where resentment is a terrifying logical response to deep divisions in wealth and power without any decent ideological defense for those differences, such acts of participation may make possible a competing psychological economy based largely on appreciating what can be accomplished by human constructive powers.

What Is to Be Done: Toward a Phenomenology of Imagination

When I call on phenomenology, I refer to a form of practical analysis attempting to clarify distinctive psychological features of imagination at work within practical experience.[3] I am not qualified to engage the ontological questions inseparable from phenomenology for Husserl, Heidegger, and their heirs. And I am concerned only with what one might call a phenomenology that clarifies how we typically use expressions such as "imaginatively" and "with imagination." This means that my version of phenomenology need not deal with all aspects of imaginative life, especially with hallucination. Instead the theory will have to take account only of how attributions about value can be grammatically inseparable from the functions we analyze.[4]

Fortunately, I can develop this practical orientation by elaborating several categories from Edward Casey's brilliant *Imagining: A Phenomenological Study* while also making some modifications to put this study in dialogue with contemporary concerns of artists and critics.[5] Then I will turn to John Ashbery's early poem "The Instruction Manual" to spell out how a writer can not only deploy the imagination imaginatively but also deliberately build a model, or an instruction manual, by which self-reflexively to elaborate in purely secular terms what the powers of imagination can produce and solicit.[6] Ashbery is aware that he is at every point in the poem undercutting a rhetoric developed by the New Critics, who were Ashbery's teachers at Harvard, about how imagination is a source of nondiscursive truth. The poem offers a daydream and not a vision. But Ashbery is by no means content with irony. If there is no "truth" in the poem, there is a great deal of significance in how it stages the activity in making the poem.

The poem deploys a manual that relocates imaginative power to emphasize control of tone and perspective and the weaving of the lyrical ego into manifestly public registers of affective life. This control offers ample consolation for the poem's lack of high seriousness because it can put on stage the engaged ego's capacity to flesh out fascination with the lives and loves of other people. In effect, Ashbery builds a model of secular imagination at work as it interprets one's pleasures in entertaining one's own bonds to society. And in the process this poem offers the possibility that its way of imagining may afford a release from the kinds of anxieties that produced romantic metaphysics: there is no need to offer elaborate reconciliations of the energies of self-consciousness and the sheer presence of the world beyond that self-consciousness because even the daydream can afford a great deal of engagement in what seems life beyond the ego.

I think there is a case to be made that Ashbery defines a post–New Critical poetics in the poem's foregrounding of an apparently thin surface and playful fascination with particulars rather than demanding the depth, compression, and complexity dominant in modernist lyrics. But here I will approach questions about imagination on a larger scale, arguing that the play of tones and surfaces in "The Instruction Manual" establishes a plausible, secular, postromantic model for how the work of imagination gets foregrounded in a wide variety of texts from Homer to Robert Hass. Given this ambition, I probably should follow my discussion of Ashbery with poems about place, from Vergil's *Georgics,* to Jonson's "To Penshurst," to Marvell's "Upon Appleton House," to Bryant's "The Prairies."[7] But this seems too predictable and not sufficiently focused on the best way to bring out the distinctive sense of powers elaborated by Casey's account of imagination.

So I will turn instead to a comparison between Ashbery's poem and Yeats's "Leda and the Swan" because I want to draw out how the two poems try out parallel functions despite their quite different subject matters and imaginative orientations. If despite their historical differences we find a significant self-conscious sense of shared resources in these two texts, we can have some confidence that we are pursuing vital features of imaginative activity worth guiding our readings of poems and of other kinds of literary texts from a variety of cultural situations.

Casey's Four Attributes of Imagination, plus a Further Consideration

Casey's book is devoted to the imagination in practical life, not in literature—so it positions us to see the many practical roles imagination can play even as it makes discourse about "truth" either impossible or reductive in relation to what these actions involve.[8] In order to elaborate the four categories I will borrow from him, I want to develop a simple social scenario as our test case. Consider two people planning to have lunch. Notice first that although such actions might seem determined in retrospect, at the moment of imagining these agents seem free from all practical restrictions—at both poles of subject and object. One can picture the couple with almost unlimited freedom to determine where they will go and what the menu might be, in contrast to all practical judgment. (Even if they know they cannot afford something, they can imagine treating what they can afford as if it were the place they wished they could attend.) Second, we see that this sense of freedom correlates with an infinite set of possibilities for composing and combining the details of the situation, in sharp contrast to the demands in typical situations, where perception shapes discourse. Think here of fourteenth-century Florentine and Siennese painting, their composition so of a piece with the fantastic dimension of saints' lives.

Perception works in terms of the logic of picturing. It activates a relation to a physical world with its own deep structure, independent of the perceiver, who contributes a perspective but not a shape. In the order of perceptions there are degrees of visibility: some properties of the scene are foregrounded; some grasped only fleetingly; and some assert pressures (such as a history of previous interactions) that are not noticed at all. The menu has both a history and a shape that determine how its particular aspects are to be read. But with an imagined situation there is no inherent logic and no pressure to recognize specific salient details. Salience is determined by the imaginers, and there is (phenomenologically) no other world that imposes underlying demands. As Jeff Blevins once put it in conversation, "imagination is the only guarantee for the shape taken by its contents." Our constructed menu might be fit for the gods.

Such freedom does not entail that imaginers will not choose to present their materials as if they were bound to the logic of perception. But these literary imaginings will usually have moments when authors revel in their freedom and simply select what feels right rather than what would be demanded were they to follow a historian's practice. Yet at the same time, the freedom itself can appear insubstantial because its world is not bound to the logic of perception. Freedom within the imagination can be both illusory and purposive. Because imaginative activity seems a mere projection, we are always tempted to locate causes for it, yet it seems also capable of treating itself as shaping what emerges.

This freedom to act without constraint and the corresponding freedom from latent structure have two significant consequences that complete my borrowing from Casey. The third feature stressed by a phenomenology of imagination is its capacity for staging infinitely subtle tonalities for situations—as perhaps every lover knows. Because there are no clear constraints on the subject or the ways details are related to one another, there are no categorical principles by which we can expect to draw out the relations among those details so as to conform to any prevailing notion of sense. Shem will never catch up with Shaun. The principles of relation are shaped simply by the details, and our modes of apprehending them as aspects of a concretely emerging set of conjunctions.

An imagined face does not have to resemble what we think faces show, so one possibility for an imaginative representation is to suggest subtle desires and demands and fears that take strange shapes as they escape our typical routes of repression. Imaginative figuration has virtually unlimited control over the play of surfaces, fold upon fold, as details breed details, gestures breed corresponding gestures, and affective tones multiply freely—think of Picasso's portraits of women. But an observer also has to recognize that this kind of imaginative activity pays a significant price for its freedom. Because they are not bound to the logic of perception, the fantasy features have no specifiable depth: viewers or readers might find the figures of imagination suggestive, but they might also find them simply unintelligible.

This issue of interpretability leads us to our fourth feature. The play of surfaces often creates the very desire for in-depth interpretation that it frustrates. Few events in the domain of the arts are as depressing as the effort to pin down imaginative flights of fancy in terms of psychoanalytic or moral explanations, as in Freud's reading of *La Tempesta* or Martha Nussbaum's reading of almost anything. Purposiveness, if it is manifest at all, need be manifest only within the arrangement of surface details and so cannot provide a discursive rationale for them, however plausible the effects achieved. I agree with Casey's claim that because of the plural surfaces imagination can develop, the only effective way to offer interpretations of imaginative activity is to grant the product the force of self-evidence. The work is replete and so can only stand beside efforts at interpretation in partial mockery and in partial yearning for what might anchor it within the interpretive models provided by a culture. As William Kentridge put it when asked how his father, a renowned lawyer, influenced his work, "I think having parents who are lawyers pushed me to find an activity in which I could find meaning with a different kind of logic that was impervious to cross-examination."[9]

I mean by the force of self-evidence simply the way the imaginative activity folds in on itself so that we can establish its significance only by accepting its terms or rejecting the episode entirely. Typically we determine meanings by the conjunction of appropriate contexts that bear on what the speaker might want to say and how that statement might be appropriate for the occasion. With imagined worlds there is a paucity of effective external contexts, so we have to rely on what we see as relations among the elements of what we observe—think about dreaming or even speculating about what one will do in a situation. We still build contexts that make features significant, but we have little justification for invoking these contexts beyond the way that the contexts proposed seem to emerge out of our concrete need to connect specific elements and ways of speaking within the act in question.[10]

I want to add to Casey's categories a fifth feature of a phenomenology of imagination that is basic to literary experience and central to the possibility of folding our awareness of qualities of experience into our typical ways of assessing imaginative acts when they are self-consciously deployed. We can use value terms such as "imaginatively" or "with imagination" when a text or an action seems to invite attention to how it deploys the four features of imagination we have been considering in order to engage actual or possible states of affairs. A range of value predicates becomes available for how we characterize where the textual crosses the existential. Then we measure how imagination is used—not by imposing general standards but by examining how a specific purposiveness is deployed.

Think again of Claudius's speech or Wordsworth's staging of memory in "Tintern Abbey." We ask how the imagining might matter to the force of the presentation or to its capacity to produce insight or to eliciting conviction that the perspective developed brings passion and compassion to the materials that it distributes. The danger here is that our concern for values pertaining to practical life dilutes our attention to the capacity for self-evidence that makes imagination so important to writers in the first place. The possible pleasure and the possible joy here are in how the conditions for self-evidence provide responses to the needs and questions dramatized in the imagined scenario. In such cases we find the action of imagination offering significant perspectives on real-world concerns and problems.

Ashbery's "Instruction Manual" as Manual for How Imagination Works

Idealist and romantic thinkers could not resist making too much of a good thing by interpreting imagination's claims to freedom and to modes of self-evidence as giving us access to "the one life within us and abroad." So I turn to Ashbery's "The Instruction Manual" as both an implicit critique of romantic views of imagination and a modeling of quite different means of accessing its substantial powers that come much closer to respecting its phenomenological qualities as elemental features of practical life. I am especially interested in how Ashbery's tone suggests the capacity to release imagination from the self-absorbed features of romantic lyricism so that it might participate more fully in a new kind of social space not shaped in accord with the authority of the poet.

In essence, imagination in this poem develops possibilities for bringing a sense of emotional resonance to bear on the world—not by interpreting that world but by fleshing out details so that they reach out both to the possible sources of feeling in the public scene and to how an audience might be expected to internalize those feelings as elements that reveal its own capacity for shared sympathy and understanding. As model, the poem becomes an instruction manual for what can be accomplished in escaping the task of writing instruction manuals. The poem's daydream becomes a mode of self-evidence both producing and referring to how imagination can do work in the actual world. In fact, in choosing the daydream Ashbery establishes a mode of lyricism where production and reference are completely interwoven. And this act of imagining is so insistently self-conscious that it merges with a meta-imaginative inquiry into what powers imagination has and does not have. It is this level of the imagination aware of its own activity that highlights the emotional complexity of the relations to the real world, on which the poem begins and concludes.

The poem opens with the speaker's wishing he did not have to write an instruction manual and envying those he sees from his window not oppressed by that task. He engages these alternatives by reverting to his typical practice of daydreaming—in this case of Guadalajara, the city in Mexico he most wants to see for the first time. So he composes the city in his daydream. At first the details seem conventional and general. How can a poem on this subject not begin with a band playing European music in the public square and the flower girls handing out flowers? It is almost as if the imagination followed a script already written and rewritten. But soon we realize that this speaker has a penchant for particular persons and colors, from one particular girl in rose and blue to serving girls in green offering green and yellow fruit, and eventually to a parade, where attention is focused on a dapper little man in deep blue:

> . . . On his head sits a white hat
> And he wears a mustache which has been trimmed for the occasion.
> His dear one, his wife, is young and pretty;
> her shawl is rose, pink, and white.[11]

The poetry here resides in the attention to made-up detail as a condition of a strange tone that at once acknowledges distance and self-indulgently tries to bridge that divide. Details bubble over in long lines because everything flows so easily from the conjunction of dream, conventional detail, and enthusiastic participation. Within the framework provided by these clichéd details, scenes take shape that seem impossible not to visualize. So perhaps what I am treating as stock elements are better seen as the effects of a cultural grammar into which the dream enters. The grammar offers at once a panoply of details and a sense of a shared world because the speaker's dream offers access to what proves a common space for fantasy. And the commonness miraculously has no deleterious effect on the sheer exuberance of what is permitted within the dream.

Now the way is prepared for treating the imagination as a complex actualizing of thoughts that Wittgenstein's understanding of philosophical grammar makes possible. The poem moves beyond seeing to envisioning full participation in this constructed world as its texture of embedded desires also becomes visible (as avowal turned model):

> Here come the boys! They are skipping and throwing little
>   things on the sidewalk
> Which is made of gray tile. One of them, a little older, has a toothpick
>   in his teeth.
> He is silenter than the rest, and affects not to notice the pretty
>   young girls in white,
> But his friends notice them, and shout their jeers
>   at the laughing girls. (*ACP,* 6)

Then, for first time after setting up the dream, the narrator intrudes as "I" because he wants to hear a conversation between a particular girl and a boy that his story has produced. It is as if the collective picture of young boys and girls matters primarily for the particular sense of romance that it might elicit. Then, perhaps weary of this "I," our narrator takes up a voice that could be essentially a native guide, now strikingly in the first-person plural:

> Let us take this opportunity to tiptoe into one of the side streets.
> Here you may see one of those white houses with green trim
> That are so popular here. Look—I told you! . . .
> An old woman in gray sits there, fanning herself with a palm leaf
>   fan.
> She welcomes us to her patio, and offers us a cooling drink.
> "My son is in Mexico City," she says. "He would welcome you too,
> If he were here. But his job is with a bank there.
> Look, here is a photograph of him."
> And a dark-skinned lad with pearly teeth grins out at us from the worn
>   leather frame.

> We thank her for her hospitality, for it is getting late
> And we must catch a view of the city, before we leave, from a good
>   high place. (*ACP*, 7)

It seems as if the more the narrator daydreams, the more he is enfolded within the details of the dream, so he becomes the only one capable of guiding us through this self-enclosing picture. Then as the role of guide takes hold, so do the pronouns "we" and "you" that make this "here" a fully social object (capable of being balanced with "there" to recapitulate in another key the situation of the entire poem). "Here" inspires a playful but profound range of indexical references—from the space produced by the dream, in which green trim is so popular, to the hypothetical that her son would welcome us if he were "here," to the mother's directing attention to the photograph, to the activities of talking and of writing with what seems utter transparency. We might also note that as "here" takes over, there is no need to rely on references to "I." How could such intense participation not establish a sense that the subject shares the world produced by the scene? And how could such detail not shape intersubjective space, even producing dialogue on the diegetic and authorial levels?

The affective power of the poem depends on its correlating two aspects of imaginative life—its productive dimensions, by which it escapes writing the demanded instruction manual, and the self-reflexive dimension, by which the poem fleshes out and takes pleasure in its own productive powers to develop a different kind of instruction manual. For Ashbery the core of imaginative life is the sheer capacity to select details in a way that elicits powers to inhabit and extend what the details bring to consciousness. The text becomes the presentation of a series of actions inviting an audience to participate in the transformation of scattered, insistently arbitrary details into a dense, coherent, and playful particularizing of elements that function as examples of life in Guadalajara. And the scene as it emerges fills out three worlds—an imagined picture of an intricate social scene, a rendering of practices by which the imagination itself becomes a manifest principle of activity, and a lightly held but intense social critique of a work life that requires using the imagination as a vehicle for escape.[12] As the speaker elaborates each of these worlds, he mobilizes for self-consciousness the processes by which we can come to appreciate what is involved in our capacities to give significance to fictional sequences—without forcing that significance into discursive intelligence.

Each choice in the poem is experienced as playfully uncaused (even though the underlying situation is clearly caused by the bureaucratic deadening of our sources of pleasure). But over time the scene takes on a level of coherence that deepens our engagement, even while we know that the only evidence for the coherence is within the imaginative process itself. There is no external arbitrator for what significance can unfold. Yet Ashbery is careful to produce an increasingly dense social world because the imagined characters find their affective lives embedded in the public details dwelt on and dwelt among by the imagination. As we develop the projected world there seems less to divide us than to unite us. And the entire phenomenon of the dream providing its own self-evidence takes on social force by offering a powerful metaphoric emblem for how this freedom of imagining can take on social weight without needing to be explained. Ultimately this playful tone affords means of reminding ourselves of our beings in common as we dwell on what begins as only an individual's escapist dream. The freedoms of imagination need not preclude putting that freedom to work in fleshing out for self-consciousness what "dwelling" might involve.

There is not much left to the poem, but what remains considerably deepens its affective intensity, in part because the poem seems intent on drawing out how the imagination comes to realize its own limitations. Then it can embrace these limitations to assert another aspect of its potential power more closely woven into the constraints of practical existence. This is where my concern for imagination's evaluating its relation to the real comes to the fore. Once the attention of "we" orients itself to the overall view of the city, there need be only a series of isolated observations based on the expression "there is." But then we almost have to ask, how can there be an interesting end for a daydream that has no inherent logic? Ashbery's response to our question is to shift tonalities and introduce concerns for the imagination's relation to several kinds of realities.

The last specific detail the poem offers is the young boy and girl "now" in the heat of the day lurking "in the shadows of the bandstand." This move to the shadows then allows the poem to turn to the past tense in order to offer explicit self-reflection on what the imagination has enabled and, more strikingly, failed to enable:

> We have seen young love, married love, and the love of an
>   aged mother for her son.
> We have heard the music, tasted the drinks, and looked
>   at colored houses.
> What more is there to do, except stay? And that we cannot do.
> And, as a last breeze freshens the top of the weathered old tower,
>   I turn my gaze
> Back to the instruction manual, which has made me dream of
>   Guadalajara. (*ACP*, 8)

In this adventure imagination cannot conquer the pressures of time and loss. And it cannot successfully evade the loneliness (or capitalist-driven isolation) that has in fact shaped the poem from the start. So at the end the poem seems to take responsibility for the fact that what seemed so casual and so free also had a drivenness to it, almost successfully resisted by the imagination's capacity to dwell in the present tense.

There is ultimately a pathos to the dream condition because, however enticing the engagement in the lives of other people, it is sadly provisional: we cannot stay in our fictions, which is probably why we have license to enjoy them so thoroughly. But the more the poem admits the limitations of its own imaginings, the fuller becomes its positive presentation of how the imagination of the writer can switch registers so that it comes to speak for the dreamers rather than for the object of the dream. One freedom the imagination has is the freedom to reflect on its escapist tendencies and to make those tendencies the focus for adapting its productions to the self-reflexive languages we typically use in characterizing our disappointments.

Pure imagination has no pathos because there is no other, no pressure of the real to impose limitation and pain. Ashbery's writing, on the other hand, is drenched in self-consciously staged pathos because he is so acutely aware that time and loss are the inescapable accompaniments of presence and pleasure. But Ashbery can still honor the freedom of imagination by treating it as the necessary condition of a perpetual conflict between the urge to flee into the daydream and the recognition that daydreams, too, have their existential implications.

The acknowledgement of necessity in "The Instruction Manual" is charmingly and imaginatively handled—by treating necessity as the literal emergence of what Wallace Stevens called "the pressure of reality." In moving toward conclusion, Ashbery deploys an extended simile of the breeze (a staple of romantic lyricism) now useful only to suspend time for a moment and to delay further the task at hand. Then, as the speaker returns to his instruction manual, we recognize in retrospect that accepting our isolation may be the necessary precondition for appreciating what we need from other people. These real-world needs provide the drive to freedom in the first place, and then freedom finds itself fascinated by what might bind it to the lives of other people—in the dream and in the need to accept what dreaming cannot accomplish. Here the freedom is not the same as in most romantic poetry because it is not the result of liberating the imagination from bondage to an epistemic process. Instead, freedom finds its grounding simply in its being woven into the ways imagination turns self-reflexive and has to encounter the limitations of its self-enjoyment (albeit with some pleasure in this encounter because it retains self-possession).

Yeats's "Leda and the Swan": Questioning as Self-Evidence

"Leda and the Swan" obviously has a very different sensibility. Yet it utilizes essentially the same four properties of imagination that Casey emphasizes.[13] And it engages in the same struggle to develop an implicit account of its own distinctiveness by playing on its differences from what any pursuit of discursive knowledge might be able to establish. Consider, for example, how important it is for the speakers in both poems to choose details that trouble our conceptual structures—if only in Yeats's insistence on sonnet compression and in Ashbery's refusal of any confessional impulse. In both poems the fact that the details are blatantly chosen projects a kind of gravity that gives a body to the intentions of the chooser. By stressing how imagination resides in the madeness of the details both poets solicit our establishing complex modes of relatedness among them. Comparing both poems can suggest that reading poetry is largely a matter of seeing in to this interplay between what choices naturalize our sense of the action and which ones stress the ultimate specificity of the shaping intelligence.

Form becomes in many respects another kind of naturalizing, this time in the domain of mind pushed into awareness of its own radical selectiveness and of its historical dependencies. Attributions of form afford a second level for the details by introducing entire explicit and often subtle systems based on choice rather than contingent features of descriptions. So we are invited to treat form as the attribution of a logic to choice that is not based on practical concerns but on the possibilities of fleshing out the way imagination affords self-referring structures providing coherence for the relations among the details. As we will see, this clearly applies to how writers manipulate fixed verse forms, use syntactic figures such as chiasmus, and foreground where structure extends features of what constitutes self-evidence. But self-reference is no less present in how "The Instruction Manual" is built on discrete units focusing on various features of Guadalajara as inviting styles and tones of address.

Finally, these productive energies become inseparable from what the poem treats as the force of the self-evidence by which it takes on a shape and even a role in the social world. The two poems diverge in many ways. Yet both poems rely for their communicative power on the reach for social significance made possible not by overt generalization but by extending and sharpening the powers of specific figures. By stressing the specificity of relational features the text can come to constitute a distinctive or singular attitude that carries exemplary force. We need not seek truth from imagination because its powers of exemplification provide an alternative way of predicating what might be possible.[14]

The efforts at intensified force and the synthetic power of images we see in Yeats's poem are almost totally foreign to the attitudes and emotions explored by Ashbery. For later Yeats, the spirit of casual playfulness would abandon the concentrative force by which the authorial ego can hope to transcend the banalities of ordinary existence. Where Ashbery wanders into the imagined world sponsored by the idea of Guadalajara, the opening lines of "Leda and the Swan" are devoted to theatricalizing a sense of the demands a single world-historical event can make on consciousness—as what is represented and as the pressure on the representing:

> A sudden blow: the great wings beating still
> Above the staggering girl, her thighs caressed[15]

These condensed, quite selective details will not allow the readers to relax but demand complete concentration. Here any spirit of playfulness would count as turning one's eyes away from this emerging tragedy—not a celebration of imagination but an evasion of its purest modes of intensity.

Yet there is much to learn from Ashbery in appreciating how this poem unfolds. Notice, for example, how the poem from the start insists on its autonomy: it is willing to engage a situation that offers no underlying rationale and whose claims for intensity can be justified only by what further evidence the poem can produce that this particular focus on the individual retains the immense consequences of the rape.[16] Notice, too, how a sense of pure event justifies a parallel to Ashbery's freedom in selecting details, combined here with a pronounced freedom in deciding on the modes of syntax that will best mobilize the linguistic surface:

> A sudden blow: the great wings beating still
> Above the staggering girl, her thighs caressed
> By the dark webs, her nape caught in his bill,
> He holds her helpless breast upon his breast. (*WB*, 214)

Even the syntax challenges the authority of understanding in order to stress the apparent arbitrariness of what happens to Leda. For there seem to be two possibilities of organizing this sentence—one as the processing of an absolute construction separate from concerns for modification and the other a series of participles that never quite connects grammatically to the "he" that is the subject of the main clause. Both remain perennially present as conditions of feeling.

Why do these alternatives matter? First, they are again signs of the absoluteness of an imagining that produces autonomous event qualities difficult to reconcile with our ordinary procedures for making sense. (Imagination seems to have strange affinities with rape.) Second, the absoluteness of the imagining links the poem's sense of the radicalness of making with a striking capacity to blend details that evoke the order of perception without submitting to it. There is no background here: all the details align with the focus on the present tense of the rape. Just because imagination has no obligations to the logic of the perceptual order, it can explore means of intensifying the present that might bring sufficient intensity and scope to constitute another order of being. And this order of being might be capable for the moment of providing modes of self-consciousness that are not compatible with practical life (although "there we cannot stay").

Finally, one might argue that the greatness of this poem consists largely in its unwillingness to be satisfied with achieving the level of intensity established by its beginning. Yeats wants to elaborate this intensity by correlating it with a radical sense of structure. It is as if the rest of the poem were an instruction manual making the freedom of self-evidence itself a domain of pure compositional intelligence that extends what we can mean by "intensity" and by "event":

> How can those terrified vague fingers push
> The feathered glory from her loosening thighs?
> And how can body, laid in that white rush,
> But feel the strange heart beating where it lies?
> A shudder in the loins engenders there
> The broken wall, the burning roof and tower
> And Agamemnon dead.
>   Being so caught up,
> So mastered by the brute blood of the air,
> Did she put on his knowledge with his power
> Before the indifferent beak could let her drop? (*WB*, 214)

Perhaps only an emphasis on self-evidence has a chance of answering this final question the poem poses because the practical understanding does not have the appropriate power. Such a serious question may demand the fecklessness of imagination.

This poem is a sonnet, but a strange one. Most sonnets, Italian and Shakespearean, assume that the form requires elaborating fundamentally argumentative strategies so that they gather and structure affective consequences. The opening quatrains pose a problem or dilemma, and the closing elements propose a redirection of the mind and feelings so that the problem proves in fact an instrument of discovery. But in Yeats's poem the thinking is charged with urgency: rather than allowing reflective distance, the details selected emphasize the immediacy of the situation, and the form is under such urgent pressures that the statement of historical consequences in line 11 is broken off, as if the details were so ominous that the poem had immediately to establish an attitude by which to confront those consequences.

Then the final lines offer two very tight rhymes followed by what is virtually an off-rhyme between "up" and "drop." This final question is not something that will be easily resolved into the pressures of form. Yet the poet does not just admit defeat. There is a brilliant supplemental formal process that makes the final four syllables parallel the five-syllable unit in the second part of the broken line 11. "Could let her drop" completely echoes "Being so caught up," so that there is another level of parallelism at least acknowledging the difficulties that the off-rhyme poses for any sense of satisfying closure.

Yeats responds to the challenge of developing an emotional stance that can adapt itself to both the shock and the scope of the initiating situation by stressing from the beginning not just the imagination's freedom in selecting telling details but also its constructive capacity to provide distinctive frames for those details. The overall structure of the poem balances two levels of statements of fact with two questions, making quite different demands on the reader. The two statements of fact try to compare what proves incomparable for consciousness—the momentariness of the rape and the general sense that a civilization is doomed because of it. But the differences in the two questions try to address and resolve this immense gap between event and the need for comprehension. The first question is emotional, seeking empathy with Leda; the second question is philosophical, seeking to develop a stance toward knowledge that can encompass human vulnerability to being raped by what drives the course of history. The more forceful the first question, the more inevitable the need for this second effort at offering a consoling generalization.[17]

Both questions do not quite allow specific answers that might count as knowledge in the practical world, in part because, as Wittgenstein might say, what would pass as answers do not appear to overcome any kind of specific doubt. We can know that Leda must be feeling something, but if we want any fuller sense of that feeling, we must rely on the kind of attunement only imagination can provide. The second question asks not for shared feeling but for a shared knowledge—between Leda and Zeus and implicitly between Leda and the audience—that cannot even be aligned directly with emotion. This "knowledge" clearly lies beyond the domain of propositions—perhaps it offers a kind of "knowing how" rather than a "knowing that."

Even Leda probably cannot say whether she can put on the god's knowledge with this power, especially because the possibility of knowledge and the pain of knowledge turn on the phrase "could let her drop." This phrase suggests that there is a power beyond Zeus, the power that undid his father and will eventually undo the Greek gods as well. What can this knowledge be?

Perhaps this knowledge can be imagined only by reflecting on the disturbing gulf between human impotence and some unidentifiable level of shaping force that makes history. Then the imagination is probably the only mental power that can dwell on this level of awareness without trying to formulate this knowledge as if it were another claim to propositional adequacy. If discursive reason is stretched to its limit simply so that it can flesh out what Leda is experiencing, it seems paradoxically far more helpless in relation to how she develops self-consciousness. So we are invited to explore the possibility that these questions do not quite ask for what typically passes for knowledge. These questions might offer a mode of affirmation, or at least of relatedness to being, precisely because of the way imagination relies on self-evidence and so can pretty much bypass the roles played by understanding. Yet there is no mysticism involved, no special world for which the imagination holds the key. Instead, Yeats suggests that issues of manner must come to the fore.

Here both questions posed by the poem invite us to ignore the entire domain of indicative sentences. They function as something closer to exclamations so that the questioning itself is the measure of intensity. And then the ability to stay within the question is the poem's suggested response to its sense of tragedy: the richest response to tragedy is to ram all of the intensity possible into the questioning that marks both our impotence and our imaginative capacity to correlate feeling and willing on levels that understanding cannot hope to provide. The self-evidence afforded by taking questions as exclamations gets raised to the highest plane of what is involved in becoming full witnesses to tragic conditions.

What Theory Can Learn from Such Sites for Imagining

Now let me refine and summarize some basic theoretical claims that I think derive from taking these readings as exemplary for a large gathering of literary texts. I cannot say that all work of literary merit emphasizes imagination as the basic constructive force of the text, fusing sensuousness with activities of reflection. But I think I can say that most work will rely to some extent on visibly nonrational processes of selection, resistance to practical interpretation, and some version of self-evidence, so that the relations that imagination provides establish the work's claim to be involved in practical life. So I derive four claims from my examples.

1) In most situations there will be several levels of embedded imaginative activity—involving how the author establishes a presence and develops personages with more density and immediacy than they would have as elements of argumentative structures.[18] The crucial feature is how the text calls attention to its manner as defining the significance of its matter. The "how" of imagining establishes the modality of what is imagined. "Leda and the Swan" is best seen, then, as not the act of an individual speaker but as an outburst that derives from a speaking position privy to Leda's vulnerability and pain. The speaking is devoted to articulating how all those occupying that position are likely to respond. And "Instruction Manual" manages a marvelous process of treating the utterly banal with an expansive compassion and a grace that invites all readers to modify their understanding of the dynamics of lyricism.

2) The selecting of details is how imagination produces a world in which it solicits our responding imaginative activity. In realist fiction we tend to ignore the axis of selection so we can devote our attention to the axis of represented action. But precisely because there are so many details available within how realism identifies with the perceptual order, there is an enormous freedom and a powerful need to control the sense of focus by careful selection. The realist text appears as already naturalized, but it does not emerge that way for the author facing a blank page.

If one goes back to oral narrative, one sees that the dynamics of choice becomes central because the audience is familiar with the options for the narrator, yet is still capable of being surprised. Seeing this, it is difficult not to register similar oral narratives enclosed within the realistic textures of the Victorian serial novel. For the profusion of sentences is dramatically and syntactically making constant modifications in the expectations and investments of its readers. And then one could say that Joyce's originality in Ulysses and Finnegans Wake consists largely in emphasizing the degree to which the author's choosing is everywhere constitutive so that only hypotheses about self-evidence will enable us to offer possible interpretations of what ties together the several levels composed by such choosings.

3) Within aesthetics this claim to self-evidence has been asserted as a special power of imagination. Imagination produces objects that are ends in themselves, while interventions in the world of givens are bound to discursive processes. Yet I think it silly to seek a single framework in which the discursive can be measured against the nondiscursive. Each activity involves a power that we have to describe and delimit. The important aspect of the imaginative power we have been considering is its capacity to put details and states together that do not necessarily cohere in ways that are bound by knowledge claims. This freedom is accompanied by an obvious weakness: we need testing before we make any existential claims based on imaginative products. But at the same time the foregrounding of choice is also an obvious strength because writers can produce states in which, among other relations, interrogatives function as exclamations and therefore bypass indicatives.

So we can imagine imagination affording affinities with persons and states of being, or even what we want to call knowledge, that we can deal with only in terms of how the internal relations establish self-evidence. Yeats's questions are so powerful because their only answers are in what the poems offer as conditions of experience embedding this strange "could" within history. And "The Instruction Manual" can compose an alternative version of instruction because it specifies how the imagination organizes what can be involved in dreaming of Guadalajara. Abstract commentary can indicate that this alternate world is being constructed, but the power of that world depends on our attuning to how it composes internal relations that stand on their own. In this case the details are not even metaphoric. They do not serve as tenors for expanding the poems' imaginative reach. Rather, the details directly exemplify the power of imagination to interpret its own productions. Here Ashbery oddly provides almost the same process Tolstoy deploys in rendering Anna Karenina's suicide.

4) We have to ask what use this responsiveness is to modes of evidence that cannot add up to any kind of propositional knowledge.

And we have to ask how this alternative to knowing can be mediated by images that refuse the logic by which picturing operates. Why care about these thin surfaces that cannot be held responsible to the levels of intricate and partially hidden depths that accompany perception? Why not relegate all imagination to fantasy and illusions about powers of mind independent of causality?

I think this very line of questioning establishes the logic of a possible answer, one that I have implicitly been relying on throughout this chapter. It is quite common to be in practical situations where we do not worry about evidence or even about responsibility to the truth latent in situations. On such occasions the important thing is not to separate imagination from reality but to preserve imagination's authority to define what kind of reality the relations among images project. Imagination is an instrument for clarifying or developing pictures rather than for applying them as knowledge-bearing propositions.

Consider, for example, how we treat feelings and emotions when we are committed to appreciating acts of imagination. We could just name the feelings if we were worried about how to act with respect to them: beware the angry person, pursue what seems possible from gestures of friendship. But instead we have been attending to how our ways of naming make possible states of appreciation entirely focused on specific situations—as dramatic moments and as figures embodying an author's modes of attributing significance to these moments. Consequently, we cannot quite say what Leda is feeling or knowing or what the characters so briefly glimpsed in Guadalajara are likely to do with their lives. Instead we seek participation in the characters' situations, even if this means dwelling in uncertainty, rather than pursuing a mode of knowing that would ask troubling questions of those details while admitting that it could draw no significant conclusions. The goal of participation perhaps requires that we be content with the intensity of our questions as the fullest measure of attunement.

I think Marx realized that the only way he could give priority to social relations was by a theory of historical determinism. Perhaps only a sense of necessity will stabilize priorities and give reasons for acting that are not limited to self-interest. Analogously, it may take a sense of the significance of pure questioning in order to free literary theory from the appeal of knowledge claims so that it can look for other, more indirect social uses for what we come to care about through individual texts. These individual texts can make assertions about truth values, just as any speech act can propose such assertions. But if we read them as assertions, we are stuck with their referential value—true or false—and the manner becomes irrelevant once it is deciphered.

The logic of perception seeks examples that illustrate concepts so that we get a sense of what is typical about the object. The logic of imagination, in contrast, seeks a different kind of exemplification based not on the concept but on how the particular activity might suggest analogical uses or significant differences as we sort out what particular constructions can be useful for projecting onto other scenes.[19] This kind of exemplification makes the manner of presentation central to the reading process. Such exemplification may emphasize the particular fullness of a powerful experience. Or it can be more generic, making present on various levels what can be compared to other literary texts, as the turn to pathos dramatizes in "Instruction Manual." In such cases the labors of imagination take on worldliness because they affect our sense of how experience impinges on our values.

Chapter 3

Where Doubt Has No Purchase

The Roles of Display

> The concept of an aspect is related to the concept of imagination. In other words, the concept "Now I see it as . . ." is related to "Now I am imagining that." Doesn't it take imagination to hear something as a variation on a particular theme? And yet one does perceive something in so hearing it.
>
> —Wittgenstein, *Philosophy of Psychology—A Fragment*

> But is it not peculiar that there is no such thing as this reaction, this confession of intention? Is it not an extremely remarkable instrument of language? What is really remarkable about it? Well—it is difficult to imagine how a human being learns this use of words. It is so very subtle. But is it really subtler than that of the phrase "I imagined him," for example? Yes, every such use of language is remarkable, peculiar, if one is adjusted only to consider the description of physical objects.
>
> —Wittgenstein, *Zettel*

For me the switch we now have to undertake feels like a very cold and very long shower. We have to shift from speculating on the nature of imaginative activity to facing up to contemporary criticism's losing sight of almost anything connected to imagination and imaginative power, except perhaps its capacity to generate escapist fantasy. I think Wittgenstein on the concept of display provides a terrific resource for reestablishing the importance of accounts of imaginative activity as fundamental to literary criticism. But elaborating that requires a further step in my argument (as does honoring what he does with "Now" in my first epigraph).

In the previous chapter we speculated on how to describe the imaginative labors fundamental to many of our literary experiences. Now we have to establish the roles these imaginations can play in our practical lives. That entails finding areas in these dimensions of our lives where we cannot operate simply by offering descriptions and positing propositions. Where do we have to use skills of attunement and responsiveness? And what other practices, beyond ones engaged in epistemic concerns, are fundamental to our negotiations with other people? In responding to these questions we can explore how works of art may correlate with these practices and help shape our capacities to participate in these real-world activities.

No literary critic with whom I am familiar takes up Wittgenstein's arguments about the limitations of what we can be said to "know" despite the fact that setting art against "knowledge" and "understanding" is commonplace in two hundred years of thinking on aesthetics, at least in Kantian and romantic traditions. Perhaps Wittgenstein can set this opposition on a firm foundation, anchored not in speculation but in a sense of how we learn very different ways in society to address our needs and participate fully in the social lives available to us. For he provides a consistent and powerful story of what kind of authority knowledge can and cannot wield in relation to our diverse linguistic practices. He does not deny that knowledge claims are crucial engines of our practical lives. And he probably would not deny that virtually any assertion can be made out to address a doubt and therefore to be working toward knowledge. Yet Wittgenstein resists the exclusively cognitive domain of descriptions and propositions by articulating what is involved in other cultural domains in which we deploy expressions, the demonstration of feelings, and the use of examples rather than assertions—all modes of display rather than description.[1]

That art involves presentation rather than description or making copies of events is a doctrine common to all expressivist theory. That is, many theorists since Kant have stressed the way the making of art objects brings distinctive states into being for the subject. Making brings feelings to bear on how objects are rendered, so the work develops fusions between sensibilities and perceptions. But not every way of accounting for such presentations is equally useful because each characterizes such modes of presence in quite different ways.

Most versions of expressivist theory explain presentation as a quality that art objects have that distinguishes them from the modes of sequential exchange governed by the practical understanding. The sense of unique presence takes the work out of the world, while establishing the work as a singular event, born of intuition and constituted by an audience's contemplative activity, where the aesthetical idea can unfold without having to deal with impatient demands for action. So it seems the only way for art to speak is for the rest of the world to become silent. Such tendencies come to a head in Heidegger's rhetoric. First he offers a powerful image of the expressive process in his characterizing art as "disclosure" of truth rather than participation in merely instrumental activity, then his settling into claims that the work of art produces a kind of *ereignis,* where an event occurs that sets language on its way to *being.* But then these artworks become isolated, singular objects, dignified out of practical existence by their power to perform the rescue of being from beings. Language takes over from any kind of specific action, and being takes priority over the dynamics of human relationships.[2]

Wittgenstein's sense of display, on the other hand, places art's powers of presentation as continuous with what persons do in other domains. Consider this passage, from relatively early in Wittgenstein's thinking his way beyond his *Tractatus:* "Feelings accompany our apprehension of a piece of music in the way they accompany the events of our life" (*Culture and Value,* ed. Peter Winch [Chicago: University of Chicago Press, 1984], 10; cited hereafter as *CV*). Feeling then joins certain aspects of life to art and of art to life.

To describe such events without recognizing the place of feeling is simply to be dealing with a species only faintly related to human beings. But to describe the feelings as we do other material aspects of the event is also to destroy their place in human lives. For just describing the feelings would have to cast them as objects. Such an act would fail to recognize how and why they are woven into human lives in such a way that they require expression and not simply observation. Expressions usually seek responses, not descriptions. To utter grief without feeling grief would be not just false but a failure to live up to the expectations embedded in how we learn to deploy and respond to such terms.

Wittgenstein on the Limited Roles Concerns for Knowledge Play

Over his career Wittgenstein develops two basic critiques of how we tend to misuse claims about the entire family of epistemic protocols—from descriptions that fix objective conditions to propositions that seek to say something true about those conditions. Both critiques insist that many language games call not for understanding but for attunement to the practices they enable. And in demonstrating how these practices work, Wittgenstein invites attention to significant literary parallels that explore what values are involved in these kinds of action.

Philosophical Investigations concentrates on specific critiques of what happens when we try to impose efforts at understanding based on criteria specific to knowledge on practices not concerned with fixing objects and discovering truths. These language games might concern sensations, feelings, events, and references to rules and examples rather than assertions about the world. As Richard Moran put it, "Wittgenstein emphasized how philosophy had to deal with more than humans considered as perceivers."[3]

Wittgenstein continued throughout his career to develop particular exemplary cases where the desire to "know" leads to serious misunderstanding. We will explore some of these, primarily because I am most interested in how his alternatives to the pursuit of knowledge make it possible to link the functions of display in practical life with the functions of display that offer plausible characterizations of what artworks can be said to make present. But it is also important to recognize how Wittgenstein developed a more abstract understanding of display by which he could refer not to specific practices but to the ontological status of all of our foundational practices.

This more general attitude toward the foundations of our practices begins with Wittgenstein's understanding of the status of logic in his *Tractatus*. One cannot argue about logic because logic is necessary for such argument. So the nature of logic can only be displayed, and the display has to reveal the complete structure of logical form. Then Wittgenstein realized that his particular analyses of what happens in our language games depended on treating the entire network of language as also something that could only be displayed: we cannot argue about the structure of language games without deploying what we would describe. So he devotes the remarks collected in *On Certainty* primarily to making clear the possible force of this level of display—not to characterize a single structure but to indicate how grammar, not logic, makes understanding possible.

Wittgenstein's first critique of the epistemic consists in a series of contrasts between the work language games do and the ways that our Enlightenment pictures of the world simplify and distort those modes of social interaction:

> In the first place, our language describes a picture. What is to be done with the picture, how it is to be used, is still obscure. Quite clearly, however, it must

be explored if we want to understand the sense of our words. But the picture seems to spare us this work; it already points to a particular use. This is how it takes us in. (*PPF*, 55)

Our typical picture is that language offers representations to be assessed as true or false: we use language to describe and to explain. And when we are confronted with cases where it is not obvious how to proceed, we manage to find ways of applying familiar epistemic strategies that allow us some kind of knowledge claim.

But for Wittgenstein this attitude drastically oversimplifies the tasks we perform as our language processes various uses of pictures in a range of situations. So he has to struggle against the reductive simplification suggested by the immediate picture, especially if he is to provide a "perspicuous representation"[4] of the human powers and needs made visible in the language games involved. Rather than find the epistemic in all these uses, we have to realize that the protocols of knowledge actually apply only when a statement can be seen as resolving some kind of doubt. In situations where doubt is not an issue, neither is knowledge. Having a variety of language games matters, then, because we have guidelines for behavior that do not depend on knowledge of facts but rather on familiarity with situations. (That one is using a particular language game may be determinable as a fact, but how to respond involves other modes of judgment.)

This argument is much easier to illustrate if we turn from generalization to concrete cases. The passage I quote now takes up a recurrent contrast in Wittgenstein between the expression of pain and its description. It seems as if the narrative voice keeps trying to find epistemic leverage for descriptions. But the first-person expression of pain leaves no space for doubt and so invites something other than recognition of the facts:

> I turn to stone and my pain goes on.—What if I were mistaken, and it was no longer *pain*?—But surely I cannot be mistaken here; it means nothing to doubt whether I am in pain!—That is, if someone said, "I do not know if what I have is a pain or something else," we would think, perhaps, that he does not know what the English word "pain" means, and we would explain it to him.—How? Perhaps by means of gestures, or by pricking him with a pin and saying, "See, that's pain!" . . .
> If he now said, for example, "Oh, I know what 'pain' means; what I don't know whether *this*, that I have now, is pain"—we'd merely shake our heads

and have to regard his words as a strange reaction which we can't make anything of. (*PI*, 288)

Pain is not an object to be discovered but a state to be revealed. Nothing can come between the self and the event of the pain, so the first person cannot formulate a doubt. We do not infer pain when speaking in the first person. We experience it and we express it: "The verbal expression of pain replaces crying, it does not describe it" (ibid., 245). The expression of pain is a means of drawing attention to the self, not to a condition outside the self (ibid., 405). So the crucial question becomes not whether the one speaking in the first person knows he has pain but whether he has mastery of the uses of the word "pain." To determine whether he has mastery we cannot figuratively look in his head, but we check whether his behavior seems congruent with his speech.

It is crucial to realize that were the agent to doubt that he had pain, he would allow epistemic concerns to outweigh expressive ones. And then the agent dealing with his sensations would be plunged in a quandary, or an aporia, which seems to require conventional philosophical analysis and to frustrate it at the same time:

> The expression of doubt has no place in the language-game; but if expressions of sensations—human behavior—are excluded, it looks as if I then legitimately begin to doubt. My temptation to say that one might take a sensation for something other than what it is arises from this: if I assume the abrogation of the normal language-game with the expression of a sensation, I need a criterion of identity for the sensation, and then the possibility of error also exists. (*PI*, 288)

There are two reasons that avowals of sensation such as "I am in pain" involve a distinctive language game. First, we have to see that we are asked not to locate the pain but to find in ourselves some mode of attuning to the person in pain. The person is likely to want comfort more than information. And, second, if we try to pursue truth concerns we have to search for criteria that we can use in overcoming doubts that I am in pain or doubts about the nature of the pain. And then we set up a wild-goose chase trying to make the occasion fit the boxes that epistemic protocols provide. (Deconstruction hovers within such confusions, as do all forms of skepticism because we can always challenge the criteria of identity forming each box.)

We should also not ignore a point I will develop later. Who is this "I" who expresses pain? This question is meaningless if we are concerned with testing propositions. When we seek to resolve doubts about the truth of the statement or the location of the pain, we have to treat the person as the empirical observable "I." But perhaps there is a self-reflexive relation to that empirical self which requires somewhat different modes of engagement. Just after speculating on how expressions of pain call attention to "myself," Wittgenstein adds this twist, in the person of his interlocutor:

> "But surely what you want to do with the words 'I am . . .' is to distinguish between yourself and other people."—Can this be said in every case? Even when I merely groan? And even when I want "to distinguish" between myself and other people—do I want to distinguish between the person L.W. and the person N.N.? (*PI*, 406)

Wittgenstein suggests here that there are some ways of feeling oneself a subject that do not refer to the social being who has a name and for whose presence there are, in fact, criteria of identity.

The reflexive "myself" can refer to the social "I." But it can also simply evoke or express the condition of feeling involved in the power of saying "I" without pointing to any empirical identity at all. "Myself," then, is an expression fraught with danger for philosophy but also with possibility. Once we take "myself" as a referring term, we reinforce the sense that the "I" has an inner reality even though we are doomed not to find its location. And once we get seduced into this effort at finding a referent for the expression, we are likely to lose our capacity to engage what the "I" is actually doing in speaking as it does. As I move toward concluding this chapter I will elaborate how this possible flexibility in determining who "I" is at any given moment allows us a fresh perspective on one of the major impulses to experiment in modernist writing.

Some Uses for the Concept of Display

Once we recognize how certain pictures seduce us into trying to adapt epistemic orientations when they are not appropriate, we are prepared to examine the many ways in which display functions as an alternative to the invoking of epistemic criteria. The crucial distinction here is between what we take as preexisting the utterance or the avowal and what we take as coming into being only through the utterance: "I do not 'observe' that which comes into being only through observation. The object of observation is something else" (*PPF*, 67). We deal with objects of observation when pain is reported in the third person. Then the pain is an object of knowledge and not a reason for continued observation. But the situation is different with pain for the first person because there the avowal of pain seems not to refer to the pain so much as to make manifest that the self is in pain.

The self is not referring to a specific sensation of pain but crying out for some kind of response to the display being offered. Correspondingly we do not say, "Yes, you are right; you are in pain." We respond to the utterance "I am in pain" by trying to react with compassion to the person displaying it and not specifically to the pain. We treat this kind of utterance as "gesture" rather than object (*CV*, 73). And in speaking about gestures that come into being as we respond to them we again approach the language of aesthetics.

If we adapt this distinction between what we can describe independently of the expression and what comes into being only through the expression, we need not confine ourselves to an opposition between conditions such as a picture of pain and a cry of pain. We also gain a way of reading how "now" and other indexicals can also take on expressive force because they become aspects of something coming into being only because of changes in the observer's stance. And then we are well on our way to seeing how central display is to our practical lives because of the many ways it hooks into our ordinary practices.

I will dwell for a moment on how Wittgenstein recuperates a possible force for the expression "now" because that expression has obvious implications for how we deal with anything suddenly taking on an aura of presence. There are many uses of "now" that have only adverbial force signifying a relation to an already observed set of details. But the "now" of calling attention to an aspect of experience seems to me a more complicated case. For in this case "now" becomes a feature framing the use of the display rather than an adverbial complement to an observation.

This "now" used for framing presents an exclamation that makes sense only in the context of utterance. And then it becomes possible to say that aspect-seeing constitutes a large domain where our imaginative activities warrant the same critique of epistemic protocols as do first-person cries of pain.

Consider the difference between "red" as descriptive adjective and "Red!" as exclamation of the dawning of an aspect (*PPF*, 70–71). "Red!" still bears traces of its adjectival use. But the primary function of the exclamation point is to shift the focus from a description to what comes into being because the person all of a sudden recognizes something of interest. The focus now is less on the object than on the conditions of the subject. For we want to address what went on with the person to elicit the shift from any kind of simple noting of the world to an excitement with that world right now.[5]

Here I can be brief because John Verdi has developed a superb account of how display is involved in aspect-seeing.[6] Consider Wittgenstein's basic analysis of possible responses to Jastrow's figure that can assume the shape of a duck and of a rabbit depending on whether one sees a bill or ears on the left side of the image. When we can say, "Now I see it as a duck," or "Now I see it as a rabbit," we introduce language games that go far beyond any understanding of the subject that depends on a causal view of perception and response. At stake is one power of imagination that is clearly not reducible to empiricist causal accounts of perception (*PPF*, 126):

> I'm shown a picture-rabbit and asked what it is; I say "it's a rabbit." Not "now it's a rabbit." I'm reporting my perception.—I'm shown the duck-rabbit and asked what it is; I may say "It's a duck-rabbit." But I may also react to the question quite differently.—The answer that it is a duck-rabbit is again the report of a perception: the answer "Now it's a rabbit" is not. Had I replied it's a rabbit, the ambiguity would have escaped me, and I would have been reporting my perception. (*PPF*, 128)

"Now it's a rabbit" introduces at least two features that are not involved in perception or the reporting of perceptions or the copying of what is perceived.[7] "Now" does not involve any causality with which science is familiar because there is no predicting from the duck-rabbit what aspect dawns for the agent. Yet there is no difference in the appearance of the object: the duck-rabbit remains the same. Only the agent changes with each utterance: "The expression of a change of aspect is an expression of a new perception and, at the same time an expression of an unchanged perception" (ibid., 130). The new perception is not a new fact about the world, only about the agent. And we expect the agent to flesh out this change by elaborating the difference that "now" makes for her.

She cannot just make a copy of what she sees because the copy would reflect only the unchanged perception. She has to make sense not just of the reported perception but of the exclamation. Developing how the agent presents the dawning of an aspect requires a model and not a copy (ibid., 131). We can imagine stories and extended metaphors as themselves aspects of following up the dawning of an aspect.[8] And we can imagine the painful spectacle of aspect blindness when there is no dawning of an aspect for certain individuals.

For, as Wittgenstein says, we have shifted from concern for properties of the object to "an internal relation between it and other objects" (ibid., 247). I think of how the speaker in "Leda and the Swan" processes the "now" of what he sees. First, there is an event of seeing, then efforts to see that event in various lights until the speaker arrives at what Leda might possibly know through this world-historical event. Were the speaker aspect-blind, there could be no such speculation. There could only be description that becomes a record of sheer victimage.

How *On Certainty* Echoes and Transforms Wittgenstein's *Tractatus*

On Certainty is not much concerned with the nature or intricacy of specific language games. It asks two prior questions: how can we recognize what is involved in any language game, and what do the roles language games play tell us about how our consciousness can be attuned to the world? *Philosophical Investigations* uses language games to develop the contrast between what can be doubted and what has to be taken as display. It uses display to criticize epistemic ambitions. *On Certainty* concentrates on what we might call the ontology of display, which extends and revises the version of logic as display that Wittgenstein elaborated in his *Tractatus*.

Display in the *Tractatus* is encompassed within the distinction between what can be said and where we must remain silent. The one domain is of saying; the other of showing. But even in *Philosophical Investigations*, this Tractarian distinction breaks down. For display is not "showing" and does not require silence. Display depends on another kind of saying with different projections of uptake.[9] So display is the means by which certain language games produce social effects. And the same model of display invites *On Certainty*'s second-order reflection on how the entire network of language games provides our frameworks for making sense.

This notion of display as articulate presentation in turn enables us to treat Wittgenstein's rendering of G. E. Moore in *On Certainty* as presenting a fictional character. It matters that Moore's commonsense philosophical realism stakes out a philosophical position Wittgenstein rejects. But it may matter more that Moore's character in the text comes to exemplify attitudes toward philosophy which are much more pervasive and more dangerous than specific doctrinal mistakes.

I think we need only Wittgenstein's discussion of Moore to illustrate *On Certainty*'s three basic critiques of all versions of empiricist epistemic ideals from verificationism to Moore's commonsense realism. The first problem is addressed by Wittgenstein's now familiar argument about the grammar of "know." Wittgenstein asks his readers what Moore is accomplishing (and failing to accomplish) when he asserts a traditional commonsense refutation of the skeptic: "I know that here is one hand" because my senses directly encounter it? Wittgenstein points out that in normal circumstances one does not "know" that here is one hand or that "this is a tree." One does not "know" these phenomena because this is not a situation where there is a call to overcome doubt, and so there is no place for the kind of guarantee that saying "I know" involves. The implication is that my having one hand and there being trees are just aspects of my world, at least as stable as any "I" that might inquire after them.

"To know" is a verb that marks an achievement rather than defining a state of mind, as "believe" does. No one not doing philosophy would doubt that this is a tree or that Moore has the hand he is pointing to. Moore is actually not reporting a discovery but indicating the presence of hand and tree as possible instruments and settings for the making and testing of truth claims. Having hands is not something we know but something that we rely on for all sorts of actions that are basic to life as we recognize it.[10]

Repeating this argument makes me feel I am in a Monty Python sketch. But we will see that the stakes are quite substantial as Wittgenstein's second and third points emerge. The second critique mounts an attack on the core of a realist and empiricist view of the world that Wilfred Sellars would later make more elaborately. Moore treats knowledge as if it were based on an accumulation of individual observations, each added to the other. But for Wittgenstein, we do not simply build up particular observations in order to produce a picture of the world as a whole. Instead, we develop early on a sense of entire frameworks that provide what certainty we can have: "Experience is not the ground for our game of judging" (*OC,* 131). In fact, we cannot describe this ground at all: "I do not explicitly learn the propositions that stand fast for me. I can discover them subsequently like the axis around which a body rotates. This axis is not fixed in the sense that anything holds it fast, but the movement around it determines its immobility" (ibid., 152). Were there not substantial fit among our expectations, there could be no inquiry at all because we could not even frame consistent doubts. Imagine thinking about mathematics on empiricist principles, which require building a system of ideas perception by perception: "Instead when someone is trying to teach us mathematics he will not begin by assuring us that he knows that $a+b=b+a$" (ibid., 113). Certainty is not a matter of proof but rather of forms of life that establish what we have to take as given.

Wittgenstein's second point then clarifies what we can learn when we cease to assume that bits of knowledge come to constitute a stable ground for our judgments. He sets the stage by asking what would be different if instead of "I know" Moore had said, "'It stands fast for me that...' And further, 'It stands fast for me and many others'" (ibid., 116). When we cease to look for the foundations of knowledge in a series of isolated propositions, we begin to get a very different sense of the role of logic.

We have to recognize how what had been the foundational role logic played in Wittgenstein's *Tractatus* is assumed now by this capacity to "stand fast" and so sanction predication. The force of logic now resides in the display afforded by stable practices:

> What sort of a proposition is: "What could a mistake here be like!"? It would have to be a logical proposition. But it is a logic that is not used, because what it tells us is not learned through propositions.—It is a logical proposition, for it does describe the conceptual (linguistic) situation. (*OC,* 51)[11]

Rather than studying how a picture secures its sense, we have to look to how the whole practice of picturing fits into other practices to compose the world as we know it. Ultimately it is social relations and not pictorial ones that teach us the roles doubting can play in our lives.

The relations that form this new alternative to traditional logic then must provide repeatable structures establishing conditions for making sense, and they must provide the examples by which we can modify our understanding of these structures. These components in turn condition all our ways of making sense. Think of how Ashbery projects implicit structures based on shared language games to gain access to an entire framework of social relations. For Ashbery the relations are imaginary, but the imaginary in his poem fleshes out possibilities of sharing based on the kinds of language games it is very difficult not to see shaping life in the United States as they do in Guadalajara.

My third critique extends beyond what Wittgenstein may have intended in this discussion. But I elaborate it because it makes the case about the primacy of display in large part by a quasi-literary use of display established by treating Moore as a dramatic character. So far we have dealt with Moore's statements as pieces of philosophy—statements about how certainty might be possible. What if we took the statements as actions, as modes of responding to particular existential situations? Wittgenstein almost forces that question on us as he concludes his engagement with this image of Moore: "When one hears Moore say 'I *know* that's a tree' one suddenly understands those who think that that has by no means been settled" (*OC*, 481).

Now we are asked to make inferences about what Moore might exhibit. And, strangely, it is Jacques Derrida who best articulates this inference in his response to John Searle that became the book *Limited Inc*.[12] Searle clearly wins the philosophical contest. But in doing it he manifests himself as so aggressive and incapable of sympathy that he calls into question the entire dream of what philosophers might do for society.[13] Here there are close parallels to how Searle appears in two features of Moore's statement. One has to ask why he insists on repeating an assertion that can do no philosophical work. And one would be hard pressed not to answer that he is relying not on argument so much as on an image of the authority of the philosopher.

In assuming that he is refuting a childish folly, Moore reveals his own anxious need to wield the authority of a parent. Worse, he seems to connect the stability of having a clear referent do the work of establishing certainty with the possibility of having a clear and discrete "I." This "I" seems assured of its own stability and its own transparency by being able to assert a similar stability for the tree. Why else insist not that there is a tree but that "I know there is a tree"? So he ends up connecting the state of his ego to his assertion about the state of the world—precisely what the spirit of realism in philosophy was developed to combat.

Moore's stumbling to reassert the connection between authority and direct knowledge sets off by contrast Wittgenstein's own alternative route to certainty. For Wittgenstein certainty is not established by propositions but by the way that the subject comes to understand what is entailed in how language provides stable frames for various actions. Moore's commonsense realist faith in simplicity leads him astray because it prevents him from recognizing the more elemental simplicity that Wittgenstein is proposing in his rendering of how certainty gets formed: "I did not get my picture of the world by satisfying myself of its correctness; nor do I have it because I am satisfied of its correctness. No: it is the inherited background against which I distinguish between true and false" (*OC*, 94).

What Moore does not see—what Moore's philosophical anxieties will not let him see—is that the same stability or certainty provided by logic might be provided also by the social practices establishing specific language games as the basic forms by which we develop shared meanings in our lives. Wittgenstein is clear that "the system is not so much the point of departure as the element in which arguments have their life" (ibid., 105). Even when we know the relevant rules, we do so not by interpreting them correctly as isolated principles but by having immersed ourselves in the "grammatical" practices that they govern (*PI*, 201). We have learned the language and so mastered techniques of going on (ibid., 199) without any explicit formulation of the procedures that we are following. Rules emerge as expectations built into practices. We can deviate, but then we are likely to generate questions or confusions and ultimately create a risk that the entire practice will cease to make sense.[14]

This transformation of logic into grammar is crucial in understanding how *On Certainty* treats the nature of language games. Language games themselves provide the possibilities of making sense. So they, too, cannot be described without trying to turn what are, in fact, something like flexible structures of possibility into objective conditions in the world. We do not quite "know" what our language games are unless we understand what is involved in participating in them. And this understanding cannot itself be pictured, although it can be shared by learning to offer perspicuous representations of how one finds a satisfying sense of being involved in particular practices as one acts. One can only illustrate the foundational role of grammar by analyzing representative instances of how it works.

Unlike the *Tractatus*, *On Certainty* does not entertain the fantasy that one can make a display that covers all of the possibilities of logic. For there are multiple grammatical frameworks that support how we can make sense. And this multiplicity in turn allows us to emphasize not pictures of the world but subjects acting on and within the world. When the emphasis had been on objective truth conditions, there was simply no place for subjectivity. The subject was not in the world as fact but at its margin, where it could only project fantasies that value might somehow inhere in what can be pictured.

But when grammar becomes what is foundational, making sense proves intimately connected with modes of valuing what one encounters. Value is no longer something separate from the world but becomes embedded in the very practices it enables. Cries of pain involve projections of possible responsiveness. And promises involve both valuing the other person's right to expect something and valuing the agent's own word as something that is not simply instrumental. The person's word becomes a bond. We could not have promises or apologies or practices of courtship in a world where values were not involved in our basic modes of making sense.

How the Concept of Display Can Make Differences in Our Responses to Art

Now we must speculate on the consequences for literary theory of giving display so fundamental a role in how certainty emerges. The most important point is the most obvious. There are clear limits to knowledge, especially knowledge based on scientific protocols, because there are significant preconditions for the roles propositions can play. Knowledge occurs within language games; certainty occurs when one grasps the nature of how the framework for those games establishes our elemental senses of being at home in the world. Therefore *On Certainty* can substantially reduce the importance in philosophy of worries about relations between the subject of experience and the object of thought. In the versions of display developed by *On Certainty*, the problem is not the distance between subject and object but the need for subjects to find their bearings amid a variety of roles they might play.

That is why it matters to determine the most appropriate language games for given contexts. And that is why aspects of actions such as participation and attunement become more important than the unblinking lucidity idealized by Enlightenment versions of scientific inquiry. Participation is recognition of where we can stand within a practice or a language game. And attunement is our adapting to what others desire or make visible by the roles they play in these language games. Both modes of attention show how actions can become intelligible and invite response without the intervention of epistemic protocols, and both involve something very close to aesthetic sensibility adapted to practical life. Both even take up the suggestion that our figures for agency, such as the "I," are more mysterious and more diverse than empiricist thinking allows.

So here emotions serve as primary aspects of what becomes present for our participation; they need not be interpretive constructs. And formal properties are inseparable from how the action finds a path to articulation: "'A picture tells me itself' is what I would like to say. That is, its telling me something consists in its own structure, in *its* own forms and colors" (*PI*, 523). For the aim is less to inform us than to "absorb us" (ibid., 524) in establishing its own particular qualities as they unfold, as if it had "assimilated its meaning into itself" (*PPF*, 294). This indeed is why interpretation in general terms seems at once so necessary for contextualizing the work and so violent in appropriating it. Interpretation by itself cannot capture the feelings in "the way we choose and value words" (ibid.): feelings typically require some mode of affective adjustment to the particular case.

Exemplary versions of these choosings and valuings, then, are likely to have the force of particulars rather than serving as instances of generalizations. The force of the example can be as a "means of representation" rather than as something represented because they indicate how language might be used in given cases. The example helps establish the nature and scope of the language game. There is a close connection between having an object serve as a means of representation and seeing something as something else that enables us to change the boundaries of speech situations. And it is not a large step from using particular means of representation to building entire models that can serve as exemplary means of representation making it possible for us to direct and complicate our repertoire of language games. Indeed, we will see in the next chapter that the ideal of modeling makes it possible to treat expressive activity as not just an avowal but a means of representation clarifying what is possible within our modes of feeling and of thinking. A model is not a description or an explanation. Rather, it is a vehicle for presenting "internal relations" (*PPF,* 247) deriving from a subject's effort to establish its own force as it adapts a public grammar for its own purposes.

On the basis of these observations I can close this chapter by elaborating three ways in which attention to the force of display (and its concomitant resistance to knowledge claims) makes a major difference in our ability to explain how the arts take on worldliness as extensions of basic human practices.

First, *On Certainty* shows how an understanding of display can change our grasp of the powers of realism, as is evident in the work that philosophers such as Sellars and McDowell do in extending Wittgenstein's critique of empiricism's "myth of the given." Traditionally we treat realism as a rhetorical mode emphasizing what can be seen through language rather than what language in the form of the space of reasons can do on its own to supplement experience. Realism is a rhetoric binding us to how people typically construct worlds by negotiating everyday objects and situations. For many readers, and writers, this rhetoric seems to put heavy constraints on the powers of imagination. But think again of what realism becomes in the hands of a Tolstoy or a George Eliot or a principle revived by means of experimental efforts in James Joyce and Virginia Woolf. Here realism is best seen as a mode of displaying collective feeling for a shareable world rather than a rhetoric setting limits on literary representation.

Realism can offer self-reflexive explorations of what is involved in leading a recognizable life in society, sharing its pleasures and its pains and, especially, its principles of evaluation, even if this sharing also means criticizing those who do not live up to its potential for developing its own celebrations of states very much like those Wittgenstein evokes in his discussion of certainty. The emphasis on manner then breaks free of a commitment to stylistic innovation in order to foreground what is involved in our valuing. And this foregrounding makes visible who we become as social beings because of that valuing, especially the valuing structured by our second-order concerns for the qualities by which we imagine what lies beyond mere imagining.[15]

My second way leads in exactly the opposite direction from the temptations to make present the values of a realist sensibility. Here I am concerned with constructivist experiments in altering our operating notions of intentionality by dramatizing forces of purposiveness that are quite different from those that might be negotiated in talk *about* a person's intention.

Correspondingly, one can imagine the display features of art as modifying our sense of our own powers within a culture because the works call on capacities that are different from those that govern descriptive and interpretive discourse. One might even say that artists like Malevich and Stein and Pound foreground aspects of self-reflection that depend on our seeing into the terms by which our own activities establish our stable place in the world.

I see the modifications of intentionality clearly visible in how Wittgenstein treats the difference between seeing the full compositional power in a drawing and just knowing what the work seeks to accomplish: "From someone who sees the drawing as such and such an animal, what I expect will be rather different from what I expect from someone who merely knows what it is meant to represent" (*PPF*, 196). The sense of the drawing as realizing a particular state is quite different from the understanding of a psychological intention to do something. And the maker of the drawing takes on a somewhat different existence just because his or her intentionality is made concrete and specific. The drawing makes accessible not just the intention to draw but the specific way that intention takes on both power and definition by modifying the object of representation. This drawing may represent, but it is not primarily a means of representation; it is a vehicle by which the artist defines an aspect of sensibility. The drawing makes visible powers of agency by which the world becomes intelligible in potentially new ways because of the kind of scrutiny it invites.

Attention to the structures composed by drawing—dramatically and thematically—becomes attention to how we take up places in the world aligned with the actions and expectations of other people. The world involves more than a capacity for making precise descriptions. The world involves myriad structures by which we can work out what we care about and in so doing make ourselves intelligible to other people, who can come to share a grammar with us. And we do that often without being able to describe adequately what engages us.

How we identify displays of feeling and how we respond to actions can be as elemental and as transpersonal as conditions that allow us to formulate and explain facts even though they involve quite different procedures. This expanded sense of the domain of display even allows us to develop a second-order appreciation of what is involved in attuning to avowals, pursuing the dawning of aspects, attributing value to how care is manifested in choosing our words, and participating in the intricacy and complexity of expressions. We relive imaginatively and self-reflexively the very conditions of sense that we share, as if our emotional lives could take up a dwelling in reflective space without losing their distinguishing qualities.

Finally, there is a tight relation between the ordinary practice of avowals and the expressive modeling of what can be forceful or memorable or especially intense within that avowal process. This is the topic of my next chapter. Even though characters and speakers in literary works constantly make use of avowals, that principle will not get us very far in understanding the nature of what the individual artist or writer does in composing a complete work. On the level of making we have only a few clear instances of avowal—perhaps in Whitman or in Ginsberg and probably in the kinds of writing intended for specific intimate audiences. But if we extend the logic of avowal to modeling of what can go into avowals, we can place texts in the world as first-person testimony while exploring how that testimony can be shaped. Writers model the particularities of avowal and atmosphere but from the point of view of one who makes the experience possible rather than from the point of view of one who undergoes it. That is, there is a close connection between classical theories of expression and how Wittgenstein describes the role of making a model to display the consequences of taking up a particular aspect of some scene or setting. We are speaking of something very close to T. S. Eliot's "objective correlative" or Joseph Conrad's "rendering." "Model" marries the subjective energies of the modes of display embedded in avowals with the compositional structuring that casts those energies as publically visible forces at work in a given imaginative environment.

Two Examples of How Poetry Can Modify Our Understanding of Agency

I realize that I am making a very ambitious and not entirely clear claim when I talk about imaginative writing actually inventing experiences that then have the possibility of modifying our practical sense of what powers we have to make identifications with modes of subjectivity. So I desperately need an example or, better, two examples—one a rather straightforward case and the other a more speculative model of modes of agency that we very rarely consider when we make claims about subjectivity.

82   Chapter 3

We could look at how Wallace Stevens's "Old Man Asleep" renders simple breathing as sufficient to evoke dignity and a demand for respect. Or we might choose Gertrude Stein's transformations of objects into psychological forces in her *Tender Buttons*. Or we could turn to the ambitions of the modernist novel in Woolf and Joyce and Faulkner. Each writer uses the principles of display to expand our sense of how features of intending agency become inseparable from our feelings for particular objects—Stevens by modifying our sense of how elemental something like imagining can be, Stein by inviting strange attention to the forces of repetition and variation, and the novelists by engaging our sense of how sympathy and judgment might be connected in ways that do not follow traditional interpretive channels positing a clear subject position and a clear object of inquiry.

Here I will develop examples by W. C. Williams and by Marianne Moore so that I can illustrate two major themes in this chapter—the force display can gather by linking imaginative presentation to analogous forms of behavior that can take place in our ordinary language games, and the possible roles such displays can have in exemplifying modes of intentional agency that are continuous with such practices but very rarely become objects of our attention. Williams's "The Red Wheelbarrow" displays a simple meditative state but does so in such a way as to bring into play the kinds of complexity in our mental lives necessary to provide models for the encounter with intricate situations:

> so much depends
> upon
>
> a red wheel
> barrow
>
> glazed with rain
> water
>
> beside the white
> chickens.[16]

The most important feature of intentionality here is the poem's capacity to project a life for the ego that is entirely free of overt self-reference. The poem tries to identify with the force of something like Hegelian substance in a life available to any subject. And it does not simply posit this scope as an ideal: the poem interprets how values might be involved in this way of seeing by insisting on the subtlety and intensity by which the mind makes the kinds of connections that link us to the world and to other people—by virtue of the meaningfulness we can share and by virtue of the rhythms that invite our participation.

Had I written this poem, I would have had each stanza consist of two-word lines, so there would be clear symmetry. But I would then have lost the intensity that emerges when there is a sharp sense of completion after enjambment. And I would have lost the possibility of making sensuously present a compelling drive for further completion because where the mind initially settles at the end of each stanza turns out to be another essentially transitional term generating a more capacious picture. Naming and joining and building seem inseparable aspects of human labor and of the pleasure we can take in that labor. The poem ultimately leads to a dramatic sense of the elemental features we depend on, complemented by a sense that only the power of poetry as radical selection and enjambment and patience will allow us to see how the mind's workings are fundamental to staging this recognition as a mode of desire. This "impersonal" mode of intentionality displays the actual work of a contemplative desiring, inseparable from our having a world at all. The poem has all the qualities of continuously avowing the dawning of aspects, but at a level of self-reflection that projects a condition of understanding approaching an elemental logic we need if we are to appreciate how making sense is at the core of social life.

My second example, Marianne Moore's "An Egyptian Pulled Glass Bottle in the Shape of a Fish," has many affinities with Williams's poem. But it offers a more complex and more radical treatment of intentionality—first, because of its self-consciousness about the relations between art and life, and, second, because of the way Moore's commitment to syllabics brings a specific quality of hearing into play as a significant condition of receptive agency.

Syllabics offer a method of organizing verse lines that depends on the counting of syllables rather than the composition of metrical feet as the basic principle of aural structure. In Moore's poem the counting of syllables dramatizes how an Egyptian glass bottle shapes attention to the fish that it depicts:

> Here we have thirst
> And patience from the first,
> And art, as in a wave held up for us to see
> In its essential perpendicularity.
>
> Not brittle but
> Intense—the spectrum, that
>   Spectacular and nimble animal the fish,
>   Whose scales turn aside the sun's sword by their polish.[17]

It is difficult to overstate the importance of this quiet opening word, "Here," which I think borders on an exclamation. "Here" points to the actual pictured bottle. But what it does is more important than what it says. The poem calls attention to the presence of both the image referred to in the title and the poet's, or perhaps the poem's, self-consciousness about what the image is performing. The speaking consciousness in effect makes present what is psychologically involved in saying "here" with reference to a work of art. It invites us to treat every element of the poem as actually producing the emotional force of presence being claimed for what the work offers as image.

The thirst literally refers to the open mouth of the fish and to the promise that the bottle will have something in it for relieving all kinds of drought. "Patience" is a more complex attribute. It refers primarily to the age of the bottle, which dates from well before the birth of Christ or the emergence of Athens. But the question of reference for each term pales in importance before the pressure of negotiating the oxymoronic relation between "thirst" and "patience." The first term inaugurates a physical impulse toward action; the second stresses the action of those who merely stand and wait. The poem has to elaborate what art enables us "to see in its perpendicularity" in order to grapple with these two competing impulses.

Oddly, the wave design which denotes the scales of the fish seems to have no relation to either thirst or patience. Instead, it brings to bear how we might understand why art might be considered in terms of "perpendicularity": the artist approaches thirst (of all kinds) indirectly so as to display another kind of seeing and another kind of force that makes possible and celebrates patience. "Here" becomes a place for displaying art's recasting of existential desire in terms of another desire to appreciate how a sense of enduring through time might affect our emotional disposition as we observe what the fish seems to evoke.

The second stanza begins with mysteriously related phrases: "not brittle but / intense—the spectrum that." Why would Moore be so obscure? I think she wants our minds to work very quickly since the swiftness of establishing relations is intended to make us feel one kind of agency art brings to the world. "Not brittle" seems to refer to the presence of the carved fish. Then the poem can switch from negatives to positives by moving from inferences about shape to the presence of color. The intense relations among colors bring the entire spectrum into play for the mind, now able to hold in balance the qualities of the fish and the disposition by which art creates those qualities:

> Spectacular and nimble animal the fish,
> Whose scales turn aside the sun's sword by their polish.

One has to proceed carefully here. The penultimate line assigns attributes both to the figure of the fish and to the past act of making this representation, now "here." So the role of the artist is never absent. "Spectacular" evokes "spectacle" and prepares us to stress how all the attributes ultimately derive from a creative source, a source sufficiently capacious to understand passions like thirst. The bottle provides a variegated surface by which the sun's force can become visible. However, the work elicits that force primarily to test the powers of art: the very polish articulating the sun's force also serves as the instrument by which the bottle can successfully resist that force. The polish gives the fish presence and composes qualities like thirst and patience, which together establish the artwork as something that can endure all of the violences that the sun might inflict.

This little domestic object has endured for thousands of years, all the time capable of giving pleasure and depth to the idea that the bottle can prove responsive to thirst. There is no large drama here, no Michaelangelesque struggle. But, as in Wittgenstein's writing, there is a patient attention making it possible to see how extraordinary that ordinary can be, so long as one can give it presence.

The syllabics play a substantial role in establishing that sense of presence—both as a condition of experience and as a model for reflecting on how awareness of intentional stances can deepen our appreciation of specific intimate domestic states. Typically in English the meter of a poem produces a rhythmic intensification of natural speech intended to stress something like Schiller's harmony of the faculties. Rhythm invites the body to align itself with the mind's labors. Why might Moore want to have no part in that reinforcement? Why might the spirit of art she celebrates not fit this kind of harmony?

Perhaps she feels that traditional metrics stresses the intentionality of our imagined bodies and underplays the possible physicality of our mental energies. In this poem the movement of sound depends on an apparently arbitrary arrangement whereby each line has a syllable count that is repeated in lines with the same position in other stanzas. Here each first line has four syllables; the second, six syllables; and the last two, twelve syllables each. In order to deal with the syllabics as expressive we have to understand how they elicit the mind's participation in what the initial "here" brings about.

In effect, syllabics make the mind dictate to the body rather than having the body expand into harmonies with speech. There are still harmonies with speech, but they occur in unexpected ways. The poem needs something like "essential perpendicularity" to bring an abstract dimension to the perceptive process. But how can one find pleasure in the Latinate ponderousness of phrases like these? First, the phrase affords a quite weighty line charged by a sense of condensation that perhaps only a seven-syllable word can provide. We have to count the syllables of the words, and after we count we have to recognize how the three- and the seven-syllable words inventively round out the line, bringing completeness to the thought while anchoring and acknowledging the abruptness of so general an assertion. Abstraction is reconciled with the poem's eye for effective detail: making and seeing and hearing and trusting our powers of seeing and hearing all come together. Then we might also recognize that the ponderousness of the phrase is substantially lightened by how "perpendicularity" provides a marvelously delicate yet pronounced feminine rhyme that affords a kind of distinctive physicality to such abstractness.

Finally we best get an ear and an eye for what syllabics can do if we contrast the leisurely prolonged run of monosyllables in the final line with the condensed force of "perpendicularity." We can feel the poem settling into its assertion as it fleshes out in what art's power can consist. There is again a feminine rhyme, but one that I think calls attention to the poem's capacity to produce a polish that acknowledges tensions with a world of thirst while also winning approval for art's mode of patience. All of the sounds in fact contribute to this sense of what polish has to acknowledge and what it nonetheless proves itself capable of achieving. The sounds in the last stanza seem to me to mime the effect of sculpture in their echoing edges—*b*, *i*, and *s* sounds play against each other from every position in the fifth and sixth lines. And, more important, Moore waits until the third line to introduce an expansive repetition of *a* sounds that open up the emotional register of response: "Spectacular and nimble animal the fish." Then it is hard not to stress all of the closing monosyllables as triumphant celebrations of the resource of polish in the art of making poems.

So what features of intentionality does the poem make articulate? First, it displays the power of the indexical "Here" to call attention to what can become present in the visible work poems do, as well as the work achieved in the art of glass sculpture. Second, the poem brings into play how first-order references can become folded into a constant second-order awareness of what seeing makes possible. Taken together, these two features make present a distinctive perspective on what can be involved in thinking about how art takes up roles in the actual world.

We can say then that Moore recovers the force of polish to transform a vehicle signifying thirst into a set of reflections on the positive force of patience and appreciation. The poem displays a sense of why its mode of agency might matter in the world and how a poem might recognize and intensify that power. And as an aspect of that mattering we can also realize the active power potential in our learning to hear in new ways. We are asked to recognize why traditional rhythm cannot sufficiently honor aspects of recognition that go considerably beyond personal speech, especially in their allying with the force of art over time. We are also asked to appreciate our own physicality by seeing it in a new light. What we hear depends on how we count. Moreover, as we count, we enter a position in which itself becomes a mode of intentionality activated by the poem. Counting syllables proves to be a mode of intentionality necessary for participating fully in the qualities of polish the poem produces as a condition of reconciling thirst and patience.

Appendix to Chapter 3

How Logic in the *Tractatus* Becomes Grammar in *On Certainty*

Classical empiricist theory sees the world built up from the senses, so that all of our elemental modes of awareness can be placed before the mind as objects of cognition, at least in principle. Our words mean because they refer, and our desires are interpretable because they embody knowable features of nature. These principles do not quite account even for Wittgenstein's *Tractatus*. He learned from opponents of empiricist psychology such as Husserl and Frege that one could not describe logic as if it consisted of discrete, knowable rules. Logic had to be systematic, and that systematic quality could not be described or justified because it was fundamental to any meaningful statements. Philosophical talk about logic has to presuppose the very thing it proposes to explain. We cannot occupy a position outside logic from which to describe it objectively.

So the power of logic as first science had to be displayed rather than argued for. This is why Wittgenstein says that one who understands him will have to treat the propositions as a ladder that he "must throw away . . . after he has climbed up it"[18] The model of logic rests on no foundation of argument because it is the foundation. The foundational force here consists in the power of logic to display how isolated propositions cohere as a system. The system is what implicates the world which the propositions make it possible to see. Philosophy "must set limits to what cannot be thought by working outwards to what can be thought" (*TLP*, 4.114). Each proposition about logic cannot claim truth but has to "show its sense" (*TLP*, 4.022) and so display its capacity to make truth statements possible.

In *On Certainty*, Wittgenstein was clearly no longer interested in repeating his account of how language can establish truthful propositions. But he does seem quite eager to extend what Matthew Ostrom calls "the logical transcendentalism" of the *Tractatus* so that he might establish a comprehensive sense of how philosophical grammar also provides a "ground" for the achieving of meaningful statements.[19] Therefore fully appreciating the force of *On Certainty*'s critique of the limits of knowledge requires spending a little time reviewing how display is understood in Wittgenstein's first work. Wittgenstein's basic critique of empiricist thinking and commonsense realism comes out most clearly in his treatment of what is involved in establishing the unity of a proposition. He recognizes that it is tempting to treat the complex sign *aRb* as saying that "*a* stands to *b* in the relation R." But "we ought to put 'that *a* stands to *b* in a certain relation says that *aRb*" (*TLP*, 3.1432).

What is the difference between these options? I think that in the first statement R preexists the elements and can be used to tie them together. But what is that third element a picture of, given the fact that it must be primarily syntactic? Because he sees this problem, Wittgenstein proposes that we can preserve the concrete picture aRb only if we do not treat R as a preexisting element independent of "a" and "b," imposed to create overall unity. Instead we must from the start take as a unity the way R simply constitutes the lines of relation between "a" and "b," as if the proposition captured just this relational whole.

This abstract argument will make concrete sense if we imagine Wittgenstein trying to capture the form of the representation of a traffic accident in a French courtroom, a scene that he characterized as fundamental to his *Tractatus*. We can make a fully concrete description only if we do not use any preexisting relational term for describing the positions of each agent in the accident. R has to be a specific relation if it is to allow definition for the positions of all the actors without becoming a term that must be positioned for itself. The entire relation aRb is the condition that must be met if the proposition-picture is to bear truth value.

Logic, then, is of a piece with the world it comes to constitute. It must display how R works in given situations. There is no aboutness to logic; there is nothing to be described because logic just is the elemental condition by which descriptions become possible. This condition defines by contrast the insubstantiality of discourses that purport to be about the world or about the place of humans in the world, such as ethics and aesthetics. Statements in these disciplines have no necessity, or nothing to display in the strong sense of the term, so they have to be seen as arbitrary constructions at the margin of a world we can know. Similarly, the generalizations made by Wittgenstein the logician also cannot be in the world because they do not picture any particular R; they only display why aRb has to be been seen as foundational. One cannot describe logic; one can only use it to display logical form and so clarify concretely how propositions can connect to the world.

Almost thirty years later, Wittgenstein again emphasizes how logic must be displayed rather than serve as an object of knowledge: "Am I not getting closer and closer to saying that in the end logic cannot be described? You must look at the practice of language, then you will see it" (*OC,* 501). He is still convinced that there is no way to represent as object the very terms that make representations possible. How can we stand outside of what makes possible what assertions can do? Yet the demands about display are very different. For the goal is not to show how pictures of the world are possible but rather to show what is involved in making any kind of sense—for expressions and avowals and the proposing of expectations as well as for propositions. In short, logic might have to be expanded to include as grounds for certainty the entire philosophical grammar that defines how the possibilities for understanding actions are encoded in our language games (see ibid.): "Or are we to say that certainty is merely a constructed point to which some things approximate more, some less closely? No. Doubt gradually loses its sense. This language game just is like that. And everything descriptive of a language game is part of logic" (ibid., 56). It is not pictures displaying specific versions of R that constitute the foundation of meaning; the range of possible activities given shape by our language games forms our sense of what has to be the case.

Chapter 4

THE CONCEPT OF EXPRESSION IN THE ARTS

> It is possible to say "I read timidity in this face," but, at any rate, the timidity does not seem to be merely associated, outwardly connected, with the face; rather, fear is there, alive, in the features. If the features change slightly, we can speak of a corresponding change in the fear. If we were asked, "Can you think of this face as an expression of courage too?"—we should, as it were, not know how to lodge courage in these features.
>
> —WITTGENSTEIN, *Philosophical Investigations*

> The sensations of sitting, standing, or running are, first and foremost, plastic sensations[,] and they are responsible for the development of corresponding "objects of use" and largely determine their form. A chair, bed, and table are not matters of utility but rather the forms taken by plastic sensations, so that the generally held view that all objects of daily use result from practical considerations is based upon false premises.
>
> —KASIMIR MALEVICH, *The Non-Objective World*

I love the first passage cited here because it seems Wittgenstein's sharpest contrast between what display can establish—"fear . . . alive, in the features"—and any discourse about knowledge. This sharp rendering of what expression can be also seems in part to resist how two of our best commentators on Wittgenstein deal with the general theme on which I have been concentrating: how Wittgenstein's later work differs from philosophy written under the auspices of Enlightenment values.

For philosophers such as Richard Eldridge and P. M. S. Hacker, the major achievement of Wittgenstein is, in Hacker's words, "to protect and conserve a domain of knowledge and form of understanding from erosion and distortion by the scientific spirit of the age."[1] Neither philosopher defends Enlightenment values. But I want to take a different path of critique by stressing instead those moments when Wittgenstein emphasizes a particularity and an intricacy that cannot be addressed by even their version of essentially hermeneutic practices made possible by language games. In my view there are aspects of Wittgenstein's thinking—mainly about moments in quotidian life but occasionally about art—that do not "protect and conserve a domain of knowledge" but lead us to explore other modes of attunement to people and to events. At stake is our picture of what powers matter to humans and how art plays significant social roles because of its ways of addressing those powers.

Hacker argues for "the autonomy of humanistic understanding" and the "repudiation of the doctrine of the unity of the sciences": "There are forms of rational inquiry that are not scientific, forms of understanding that are not modelled upon the scientific understanding of natural phenomena" (*AHU*, 44). For science simply cannot factor in the importance of humans coming to master "developed" languages (ibid., 58). Such languages become "partially constitutive of the form of life and culture of its speakers" (ibid., 59). So understanding must take these constitutive factors into account. We cannot simply read behavior as responding to causal forces in nature. Instead, the criteria for understanding expressions by human beings require attention to established rules of use, adapting the expressions to reflect the context in which they are uttered, and acknowledging a history of uses by other people that can impinge on interpretation (ibid., 60).

Rule following becomes an especially important consideration because if we are to honor such practices we need sharp distinctions between causal relations, which can establish only the "correlation of stimuli and response," and internal or logical connections, which adapt the distinctive resources of "rule-governed connections within the network of language" (ibid., 61). Language makes available the "logical devices signifying negation, conjunction, implication, and disjunction," which make reasoning possible (ibid., 63).

Reasoning has a practical dimension because it establishes the possibility of "intentional action," where causal analysis must give way to asking for the reason that the agent performed the deed. And "to specify the agent's reason for his intentional action is to give one kind of explanation of his behavior" (ibid., 65). Then we have to we deal with two worlds—the domain of nature, which is governed by causes, and the domain of culture, which depends on "the space of reasons" (ibid.,). This space consists of both "agential reasons and motives" and the social forms of conduct that the reasons negotiate (ibid., 70).

Consequently, we have to recognize not just that scientific explanation has its limitations but also that the domain of cultural explanations itself does not authorize only one model. So Hacker can offer what turn out to be familiar pieties about art:

> To understand the latter [situations and reasons defining individual choices] requires attention to the specific agent and his unique life, to the way he views the world, to his beliefs and goals, to the reasons that weigh with him and to the values he embraces—which is why the greatest of psychologists are the great biographers and, above all, the great novelists (we understand more about Emma Bovary or Anna Karenina than about anyone we know). (ibid., 72)

This is impressive prose even if it is perhaps too aware of its nobility. And the arguments present a refreshing change, allowing us to focus on how Wittgenstein's work may affect our practices of judgment and our sympathies with an immense range of possible actions. Yet for me those arguments ally too readily with the best of instrumentalist literary criticism because their focus remains on explanation and the kinds of knowledge explanation can sustain, extending to what becomes intelligible in cultural rather than in causal terms. Even when Hacker rises to rhetorical heights in his praise of human individuality, he provides a very limited range of actions by which to honor and respond to that individuality. His emphasis is on understanding and hence on what can be explained about human character and human actions. But I think it may be equally important to foreground those passages in Wittgenstein where the choice is not between modes of understanding but between the possibility of understanding a person's reasons and the need for other responsive attitudes better adjusted to subjective performances and conditions that invite our attention to the specific actions of concrete individuals.

Among other possible consequences, this perspective I prefer has substantial implications for how we value the powers cultivated by distinctively literary concerns with expressions of emotion. Expressions are not features of the world we can describe independently of the particular way that the subject presents the object. And because of this intimacy between subject and object, what solicits attention calls for attunement rather than just an account of its objective properties. Expressions connect epistemologically to display; pragmatically to example; and aesthetically to ideals of realization. Expressions are vehicles for how the imagination calls upon self-evidence.

How Can We Talk about Affective States Alive in Facial Features?

Wittgenstein usually invokes concepts of expression when he talks about how gestures or objects take on significance, as was the case in my epigraph. Here I hope to show how his comments on art elaborate the same issues and in the process clarify a full range of powers we use to explain why expressive activity of all sorts can play important roles in human behavior.

We have to begin with avowals because these are the most fundamental modes of display in which the subject calls attention to a specific state of mind or emotion. Avowals can give information, so there can be cognitive judgments involved in how we respond to them. But avowals are not in themselves descriptions or propositions about the state of mind or emotion. Nor can we quite treat typical avowals as expressions, at least in comparison to what counts as expressive activity in works of art.

Expressions are also modes of display. But they differ from many forms of avowal in their possessing some of the features that make concrete what are the relevant states of the agent. Hence my second epigraph. Avowals display states of subjects, but they need not possess the attributes they refer to. We can easily imagine someone saying "I am sad but am good at not showing it." In that respect saying "I am sad" is quite different from drawing a frowning face or introducing a metaphor as a figure attempting to characterize that sadness or recognizing chairs as realizing attributes of plastic sensations. As Wittgenstein notices in the epigraph to this chapter, expressions possess what they refer to—in the qualities of voice or the physical appearance of the speaker or the tone or the rhythms of the speaking.

Let us imagine a few examples of acts of expression that cross boundaries between life and art in ways that challenge the capacity of understanding to encompass what becomes visible. If we stick to faces, the obvious example is the history of portraiture. One could even say that this history teaches us how faces can seem to possess the attributes to which responders direct their attention. Another interesting possibility is the way artists can treat other objects as if they were faces, in the sense that the properties possessed by the display lodge emotions and states with which we expect human beings to grapple. The most famous and best example of such transfers is Van Gogh's *Pair of Shoes*. Heidegger's reading of this painting in "The Origin of the Work of

Art" brings out the degree to which the material features of this image solicit the kinds of compassion and respect that a portrait might, but without the theatricality and evasiveness created by how humans can stage what they exhibit. And then there is John Keats's "This Living Hand," where hands become repositories of need and desires and forms of threat.[2]

Hegel might consider the hand and the shoes as instances of substance inviting a mode of self-consciousness capable of encompassing every suggestive element in the represented detail. And eventually I hope to adapt this way of thinking because it provides powerful means for motivating self-consciousness to the task of responding sensitively to the expressive features of its environment. But for now I will just call attention to "Face," a poem by Jean Toomer that renders both the expressive features characterizing a face and the self-conscious temptations in the writing to evade that very reality.

Here the discourse gets immediately complicated because the poem dramatizes two kinds of substance in the process of being expressed—what the face can be said to make manifest and what the writing reveals about the speaker as it explores means of coming to terms with its understanding of the face:

> Hair—
> silver-gray,
> like streams of stars,
> Brows—
> recurved canoes
> quivered by the ripples blown by pain,
> Her eyes—
> mist of tears
> condensing on the flesh below
> And her channeled muscles
> are cluster grapes of sorrow
> purple in the evening sun
> nearly ripe for worms.[3]

It is crucial to recognize how the poem has these two modes of expression reinforce one another. We adapt to the qualities of the face both because of the metaphors and because of what is revealed about the maker of those metaphors. The metaphor transforming the gray hair into streams of stars seems mostly a means of denying the pain visible in the face. And even the second metaphor, this time for the brows, seems excessively pretty, again creating an alternative to the pain that is referenced.

Only when the condensed structure of this poem arrives at the core of the suffering can it finally adapt the metaphor-making to acknowledging the impact of how a very hard life is now lodged in the face. That acknowledgement takes not one but three metaphors, working in conjunction to "realize" all that is entailed by the pain etched in the face.[4]

The grapes of sorrow bring out the purple of the evening sun in her face. And the mention of evening reaches out along several threads of meaning not just to define the end of life but to characterize it in the bleakest terms possible. The final figure, "nearly ripe for worms," suggests that this person's life will be fruitful for something—but not anything connected to her personal desires. Her life is purely sacrificial, a condition irreducibly etched in an appearance the poet cannot keep evading. The poet engages the difficult problem of making us feel these qualities embedded in the face largely by tracking the speaker's struggles to come to terms with a quite complex emotional curve, finally gaining access to all that "ripe for worms" can make articulate.

Important Differences between Expressions and Avowals

On the basis of these observations I think we can say that expressions differ from avowals in three fundamental ways even though the two modes of display obviously have a great deal in common. First, an expression can be a capacious mode of activity not reducible to a single intentional act by the agent. For instance, expressions can evoke aspects of the past and deliberately call attention to aspects of character. And there can be a temporality or dimension of slow emergence as the expression takes on force.[5] Toomer fully utilizes the pressures of time as the metaphors gradually adapt to the nature of this face. But even in Wittgenstein's example, a face can display a kind of fear that leads us to question whether the agent in fact knows in what it consists or where it is leading. As the face changes, the fear itself is modified. The fear may not be completely contextualized or understood if we look only at the conditions by which it seems to emerge.

Second, we often are not called upon to respond to expressions in the direct way we are when dealing with avowals. Instead we can attune ourselves to what expressions display in a somewhat more distanced and self-reflexive mode, perhaps because of the fact that expressions possess some of the conditions to which they refer. More important, these possessed qualities can be puzzling and require reflection. Notice how in English "expression" takes both the subjective and the objective genitive: the face may express fear because the agent aligns with this emotion, or it may betray fear that the agent is trying to cover up, or, as Nicholas Gooding pointed out to me, the expression can be indeterminate with regard to whether it is something the agent does or something that is simply revealed in the actions.

Is Toomer responding to his impression of the face or contouring his language to get a glimpse of what it might have been like for the person to bear the consciousness the poem makes present? The first option casts the face as object positioned by the subject's expressive energies. The second option focuses on what drives the subject to speak this way. To respond fully to an expression is to take a position with sufficient distance to allow room to determine how these versions of the genitive might interact with each other.

Finally, because of these uncertainties, expressions have a kind of objectivity, a sense of independent being in the world that is missing when we deal with avowals. Avowals are dependent on what the subject is feeling. Expressions offer a subject's feeling as embedded "hereby" in concrete facts in the world.[6] So, rather than involving a distinctive language game, the expressions on a face seem to invite, and to test, the capacities of diverse language games (cf. *PI*, 538). We "read" such expressions before we respond to them, but we respond directly to avowals insofar as we treat them as avowals. Were we to "read" the avowal, we would treat it as an expression like the expression of the face because we would have to grapple with whether its mode is objective or subjective genitive. An avowal offers signs of emotion, while a fully subjective expression often works at making some affective state into a rendered experience.

This last distinction matters a great deal to me because the relative distance from the event qualities of avowals brings expression close to what I have described in my last chapter as Wittgenstein's distinctive use of the concept of a model. Toomer's poem is not a copy of a face but an expression of how an agent can come to terms with the striking features of this face. Not all expressions are models because we find expressive features that are not the result of conscious activity. But we have to speak of models when self-consciousness is foregrounded because the expression then contextualizes the dawning of an aspect.

Why These Observations Might Matter for Philosophy

I will treat expressive activity in art as building in to avowals and other modes of display an implicit effort to read what is also presented. In Hegelian terms, acts of self-consciousness prove capable of making substance articulate and even taking responsibility for what then takes shape. I think Wittgenstein thinks that even the simple expressive face bears potential for self-consciousness—of showing something about the agent's condition if not evoking a complete grasp of what the feeling is. And then self-consciousness is heightened when we encounter modelings of such expressions in drawings or theatrical performances or instruction manuals. It is as if the model took on the task of self-reflexively exploring the possibilities of what can be lodged concretely in a face. The model might even explore at what point fear can coincide with courage.

My concern for the conjunction between expression and modeling will lead me to aspects of the concept of expression which are largely ignored in contemporary aesthetics (and largely misappropriated in poststructuralist theory).[7] Contemporary analytic aesthetics quite reasonably assumes that expression is emotive personal utterance that is given the force of expressiveness by the skills of the artist. But for the idealist traditions within which the concept of expression first took on imaginative life, expression is not quite of the person. Rather, expression is a means by which spirit seeks to reconcile its potential for self-consciousness with its embodiment in particular historical circumstances.

Our criteria for effective philosophical argument do not allow talk of any spirit seeking to reconcile anything. But this does not mean we ought to dismiss Hegel's claims rather than explore how we might state them differently. Minimally, we might think of how complex the subject of expression is even in ordinary language. We speak of expressions of emotions or expressions of groups of people or expressions of immediate states or expressions as artists' performances (most often in dance or music)—all of which do not correlate with a notion of an individual subject focused on his or her inner life. There is too much respect for how the expression calls on complex aspects of our own sensibilities.

So we might be able to make sense of the idea that expressions do not just derive from this inner life but engage some kind of intelligence in relation to making manifest what seems a force that is being experienced. Our interests in expression drive the work by which we seek metaphors or other figures that can be at once accurate to what we see and capable of defining how we feel about what we see. Artists respond to this interest by anchoring feeling in observable objective conditions, so the act of making or rendering is in effect what establishes the possibility of a shared interest in the particular work.[8]

I will argue that Wittgenstein is the philosopher respected by Anglo-American philosophy whose intellectual involvement in the notion of expressive activity proves most amenable to straightforward practical explication that can honor the complexity of what artworks realize. I think he adapts much of what these idealist traditions saw in the concept of expression while forging an account that is blessedly free not only from the language of spirit but from the straining against practical intelligence required to justify such a vocabulary. He can reconstitute expressive thinking because he understands that this mode of thinking cannot be characterized simply as effusions of specific psychological agents.

Instead, Wittgenstein allows us to develop a case that expressive actions articulate how a subject might make visible the way self-consciousness fuses with sharp attention to particular details. Even in the epigraph to this chapter we can see him working toward a complexity and precision of awareness that will require aesthetics to adapt terms such as "realization" and not settle for "description" or "avowal." For the energies of the subject are transformed by how it encounters the object and by how the encounter in turn modifies the self-consciousness of the subject because it demonstrates what in fact the subject was capable of articulating.

Put more simply, Kant and Hegel thought that the category of expression (or the work of genius that gives the rule to nature) allowed philosophy access to a mode of authorial agency that produced something different from our standard assumptions about what people do in expressing emotions and in characterizing objects of attention. Artistic expression composes objective sites with significant subjective consequences. For the making has the potential for eliciting the creative capacities of other subjects while locating those capacities in what seems the force of the object rather than in subjective interests.

Therefore I have to show that the concept of expression allows a place in discourse by which to characterize how affects modify consciousness while also stressing how consciousness can establish modes of purposiveness, creating structures for reflecting on those modifications. Expression calls attention to aspects of worldliness that have objective force as actions in the world. Yet in their dense concrete fusion of subject and object these works do not yield easily to epistemic protocols derived from Enlightenment schema for how to represent knowledge. Instead they bring aspects of "imponderable evidence" into play (*PPF,* 360).

So if we can honor this constructed concreteness, we may be able to establish an entire vocabulary for responsiveness to art that is now missing in academic discourse, not only in aesthetics. We can develop richer languages for the production of artworks. And if we do that, we also perforce demand richer languages for the kinds of responses invited by these productions. For me this language of responsiveness entails figures of participation that involve coming to see into the work. And the more we stress aspects of participation, the more we reduce the roles of interpretation and explanation in aesthetic experience. It becomes possible to focus on how the text realizes new possibilities for experiencing the relation of self-consciousness to what sets it in motion. We put on stage exploratory aspects of subjectivity that need not respect our empirical sense of the boundaries forming isolated private persons.

What Can Happen When Philosophy Ignores Hegel on Expression

I want my arguments to make it possible for criticism to rely on a robust concept of expression. But we do not now have such a framework. So let me try to set the stage in two ways, in part so that I can explain also some of the limitations of my account. I confess to steering away from what I consider the best of current work on the concept of expression because it is all about music, and I do not know how to transfer it to literary studies.[9] I also have chosen to concentrate on an essay that is not among the best work in contemporary analytic aesthetics. But I think its weaknesses bring out symptomatic features of the discipline at large, especially when aestheticians are not talking about music. The essay in question is by Jenefer Robinson, a thinker whose obsessive clarity and concreteness prevent any trace of speculative intensity.[10] The obsession with clarity ends up blocking both the possible complexity in the ideas and the possibility of challenging the audience to address that complexity.

The first way I will set the stage is by offering very brief remarks on what happened to the concept of expression after Hegel in mainstream aesthetics. That in turn should help show why I think Robinson's essay is important in large part because of its limitations.

Modern thinking on the concept of expression takes shape from the arguments posed by Benedetto Croce in his *Aesthetic*.[11] Croce tried to defend expression against increasingly vapid equations of it with the statement of lyrical feeling by setting expression against feeling. He equated the work of expression with composing an object that could display the powers of intuition, as if all expression could be equated with expressiveness. This argument was based on separating willing and valuing from knowing. Then, within knowing, Croce isolated intuition from concept so the difference from the conceptual order basic to expressive activity had to be located in the status of the object rather than in what the subject might have contributed to the making of the object.

By this work Croce laid the foundation for formalisms new and old. Then Guy Sircello tried heroically to restore expression as a condition of subjective agency.[12] Sircello showed how many of the properties we associate with expressiveness require attributions of the modes of subjectivity involved in making and in projecting affective consequences for what emerges as the world within the work. For one needs an expressive maker to account for meaning. Otherwise, purpose would have to be located in the audience, and that is not how we experience art.

We recognize in works of art qualities visible to everyone. These qualities, such as rhythm and aspects of brushwork or diction, then need a locus that has more stability and generality than can be provided by any theory based on audience response. Yet these qualities are not objects of knowledge. They invite responding to the work as a particular set of demands—again as if the making were crucial to the response. Yet Sircello would not use idealist frameworks for his account of agency. So his account of agency remains pretty thin, leading him to overcompensate by problematic claims about heroic lives in the concluding chapters of his book. Such claims left the field for discussing what is expressed in verbal and visual arts to "reasonable" theorists such as Robinson.

Robinson's basic move is to insist on a sharp contrast between the expressive act of an empirical subject and the "expressiveness" by which the art object gains its power. She insists, correctly in my view, that both "expression and expressiveness have their home in ordinary life and then are extended to the arts" (*EE*, 19). But for her having a home in ordinary life means being accessible analytically to commonsense attitudes about this key distinction: for her, expression covers only a limited range of personal emotional stances while it is the expressiveness of the work that affords the possibility of cognition for an audience.

In Robinson's terms, expression is an author-centered rendering of a point of view (ibid., 23); expressiveness is audience centered (ibid., 19). Expression issues from somebody who is actually experiencing an emotion so that other people can perceive the emotion in their response to the work: "The work provides evidence that the person is experiencing (or has experienced) this emotion" (ibid., 20). But the rendering of emotion can make an impact on an audience only if the artist can endow the art object with expressiveness.

When expressiveness is achieved, the art object can reveal something about the nature of the emotion and therefore serve cognitive functions: "If the expression is relatively expressive, we are also shown something about what it is like to be in that state" (ibid., 30). For example, if the speaker says "slimy snake," you get a better picture of how that person regards the person referred to (ibid., 31). Ultimately Robinson sees herself differing from other expression theorists because she argues that expressiveness does not have to be grounded in expression. Rather, expressiveness is the condition of how any work of art makes visible states of being for reflective consciousness (ibid., 32).

There are three basic problems with Robinson's arguments: expressive activity need not be just the presentation of emotion; the expressive object is probably not so simply cognitive as to offer "knowledge" of what authors or characters feel or even how they feel; and her pursuit of a strong concept of expressiveness has to rely on a weak concept of expression. Let me address each in turn.

I think rooting the idea of expression in the picture of a person expressing particular emotions is a disastrous oversimplification of how the best art produces models of human agency—because most artists stage their characters, including themselves, as facing up to all sorts of existential pressures that complicate what can be expressed as straightforward emotion. It is the rare artist who is unaware of how expression takes the double genitive. More important, the best work (considered in terms of what makes for canonical status) does not quite express recognizable and nameable emotion. Expressing in art is making, not speaking—a making that binds subject and world and so allows desire to emerge into meaningfulness while bypassing concepts. Expression composes a world in which affective intensities of all kinds interact in order to make present distinctive and complex states of mind so that the work can entice levels of participation not called on in standard versions of cognition.

This indeed is why Wittgenstein's model of a face is so effective—for our appreciation of life as well as our appreciation of art. To ignore this complexity and this potential density at the expressive pole is also necessarily to develop strikingly thin concepts of expressiveness. For Robinson that role in art is to let us know what someone is feeling in ordinary life. Cognition becomes possible through art, but this kind of cognition parallels what a coffee klatch can provide.

Such poverty of vision is most disturbing in Robinson's image of what the audience seeks from the artwork. The audience seems to be an eager group of naïve philosophy students seeking knowledge of how speakers reveal the nature of typical emotions one also finds in ordinary life (*EE*, 27). There is no sense of a possible audience eager for complex states of mind that they do not find in "ordinary life" but might discover if their imaginations could actually be modified by what they encounter as continuous with that life. Robinson has very little respect for the full energies of imagination.

Charles Taylor on the Concept of Expression in the 1790s

Charles Taylor makes a compelling case that, in Germany during the 1770s because of Herder and then again in the 1790s because of idealist philosophy, there developed a coherent worldview around the differences between representing the world as Enlightenment philosophy imagined it and basing thinking on how worlds are produced within the expressive activity of spirit trying to make its self-consciousness visible and so an object of knowledge.[13] Standard views of cognition became the enemy because they sanitized desire and separated the objects of knowing from the modes of experience that modified these objects.

Taylor's story provides a first step for making secular sense of expressivist ideals. It shows how these ideals can be presented as alternatives to prevailing dispensations that treat philosophy as primarily a practice for characterizing how the world can be represented accurately and truth statements articulated. Taylor's account matters first because it shows how Herder, Hegel, and others rejected the idea that the primary task of the intellectual was to present a world stripped of tendencies to project meanings onto things (*H*, 7). If we pursue only a scientific observation of things, we necessarily have a disenchanted world unable to sponsor feelings or loyalties (ibid., 9).

Second, his account shows how this disenchantment leaves the subject in a difficult position. For while the subject gains freedom from religion and state authority, agents find that victory always threatened by a sense of empty or purposeless will. The agent is free, but then what happens to loyalty or a sense of common purpose? Here Taylor can emphasize his sense of the limitations of Enlightenment political theory: "An atomistic science of nature" matched "a political theory whose starting point was the individual in a state of nature" (ibid., 10). A philosophy of expression had to (and for Taylor still has to) change our view of both subject and object without reinserting religious meanings into things and traditional authority into politics.

For Taylor the key move was to insist that the subject-object model for stabilizing cognition be replaced by attention to the nature of the actual experience by which we construct what can satisfy as knowledge. This move entails recognizing that in many situations the subject does not simply want to form an object of knowledge. Instead it cultivates the self-consciousness to appreciate itself in action as it inquires into what knowledge can involve for the self. This activity in turn changes the object of knowledge because that object becomes now robustly caught up in various modes of existence for the subject.

Then we can say that because expression foregrounds the activity of the agent in a way that fuses its agency with what elicits that agency, feelings become not facts about persons but aspects of the person's engaging with the world (*H*, 23). The self is modified by what it engages. Taylor puts it this way:

as the self unfolds, it recognizes how it participates in "the act of a universal life which was bigger than any subject, but qua self-unfolding life very subject-like" (ibid., 16). This subjectlike quality consists in how the expressive subject makes "determinate, perhaps for the first time, what he feels and wants" (ibid.). Imagine seeing your own sadness, identifying with it partially, but also partially rejecting it so you have to reconstitute what emotion you are really feeling.

But as clear as Taylor is, there is something that blocks my assent. Perhaps it is the confidence of his assertions. He attributes so much existential power to ideas such as "universal life," even though such notions can at best be only ideals related to what expression might become, that I begin to doubt that such ideals can provide an adequate account of knowledge or of how what freedom we have as humans in fact gets enacted. And I am not quite willing to accept how expression promises to value community over the range of options available to individuals, however disenchanted they might become with our dominant scientific ways of dealing with objects. (Nietzsche is one of the heirs of Hegel on expression.)

Yet I do not think I have to share these beliefs in order to rely on Taylor's work to clarify both why artists think expressive activity is important and why when it does occur it makes distinctive demands on us. Many claims within idealist philosophy can make sense for artworks because there we can entertain what might be involved in the fusion of subject and object for the duration of the work. We need make no claims about what the world is beyond what can enrich our participation in the work and in the work's projected efforts to alter the sensibilities of those participating in it. And we need make no claims about universal features of what is involved in feeling oneself a subject.

In the aesthetic domain we can plausibly believe that an individual agent can seek fuller self-consciousness by two separate means. The agent can come to appreciate what is involved in seeing objects as carrying the marks of the subject's disclosing activity. And the agent can come to understand how participating in the work of art allows identifications with other subjects and perhaps even with the idea of what it takes for all subjects to experience themselves as subjects.

We have these freedoms because the central task of art remains not to explain the world but to intensify our individual relationships with it. There is no intensifying a world that readers will not take as a plausible one. But establishing that plausibility is not necessarily a matter of demonstrating true beliefs, especially because most art is less concerned with the nature of the world as such than with the various ways in which the passions both stage and distort what might be the case. Most significant works of art promise only to mobilize and thicken experience so that the world becomes a more vital place for habitation, making the self feel itself an adequate locus of responsiveness to what the world can offer.

Hegel's Arguments about the Expressive Subject

The expressive subject for Hegel is emphatically not just an agent who offers up his or her emotional response to some phenomenon. Hegel's fullest argument about expression in art occurs toward the end of his *Phenomenology of Spirit*, beginning with his mapping of what the religious spirit can entail for artists' understanding of what their work can become. Hegel's central task here is to articulate how substance can be "charged as Subject with the at first only inward necessity of setting forth within itself what it is in itself, of exhibiting itself as spirit" (*PS*, para. 802; see also para. 757).

This statement might at first boggle the mind. But it is fairly easy to unpack once one recognizes that for Hegel there are two fundamental aspects of spirit which must eventually recognize as fully as possible the implications of their interdependence. Expression is the basic vehicle for such recognition. One aspect of spirit is the life of self-consciousness striving to expand an initial inner sense that life takes on fuller meaning as the "here" of self-consciousness seems to take on scope and power.

But this "here" has to engage something that is not directly within these states of self-consciousness because it must appear as its other, as the target of thinking rather than as a state of the thinker. Yet this other must be intimately connected to self if this knowledge is not to be just the distanced observation of Enlightenment science. So Hegel treats the forces that confront self-consciousness as another aspect of spirit and hence of the self.

Substance is that aspect of our existence through which we encounter forces—from nature and from society—that seem to determine our lives. But aspects of those constitutive factors have not yet been made explicit for self-consciousness. Substance is for human life everything that an ideal science might point out as necessities resisting the senses of power and possibility characterizing the stances that self-consciousness takes up. Then Hegel can argue that expression is the effort on the part of self-consciousness to possess this otherness by turning what is inchoate material into conditions for which self-consciousness can provide forms of recognition. The more densely this self-consciousness can abide within its emerging sense of substance, the richer the accuracy of what it can offer as the theater in which spirit produces forms for itself.

We can purge much of the idealism here if we isolate and flesh out three central figures that are crucial in Hegel's discussion of expression. First there are his criticisms of picture-thinking, which bring Hegel quite close to Wittgenstein's distrust of empiricism and behaviorism. In Hegel's *Phenomenology of Spirit* the core problem with picture-thinking is that it proves an inadequate model of what constitutes objects for self-consciousness: it offers only objects apart from the experiencing of them. So picture-thinking must be superseded by modes of awareness of the forces that underlie pictures and sustain relationships rather than images. This is why for Hegel the most sophisticated art, romantic art, has its ground not in observation but in the inner life, whose force derives from a sense of relationships that can be figured but not pictured. This inner life is one domain which constitutes the complex substance making demands on self-consciousness.

The limitations of picture-thinking then provide grounds in Hegel's thinking for a second figure, which tries to capture the nature of the relationships that "realize" how self-consciousness comes to terms with substance. This is the figure of the variable copula "I=I." Imagine one "I" as self-consciousness; the other as substance. The richness of their relationship to each other is measured by the scope and precision of the sign for equality.

Picture-thinking might be content to construct images of the events when the members of the Third Estate took the Tennis Court Oath and formed the National Assembly of France. Such an image would provide the agents a distinct identity and so would establish a vehicle for transforming the substance of the event into self-consciousness: these are those who formally stood in opposition to Louis XVI for the first time. But while the images provide some substance, they do not adequately render the substance of what the members of the National Assembly accomplished by signing this oath and forming the assembly. Both the "I" available to the agents and the "it" available to observers of the scene are relatively thin. Indeed, this level of analysis relegates self-consciousness to a version of picture-thinking about the self: at best it affords an emblem of the ease with which statements of feeling induce banal cognitive claims.

Picture-thinking offers only pictures because it ignores the relational forces that are a basic feature of our experience of substance. The episode of the Tennis Court Oath is not only a historical scene. It is enmeshed in complex relations among agents and textures of resentment crossed with competing ambitions. So a historian tracing those relations would be able to offer a much fuller rendering of how people were positioned in the scene. This kind of knowledge would provide the material for a much richer equation. The self-consciousness for the agents would include awareness of their places in those relational forces. And the substance would be radically transformed to include everything the historian sees—not just as object but as potentially what the subject has to include in self-consciousness if that consciousness is to embrace an intensified reality for the situation.[14]

Now think of what the situation would be if the agents themselves were to have participated in the historian's knowledge. They would then be in a position to develop a third figure stressing not physical identity but a full imagining of how the self strives to take responsibility for a particular sense of being just this person. Coming to a fresh sense of identity also involves willing that identity as one's realized situation. Were this condition of agency to find expression, it would establish what it can be like to have self-consciousness align with substance as each displayed its own sense of the fullness of its being.

For Hegel this sense of equivalence transforms the quality of the copulative verb. Now "I am I" or "I=I" asserts a dynamic synthesis between what happens in self-consciousness and what happens to the sense of substance constituting the grounds of that mode of awareness:

> Only after it has externalized this individuality in the sphere of culture, thereby giving it existence, and establishing it through the whole of existence . . . only then does it turn the thought of its inmost depths outward and enunciate essence as "I"="I". . . . In other words, the I is not merely the Self but the identity of the self with itself; but this identity is complete and immediate oneness with Self, or this Subject is just as much Substance. (*PS,* para. 803)

The goal of expression is to bring to full self-consciousness what one comes to know and therefore to feel about one's mode of material existence, *as* one takes responsibility for it. Self-consciousness attunes more richly to what it inhabits because it makes articulate how substance can bear language and carry the affective charge of what recognition involves. The face in Toomer's poem becomes a challenge to the reader to recognize all the history contained there and to see what the speaker will need to do to accept responsibility for that face as an element in the speaker's world.

There emerges a dynamic equivalence between what one thinks one knows about the self and how the self is actually positioned as a given historical entity: "Each meaning therefore completes itself in the other" (*PS*, para. 782). This sense of completion is not just cognitive but involves the will. "I=I" can just be flat description; it can be a statement of excited participation, and it can be a literal affirmation that the self wants to be no one else or nowhere else because its fulfillment is in recognizing how the equation affords full terms for identity (hence the Hegel in Nietzsche). This degree of identification must be accompanied by the will's affirmation of responsibility for what consciousness undergoes.[15]

We can summarize this account by suggesting that Hegel's break from picture-thinking affords a model of expression marked by capacities for extraordinarily complex structures of identification. At one pole there is the pull of intensities from within self-consciousness as it expands the conative field of actions for the self. This is in constant creative conflict with finding identification in terms of actual substance that spirit has accomplished over time—for which self-consciousness must take responsibility.[16] One is continually discovering oneself a fool as one manages at the same time to satisfy deep desires to clarify further the mistakes that ironically give one access to the force of history.

This motion, this expansion and contraction of self-consciousness as it encounters itself in the form of substance, provides a powerful alternative to any version of knowledge based on representing the facts of the case. Here the modes of the subject produce a display of relatedness, or of variable equivalence, for which no concepts can prove adequate. Expression is realization through and through because it cannot be characterized except as an activity by which subject and substance engage a process of completing the copula that reveals their underlying identity as each the active negation of the other, as each searches for fulfillment in the other.

Toward a Wittgensteinian Version of Expression

I think Wittgenstein proves a fitting heir to Hegel on the concept of expression even though he rejected every element of Hegelian philosophy. There probably cannot be philosophers more distant from one another. One sought a science capable of incorporating the stations of the cross revealed by historical experience into a cogent system. The other came to distrust almost every effort to think systematically. Instead he sought out the rough ground so that thinking could honor the multiple differences that our grammars make manifest.[17] Yet Wittgenstein's approach to philosophy seems to provide a mode of thinking capable of making concrete much of what is most forceful in Hegel's account of expression. Where Hegel concentrates on the essentially heroic content of expressive activity, Wittgenstein attends to expression's place in typical human experiences so that we recognize our own capacity to participate in a grammatical arena for working out the complexity of identity and identifications. Picture-thinking, on the other hand, is locked into empirical analyses of individual propositions. Combating picture-thinking for Wittgenstein requires staging self-consciousness as the mind elaborates its places in the experience of what grammar affords.

I want to trace some of the moments where Wittgenstein's thinking dwells on the same kind of experiences that elicited Hegel's formulations. But I also want to honor the way Wittgenstein is not interested in producing a theory of expression but simply in establishing a framework capable of helping us find our way in attuning to the range of practices by which the features of expression enter our lives. He was fascinated by how human beings make complex adjustments in their sense of who they can be as they try to go on without falling into the traps philosophy sets for us. So I hope that we can adapt his thinking to show that expressive behavior is not confined to the enactment of emotions but extends to how we stage the dawning of aspects and utilize the power of language to adapt examples for illustrative purposes. For that dawning involves not only what is pictured but also the position of the one who responds to such psychological activities by making models clarifying the relation between the person and the seeing (see Ludwig Wittgenstein, *Zettel*, ed. G. E. M. Anscombe and G. H. von Wright [Berkeley: University of California Press, 1970], 158, 67; cited hereafter cited as Z). And the use of examples is a basic way that we can display our own activity in our renderings of experience.

Now we will have to work in the opposite direction from what we were doing with Hegel. I was continually paring Hegel down in order to minimize the idealist implications of his account of the relations between subject and substance. We have to be continually building Wittgenstein up by adding a speculative dimension to his minimalist reticence and suspicion of all conceptual work not devoted to philosophical grammar. Eventually we will be extending what Wittgenstein was doing rather than commenting on him. But before that I want to quote several passages to test how they might take on significance in a context shaped by Hegel's very different language.

The first and most important parallel with Hegel's view of expression is Wittgenstein's insistence that expression and expressive behavior occupy a distinctive and observable realm in human life for which standard epistemic protocols are not appropriate. Think, for example, of a second Wittgenstein passage characterizing facial expressions:

> "We see emotion." As opposed to what?—We do not see facial contortions and make inferences from them (such as a doctor framing a diagnosis) to joy, grief, boredom. We describe a face immediately as sad, radiant, bored, even when we are unable to give any other description of the features.—Grief, one would like to say, is personified in the face. This belongs to the concept of emotion. (Z, 225)

Wittgenstein could have been reading Jean Toomer's "Face." Expression is typically concrete and immediate. We do not gather data, then fit it into a schema. We might say we directly see the face as sad, or it dawns on us as sad, because the sadness lodges in the features (*PI*, 536). The emotion is not added to the face: the emotion becomes visible in the face. We can say then that the face literally possesses the emotional attribute it signifies as the person's emotional state.

The second parallel with Hegel derives from Wittgenstein's realization that the figure of the face can take us beyond what is displayed in avowals. Avowals can present cries or statements of surprise or hope that evoke immediate response: "one does not comfort the hand" that is in pain, but one comforts "the sufferer: one looks into his eyes" (ibid., 286).

We can offer this comfort because the face expressing pain has an objective presence occupying space and time. This is where avowal takes on the properties of expression. The avowal of pain here not only makes visible an affective state but invites treatment as an object in its own right because it possesses the traits we attribute to the agent. So we can treat the expression as producing a set of internal relations among the features of the face that we recognize but find difficult to name in any precise way. One might say that we recognize specific aspects of sadness even though we think we have to use the generic term "sadness" for a variety of manifestations.

This tension between what grammar can name and what seems concretely to have a density resisting names then extends to Wittgenstein's understanding of art. So here we have a third possible comparison. Wittgenstein in effect follows Kant and Hegel in suggesting that the expressions solicit a flow of thoughts without being summarized by any definite thought: "When do we say: 'the line intimates to me like a rule always the same'? And, on the other hand, 'It keeps on intimating to me what I have to do—it is not a rule' " (Z, 279). The intimating depends on concrete properties that carry a promise of meaning but of a kind that wants to become a rule rather than follow one. A gesture has been made available for other possible contexts (ibid., 158). Hence Wittgenstein proposes this version of worldliness for expressive activity:

> For me the musical phrase is a gesture. It insinuates itself into my life. I adopt it as my own. Life's infinite variations are essential to our life. And so too even to the habitual character of life. What we regard as expression consists in incalculability. If I knew exactly how he would grimace, move, there would be no facial expression, no gesture . . . (CV, 73)

The crucial point here is that because expressions can be deliberate and deliberated upon, we have to honor their makers as capable of wielding that deliberation in highly intricate and suggestive ways. Expression is not just a view of how emotions are displayed, nor is it only the basis for making claims about internal relations in works of art. For Wittgenstein, as for Hegel, expression entails a full sense of the powers agents can exercise. Expressive activity challenges models based on behaviorist and empiricist models of human action because the roles played by the subject are complexly and variously embedded in the activity.

Where Art Comes into Wittgenstein's Treatments of Expression

Wittgenstein's awareness of these possibilities for complex and fluid performances of subjectivity are clearest in his comments on art. His resistance to epistemic protocols, for example, becomes an emphasis on the irreducible concreteness of internal relations within the work. Wittgenstein contrasts "thought in a sentence" that is "common to different sentences" with "something that is expressed only by these words in these positions. (Understanding a poem.)" (*PI*, 531). And he has the same respect for the absoluteness of picture space: "'A picture tells me itself' is what I'd like to say. That is, its telling me something consists in its own structure, in *its* own forms and colors" (ibid., 523).

Here we can notice that the picture elicits the same kind of focused range of reflection as what takes place in responding to a face. But we should also pay attention to the logical sophistication Wittgenstein can bring to the understanding of pictures, as in the following sharp distinction between elements that refer outside the work and elements that are constructed by the work as "one-place predicates":[18] "Mustn't someone who is painting be painting something—and someone who is painting something be painting something real?—Well, tell me what the object of the painting is: the picture of the man (for example) or the man whom the picture portrays" (ibid., 518; see also ibid., 683). The picture of the man derives from the painting's own structure and so constitutes a distinctive experience expressing embodied qualities, while the picture of the man whom the picture portrays relegates the picture to epistemic purposes, which involve the two-place concern for how a picture can conform to its referent.

Second, even when Wittgenstein states romantic commonplaces, there is a constant inquiry into what this specificity of focus can mean for our understanding of understanding. For example, Wittgenstein follows this description of the language of a poem with two sections reflecting on what constitutes understanding:

> Then has "understanding" two different meanings here?—I would rather say that this kind of use of "understanding" makes up its meaning, makes up my *concept* of understanding. For I *want* to apply the word "understanding" to all this. (*PI*, 532)

> But in the second case, how can one explain the expression; communicate what one understands? Ask yourself: How does one *lead* someone to understand a poem or a theme? The answer to this tells us how one explains the sense here. (ibid., 533)

I think one explains the sense here by replacing a view of understanding based on interpreting the particulars as discrete elements with one that emphasizes how gathering the whole into a one-place predicate can serve to produce fresh possibilities for experience that it can exemplify.[19] Think again of how we could best read Claudius's opening speech or Toomer's "Face." The crucial process is seeing the work as a single complex act. So we understand it not by explaining it but by showing we can use it as an exemplar that fits with or illuminates other particular ways of responding to experience. (I offer a much more elaborate account in my next chapter, which elaborates how exemplarity affords a vehicle for complex and affective understanding while preserving the specificity of the expression.)

Third, because he can redefine our understanding of understanding, Wittgenstein can make a major break from most of the modern theorists of expression, with whom he shares this emphasis on the work constituting its own reality. For Wittgenstein the fact that art involves a distinctive kind of understanding does not warrant any language about the uniqueness of the artwork as an artifact disdaining mere life, such as Yeats's golden bird. Rather, he is interested in how the incalculable dispositions we learn through art can "insinuate" themselves into our everyday situations, showing us how "what is ordinary is here filled with significance" (*CV,* 52).

This passage from *Culture and Value* offers an extended meditation on what is experienced when one follows a theme intensely in a piece of music:

> A theme, no less than a face, wears an expression.... Sing it, and you will see that only the repeat gives it its tremendous power. Don't we have the impression that a model for this theme already exists in reality and the theme only approaches it, corresponds to it, if this section is repeated? ... Yet there just is no paradigm apart from the theme itself. And yet again there is a paradigm apart from the theme: namely the rhythm of our language, of our thinking and feeling. And the theme, moreover, is a *new* part of our language; it becomes incorporated into it; we learn a new gesture. The theme interacts with language. (ibid.)

I let myself quote at length here because this passage offers a truly remarkable interplay of what we might call "the inner and the outer." It stresses how our very feel for the rhythms of our thinking and our feeling gets modified as we not only absorb the theme but find it mutating into a paradigm for possible worlds we can discover. We see Wittgenstein transforming what had been the idealist theme of the interplay between subject and substance into useful models for attending to the complexities of ordinary experience.[20]

Notice, for example, how just below the quoted passage Wittgenstein turns explicitly to how words can engage such experiences. And notice as well his own metaphors of acorn and oak that involve the direct containment of emotion in the figures language elaborates. Expression is not a matter of reference:

"Fare well!"

"A whole world of pain is contained in these words." How *can* it be contained in them?—It is bound up with them. The words are like an acorn from which an *oak* tree can grow. (*CV*, 52)

Fourth, where such embodiment is possible, questions of value cannot be far behind. I think Wittgenstein reserves for the place of art in life a language of explicit valuings that his *Tractatus* had banished from the empirical world—this time by stressing how these rhythms and choices of words modify our senses of that world. One might say that these rhythms and verbal formulations produce a sense of the distinctiveness of my world that nonetheless remains continuous with the facts of everyone's world. I feel I do not only occupy my world but come actively to inhabit it. And the powers involved in such habitation are shareable across empirically different worlds.

These are large claims for so careful and cautious a writer as Wittgenstein. Yet how can one not use some version of them to provide a gloss for the enigmatic precision of this comment from *Philosophy of Psychology—A Fragment:* "The familiar face of a word, the feeling that it has assimilated its meaning into itself, that it is a likeness of its meaning—there could be human beings to whom all this is alien. (They would not have an attachment to their words.)—And how are those feelings manifested among us? By the way we choose and value words" (*PPF*, 294). One basic claim about value here involves the sense of fit that assimilates words into their meanings. "Fit" is a crucial value because it leaves no place for doubt or irony: what complexities of tone and judgment are involved become necessary for adapting to the situation. A second value is projected in how the quoted statement turns self-reflexively on itself. Not only can the words fit the situation, but there can be a sense for the speakers that their energies also do not overflow the situation but find a home in the words that have been chosen.

Wittgenstein on Subjectivity

This self-reflexive valuing introduces a new and final turn for my discussion of expression. I think Wittgenstein shares Hegel's concern to blend a sense of rightness built on feelings that words can fit the emotional feel of situations with another, self-reflexive concern for the powers that are displayed in such moments. Both philosophers ask who one can see the self becoming by virtue of how one deploys language or any medium? The possible answers to this question go beyond the individual to the appreciation of what is involved in possessing the powers we need to adjust to the potential complexities that call for expressive makings in first place.

I have argued that most aestheticians share Jenefer Robinson's equation of expression with avowal. Then, as is the case with Robinson, they have to bend over backward to separate the meaty material of art, the "expressiveness," from the one whom they presume does the expressing. And in so doing they lose the distinguishing historicity of the expression because they can treat the author only as a biographical agent rather than as maker discovering an identity by virtue of how that making is performed.

These aestheticians also lose what we might call "the modality of expression." I take "modality of expression" to be the sense of agency constructing itself to be adequate to the demands made on its powers. And I stress the idea of modality because this seems the only adequate way for us to characterize how the equation "I=I" plays out as an internal dialectic between those demands and the accomplishment of the making subject.

Milton did not write *Paradise Lost* to express the opinions of John Milton, British citizen, but to inhabit a concrete position where it became possible to "justify the ways of God to man." And Dante puts at the center of his text the transformations of empirical agency that make it possible for a moment to identify with divine love. Last and least, when Charles Altieri writes love poems, he is decidedly not the same person as the author of this book. (Or, perhaps because he is not a good poet, he both is and is not the same person as the author of this book: empirical personal identity haunts a person, but it does not completely block the exploration of possible selves.)

The stakes here go well beyond aesthetics because philosophers working on Wittgenstein's psychology and the possible ethical implications of his thought also tend to equate the expressivist subject with the one who avows rather than the one who can dwell in differentiating "a feeling" from exploring the kinds of understanding the display of "feeling" might involve. David Finkelstein provides a test case. His book offers an intriguing attempt to navigate between two views of what kind of authority the subject has in relation to "his own hopes, fears, desires, beliefs, moods, emotions, sensations, and passing thoughts."[21] One perspective treats the agent as having a privileged position to detect such conditions by some mode of "inward observation." The second view, often attributed to Wittgenstein, is that the experience of hopes, fears, and so on is not inner observation but a mode of awareness continuous with the production of these states.

Ultimately Finkelstein rejects both "detectivism" and "constitutivism" for the view that "to call attention to the fact that some utterance is, or is akin to an expression needn't be to deny that it is an assertion as well" (*EI*, 5). And such assertions have truth value because they can either be accurate descriptions or mistaken projections. So Finkelstein extends avowals to expressions, then claims that avowals are to be treated as modes of self-awareness that are "truth-evaluable" (ibid., 96).[22] The avowal is not literally a description. But when one understands what the expression is asserting, one can judge whether it, in fact, captures who the person has become in the relevant situation.

These claims seem worth examining because if Finkelstein is correct, Wittgenstein makes his peace with those who want to absorb expressivity into assertions that do or do not work out to have truth value. And Finkelstein is almost certainly right that if a person understands an avowal, one can successfully describe the state of the agent. But is this mode of description what the agent wants, or why he or she produces the utterance in the first place?

It is probably the case that even with simple avowals, the description cannot quite capture the event. Imagine telling the agent: "Yes, you are right that you are in pain," or "Yes, you do expect him to come." I cannot see how that would satisfy because the relevant quality of the information is not the content of the message but the state of the speaker. The force of the expression can bring into play aspects of the making energy that simply do not fit within the limits of the self, whom one might try to describe in historical terms. The relevant self in the avowal is what the context allows one to construct in relation to how the feeling unfolds as a property of what becomes articulate.

This seems to be a very important debate because if the theory of expression is to get anywhere near Hegel's claims about the struggle to bring spirit to substance, it has to have a capacious and dynamic view of subjectivity. It cannot be limited to the empirical subject that we picture from the outside. With this in mind, I want to return to the Tractarian view of subjectivity as incompatible with empirical observation because I think Wittgenstein held aspects of this view throughout his career.

Indeed, without this sense of continuity I do not think we can explain why "confession" becomes so important a concept for Wittgenstein (and ethics so unimportant a concern) late in his career. Confessions become the elemental mode by which subjects take responsibility for all that they cannot picture about themselves, yet must express to find any stable place in the world of facts. Knowledge categorizes: "this is a version of that." But confession for Wittgenstein has to individualize and so has to deny all versions not just of representativeness but also of justification. The person must just be there, like forms of life. And, like forms of life, this thereness can elicit modes of responsiveness that do not require "knowledge" but are content to adapt to what seem to be specific needs and desires.

We have already seen how in Wittgenstein's later writing grammar plays the same role as logic and has the same dependence on being displayed rather than discovered through argument. Language games, like logic, do not "rest on some form of knowledge" (*OC*, 477) but are the indispensable medium in which to formulate what can count as knowledge.[23] But unlike language games, logic has no place for expressions of subjectivity such as attitudes or assertions about values.

When Wittgenstein rejects the primacy of logic and establishes the foundational roles of grammar, how does he also adapt to the ways that logic in the *Tractatus* simply abandoned subjectivity to the domain of an often powerful, irrational, and unintelligible force? What place does subjectivity have in the scheme of *On Certainty*? Is it just a feature of how we use language, with nothing more substantial at stake? Or is there a strong sense of the individual subject that can be manifest in various language games but not described?

In order to answer this question we would have to know what "a strong sense of an individual subject might mean." I propose that a strong sense of a subject refers to the feeling that there is a power persons have to endow situations with values important to the agent and to draw out from the encounter what had been implicit aspects of those values. One makes visible both the values and the working out of the implications by the style with which the agent takes responsibility for any particular stance. If this attitude toward subjectivity makes sense, we can insist that we can recover the force of making basic to expressive activity without any need for the language of spirit and substance.

It is important then to realize that Wittgenstein probably never rejected this fundamental view: "The sense of the world must lie outside the world. In the world everything is as it is, and everything happens as it does happen: in it no value exists, and if it did, it would have no value.... What makes it non-accidental cannot lie within the world, since it if it did it would itself be accidental" (*TLP,* 6.41). Values occupy the same marginal status as attitudes because they do not derive from propositions or descriptions. Thus, "ethics cannot be put into words"; rather, that domain is "transcendental" (*TLP* ibid., 6.421).

Early Wittgenstein was no positivist. He was fascinated by how this transcendental domain continued to haunt him because there resided the ultimate questions about the shape of a life: "If good or bad acts of the will do alter the world, it can only be the limits of the world that they alter, not the facts, and not what can be expressed by means of language.... The world of the happy man is a different one from that of the unhappy man" (*TLP,* ibid., 6.43).

This picture had to change once grammar took over the constitutive roles logic played in the *Tractatus.* Now the subject has many roles to play, in part to appeal for attunement if not for understanding. For the solipsism of the subject in the *Tractatus* gives way to the subject, which is always in a social position within a language game, although not necessarily understanding what that position might entail. Yet the "I" so positioned by language games remains in a marginal position in the sense that it does not determine the values that the games structure. The self that has a feeling for "myself" is still at the boundary where he or she can alter only the limits of the world: "The way we choose and value words" is not a feature of our language games but of our relation to those language games. There is still a mysterious gap between the language games and the force that determines whether a happy or an unhappy life takes shape.

Let me take a seemingly simple contrast from section viii of part 2 of the *Investigations* to show how insistent Wittgenstein remained about that marginality. Notice here a surprising continued skepticism about knowing what other people feel emotionally (in contrast to knowing whether they are in pain):[24]

> I say, "Do *this*, and you'll get it." Can't there be a doubt here? Mustn't there be one, if it is a feeling that is meant?
>
> *This* looks *so; this* tastes *so, this* feels *so*. "This" and "so" must be differently explained." (*PPF*, 64–65)

The primary point is grammatical. "Feels" in the sense the sentence gives it involves a language game that is different from the apparent form of description the sentence seems to take at first. Initially we have to interpret "this" as a demonstrative referring to some observable particular. But the phrase as a whole gives immense force to "so" as the complement of "feels."

Therefore the sentence requires recasting the force of "this." Only a "this" specified intentionally by the subject's "model" can flesh out this "so" because that task calls not for description but for illustrating how some aspect of the situation dawns on the agent. And once the agent takes on this degree of importance for determining the sense of "so," there must be doubt that one agent can understand what the other feels. This situation demands display rather than a picture, but the display does not secure lucid communication. There can only be an effort by each individual to clarify what "so" involves.

Now at least two enigmatic passages in the *Investigations* can take on relevance for my argument because of how they honor the complexities of subjectivity. The first is a remarkable series of reflections on who the "I" is who utters "I am in pain." Wittgenstein sees that "I don't point to a person who is in pain, since in a certain sense I don't know who is" (*PI*, 404). One hears the "I." But what criteria of identity are possible in this situation? The "I" is focused, after all, on the pain and not on matters of identity: "I don't name anyone when I groan with pain" (ibid.). So we return again to the ineffable "myself":

> "But . . . when you say 'I'm in pain,' you want to draw the attention of others to a particular person."—The answer could be: No, I just want to draw their attention to *myself.* (ibid., 405)

Here "myself" becomes a self-reflective expression that has a function that is different from referring to the person others can observe: "And even when I 'want to distinguish' between myself and other people—do I want to distinguish between the person L.W. and the person N.N.?" (ibid., 406). Perhaps we can refer to this difference as invoking the "myself function," which is not visible directly but can enter behavior when self-reflection is called for, especially in the domain of values.

Wittgenstein could be simply making a point about the gap between expressions of self-awareness and criteria for personal identity. He is certainly not speculating about the intricacies of how spirit consumes provisional identities. Yet as the reflections continue, he becomes surprisingly general, as if the tension between what we can name and what we can experience as concretely significant had to be a basic consideration in our talk about expression. We have seen this passage before, but not quite in the context now being developed: "'I' doesn't name a person, nor 'here' a place, and 'this' is not a name. But they are connected with names. Names are explained by means of them. It is also true that it is characteristic of physics not to use these words" (ibid., 410). The crucial point here is Wittgenstein's locating the problem not in logic or ontology, not in the nature of subjectivity, but in the languages by which we try to understand what kind of entities "I" and "here" can be. We need to try out different perspectives.

To illustrate the problem of locating subjectivity, Wittgenstein turns to William James, perhaps because James shared what had been Wittgenstein's dilemma of wanting to stress the powers of self without making claims that go beyond the limits of empiricism, albeit a "radical" version of empiricism. Yet turning to James will not provide the necessary help except by contrast because James felt that radical empiricism justified adding to the instruments of scientific research the practice of careful introspection. Then the "myself" function could become visible by shifting the object of attention.

But notice what Wittgenstein thinks happens to the "self" as observed by introspection. What appears as 'self' consists "mainly of 'peculiar motions in the head and between the head and throat'" (ibid., 413). This is because Jamesian "introspection" did not clarify "the meaning of the word 'self' (so far as it means something such as 'person,' 'human being,' 'he himself,' 'I myself),' or any analysis of such a being." Instead, introspection could offer only "the state of the philosopher's attention when he says the word 'self' to himself and tries to analyze its meaning" (ibid.). Whatever this aspect of "myself" might be, it cannot be the object of Jamesian introspection, which proceeds as if it, too, had the descriptive power of physics.

Style and Confession: The Force of Expressive Making

So far I have at best managed to isolate a feeling for "myself" that does not conform to criteria for public identity. And I may have developed this "myself function" sufficiently to connect it with the transcendental aspect of subjectivity, which ultimately determines whether subjects can see themselves as happy or unhappy. Now I want to make more positive assertions because I think Wittgenstein's remarks on style and on confession offer a rich sense of what might ultimately be at stake for an individual in the efforts to produce and to model expressive activity.

For example, it does not seem a huge leap to ask how an agent might go on to elaborate "this feels so" even though there is no specific content beyond the avowal that will allow us to map this "so" onto the world as physics deals with it. And then we enter conditions where confession or the making of a model must supplement the avowal so that it can give substance to an attitude.[25] In such situations we want not just to know more about the agent's reactions but also about her dispositions and sense of personal history that might be affecting what "so" entails.

Style is for Wittgenstein one basic means by which the agent elaborates this "so": "'Le style c'est l'homme,' 'Le style c'est l'homme même.' The first expression has cheap epigrammatic brevity. The second, correct version opens up quite a different perspective. It says that a man's style is a picture [Bild] of him" (CV, 78). In effect, style conveys how an agent frames the world by composing it. This is why style creates a particular kind of picture of a person.[26] This picture (which is not an empiricist picture) defines a self-reflexive dimension in which the agent stages the awareness involved in framing the world by making visible how the language has been worked (just so).

One might say that style implies ownership but does not entail discursive self-consciousness about ownership or the possibility of describing the terms of that ownership.[27] Style accomplishes this framing by accepting and displaying the individual's differences from others and not seeking any normative justification: "You have to accept the faults in your own style. Almost like the blemishes in your own face" (CV, 76). Therefore while this "feels so" invites further elaboration, it is by no means clear that producing descriptive words will add more than they subtract from what "so" displays. Claiming knowledge or self-knowledge through these words only imposes another framework beyond the framework of language, one that is rife with normativity and temptations to make judgments. Such frameworks present "so" only in the terms that are appropriate for knowledge claims.

An intentional act need not be something shaped by meaning or overt purpose that can be stated. Agents may surround acts with reasons, but we cannot take the reasons as explanations as we would if we could treat the person as an object that explanation would suffice to clarify. Instead all we can do is honor the relevant acts by taking them, and the models that might incorporate context, as a display of purposive agency. This is why there is an obvious and strong connection between style as a condition of action and style in a work of art. But this is also why the "myself" function must depend on conditions of labor by which the agent can only make that display and hope for responsiveness.

Style reveals the person. The relation between "confession" and "truthfulness" does something more. I want to say it gathers the person's most intimate sense of personal being and offers it to an auditor. Wittgenstein must have been worried about the melodramatic theater made possible by such terms because he uses them only in conjunction once in the *Investigations* (*PPF*, 319–20) and mentions "confession" in the context of religion two crucial times in the remarks collected in *Culture and Value* (*CV*, 18 and 46).[28] He very rarely allows figures of personal neediness and possible justification to enter his philosophizing. So we can dismiss these rare occasions as not typical, or we can pay special attention to such remarkable occasions.

It should not be surprising that I find the special attention the more attractive option. The relevant passage in the *Investigations* is quite extraordinary, if only because it reveals Wittgenstein's need to posit in "truthfulness" a positive, explicit alternative to the language of truth that for him is a constant object of suspicion:

> The criteria for the truth of the confession that I thought such and such are not the criteria for a true description of a process. And the importance of the true confession does not reside in its being a correct and certain report of some process. It resides rather in the special circumstances which can be drawn from

a confession whose truth is guaranteed by the special criteria of truthfulness. (*PPF*, 319)

Confession is not avowal. It is concerned with thinking as well as with feeling. And confession does not seem to involve the same kind of relation to a particular "process." Rather, confession is a deliberate, self-reflexive activity. And the "truth" involved is not resolved by an immediate adjustment to a person's needs or desires. We have to explain how confession could require special criteria of truthfulness.

Wittgenstein does not tell us what those criteria might be. But it seems reasonable to assume that the relevant criteria involve measuring the confession by what we know about a life—not to explain it but to determine the degree to which the words fit that life. "Truthfulness" is not "truth" because the criteria are not what the case is in the world but what the case is for the person speaking; the words that fit a life are not the same as those that might describe it. The words that fit a life involve taking responsibility for elaborating that sense of fit. Truthfulness adds a dimension of willing to the activity of description.

To say more on how "confession" matters for Wittgenstein one has to bring in the much more unguarded and elaborate rendering of the same principle in *Culture and Value*. Here Wittgenstein makes clear that the expressive exposure is not part of any human dialogue but a revelation of a painful individuality that bids to be accepted as such, so close and yet so far from how Stanley Cavell subsumes confession within his overall perfectionist orientation:

> The Christian faith—as I see it—is a man's refuge in this ultimate torment. Anyone in such torment who has the gift of opening his heart, rather than contracting it, accepts the means of salvation in his heart. Someone who in this way penitently opens his heart to God in confession lays it open for other men too. In doing this he loses the dignity that goes with his personal prestige and becomes like a child. . . . A man can bare himself before others only out of a particular kind of love. A love which acknowledges as it were, that we are all wicked children. We could also say: hate between men comes from our cutting ourselves off from each other. Because we don't want anyone else to look inside us, since it's not a pretty sight in there. Of course, you must continue to feel ashamed of what's inside you, but not ashamed of yourself before your fellow men. (*CV*, 46)

The words of confession summarize a life by exposing a sense of responsibility that cannot take the form of ethical judgment. Ethical judgment engages concerns for justification. Confession offers a mode of responsibility seeking the kind of understanding that might produce forgiveness or, at the least, recognition of the effort to match expression to a felt human condition. Ethical judgment makes a just society possible because everyone can seek approval on the same terms. Confession makes friendship possible precisely because one replaces the appeal to justification by an effort to take responsibility for a life so that one can offer a genuine appeal for forgiveness to particular people whom one allows to matter for their sense of identity.[29]

How Wittgenstein Reads Literary Texts

Now we are prepared to recognize how rich Wittgenstein's remarks in *Culture and Value* can be as demonstrations of how aesthetic values involve a distinctive sense of subjectivity. The following rather lengthy passage uses the concept of expression to flesh out the kind of feelings possible when we can imagine personal utterance as leading beyond empirical identity:

> There is a lot to be learned from Tolstoy's bad theorizing about how a work of art conveys "a feeling."—You really could call it, not exactly the expression of a feeling, but at least the expression of feeling or a felt expression. And you could say too that in so far as people understand it, they "resonate" in harmony with it, respond to it. You might say: "the work of art does not mean to convey something else, just itself. Just as, when I pay someone a visit, I just don't want to make him have feelings of such and such a sort; what I mainly want is to visit him, though of course I should like to be well-received too. (*CV*, 58)

One might say that Wittgenstein replaces idealist philosophy's lucubrations on the status of subject and substance by simple (and effective) analogies between the work and the person—both considered in terms of how they might establish a sense of actual personal presence. Certainly the work is not the communication of the feelings that the author had "when writing to be experienced by someone else who reads his work": "what *he* may have felt in writing it doesn't concern me at all" (ibid., 58–59). Wittgenstein wants the intensity of the visit, not the rationale for it. We approach the worked quality of the text by treating it as producing its own complex of feelings that makes dynamic an imagined world, capable of redefining who the subject becomes.[30]

There are two basic ways of establishing the kind of presence Wittgenstein sees Tolstoy seeking. An author can directly express what is involved in the dawning of an aspect so that the "Now" of realization takes on the permanence of an art object. This should not require further comment. Nor should my second way because it involves the concept of building a model that I have belabored. But I want to stress again the contrast between copy and model in the context established by Wittgenstein's reflections on Tolstoy:

> If I know the schematic cube has various aspects, and I want to find out what someone else sees, I can get him to make a model of what he sees in addition to a copy, or to show such a model . . . What before perhaps seemed, or even was a useless specification once there was a copy, now becomes the only possible expression of the experience. (*PPF*, 135)

The model here is a crucial concept because it establishes a distinctive role for the maker who wants to elaborate within the work those decisions that bring out the significance to the person of how he or she responded to the dawning of an aspect. A confession seeks to be a direct expression of the person's truthfulness. But what if an artist wants to render what it might feel like to make a confession (in Wittgenstein's sense)? Then the author might need to produce a model which brings out some aspect of the confession that engages the maker's specific interests.

Now the concept of expression gets quite complicated, but the logic of display still prevails, albeit as an appeal to a kind of understanding best articulated in the arts because the model manifests its own way of composing sense. On one level the making of the model is still an expressive act, still a rendering of the subject's stakes in a series of particular choices of aspect. But the model is also *of* an expressive act. This model then establishes a character, fictive or historical, who is trying to achieve the kind of truthfulness that would constitute a successful confession.

The model can call attention to two different displays of subjective intensities—the maker's and the designated figure's within the constructed case. But the model can only be said to clarify the two orientations: it does not offer a more general concept by which one can explain that orientation. One builds a model to elaborate for others and so make objective (but not necessarily cognitive) what elicits the speaker's involvement. Models allow an appeal to understanding that has to exhibit its own way of making sense.

Finally, the model functions as a particular kind of example—not an example *of* a rule but an example *as* something we can deploy when we are trying to sort specific options in a particular situation.[31] Again indirection may find direction out. Wittgenstein asks, "When do we say: 'the line intimates to me *like a rule* always the same'? And, on the other hand, 'It keeps on intimating to me what I have to do—it is not a rule'? In the first case the thought is: I have no further court of appeal for what I have to do. . . . The other proposition says I do not know what I am going to do: the line will tell me" (Z, 279). If we imagine the model providing this second kind of line, we can see how it might not only specify what the maker composes out of a given situation but also how we might apply that composition to our own reflective lives: "Just this gesture has been made accessible to you" (ibid., 158). Now we have something like a grammatical function for art because the model casts the work as mediating between the actual dawning of an aspect and how an audience might imagine situating that dawning in relation to other experiences. The particular model offered by the agent establishes conditions where one can devote oneself to taking the time and giving the care necessary to call fully on the resources of language games involving states such as participation, expectation, surprise, realization, and sympathy.

Summary

The last thing this chapter needs is more words. But having indulged myself in the details of how expression theory correlates with Wittgenstein's thinking—about life as well as about art—I think it would be best if I boiled this down to usable generalizations.

1) Because expression resists the authority of description and representation, it can sponsor claims about concrete features of art that are continuous with how we engage in a variety of practical situations. Expressions possess various properties that call attention to the manner woven into the presentation and therefore make the

experience irreducible to any cognitive description. This is why Wittgenstein insists that expressive works of art are not copies derived from experience. Then we can adapt his concept of model to suggest that an author composes the particular object to specify how a particular point of view takes up the dawning of the aspect or the felt need to find language for situations. The model differs from the copy because it includes the presence of the subject and therefore suggests contexts that interpret how the maker can elaborate the stakes in what style can produce.

2) Because expression is opposed to description, it sponsors versions of subjectivity very different from anything that might serve cognitive ends. Expressions are our most capacious challenge to picture-thinking. And because the making and the perceiving interact with each other, they are living versions of how the equation "1=1" can expand in power as each of the participants gets more fully developed.

We prepare the way to appreciate this shift in how the copulative verb establishes equivalences by refusing to settle for avowals as the primary concept for how subjectivity is defined within expressive acts. Expressive faces are one useful analogue for placing subjective factors in the world as objects that can endure for our attention and scrutiny well beyond the event of their emergence. At the other pole we can dwell on the work models do in order to meld the concrete with making and even with willing because the model can suggest by its structure that it takes responsibility for itself as an action. Ultimately the concept of model clarifies the work done by style and by confession—our two primary modes of appreciating how self-consciousness struggles to realize inchoate aspects of what ties us to the world.

3) Because expressive art denies the copying function, we need more intricate means to connect what happens in the work to what can happen in the world beyond the work. So we have to speculate on treating art as relying on the function of exemplification to handle such modes of connection. In that regard Wittgenstein provides a rich and subtle vision of how art can be remembered and discussed without turning it into concepts. Wittgenstein's model of uptake for expression invites careful attention to the particular and then, in the

place of interpretation and explanation, to how the work invites distinctive forms of participation in what it renders. The emphasis on exemplification eliciting participation then allows us rich ways to talk about identification and hence about aspects of subjectivity solicited by how the world gets disclosed in the work.

4) Stanley Cavell, and then Ralph Berry on Stanley Cavell, have pointed out that modernist art gains a great deal of its scope, power, and intensity from the fact that an audience always has to be worried about the artwork being a fraud.[32] For if the work claims to reject tradition and set its own terms for being valued, we are likely to have difficulty trusting those claims: we simply do not have any categories or criteria by which to assess them. In effect, one crucial task of the art object is gradually to dispel this fear by providing the relevant terms for new ways of valuing how art stages its relations to the world. From my perspective such valuing is inseparable from just learning how to respond to works such as Beckett's dark comedies or Ashbery's anti-lyric lyricism or Pollock's ways of making marks on a canvas.

I think this conversation about possible fraudulence makes clear how ultimately Wittgenstein's account of expression elaborates the logic underlying the basic social position modernist art occupies, just because that position is so wound up in expressionist ideals. One of the most powerful pleasures for audiences of this art is their continual sense that they are exploring activities for which there are no stable criteria—for the work or for how the self might present itself in the work. We have to imagine that the work takes on the responsibility of saying itself in order to push past what might be predicted by traditional concepts of art—and of life. We are asked to allow the world to display new possibilities for what it can become for consciousness and what it can demand from self-consciousness.

Chapter 5

Expression and Exemplification

> The return to life cannot come about by talking. It is an act; to make you return to life I must set an example for your imitation, I must deafen you to talk, or to the importance of talk, by showing you, as Bergson does, that the concepts we talk with are made for purposes of *practice* and not for purposes of insight. And I must *point,* point, to the mere *that* of life, and you by inner sympathy must fill out the *what* for yourselves.
> —William James, "The Continuity of Experience"

> "A picture tells me itself" is what I would like to say. That is, its telling me something consists in its own structure, *its* own forms and colours.
> —Wittgenstein, *Philosophical Investigations*

Despite the characteristic contrast in degrees of volubility, and despite James's characteristic reliance on "inner sympathy," both these epigraphs convey the same basic principle: if philosophy is to reduce the role reference plays in our understanding of how language works, it is likely to have to rely on example as a basic principle in our learning to communicate. Practices provide examples for how to go on under various conditions. Neither descriptions nor propositions will suffice for the necessary guidance.

The arts learned that lesson long before philosophy did, probably because they had many fewer options for linking imaginative labors to actual states of affairs. Insofar as artists locate value in the particular manner by which the work solicits participation, that manner can only take on generalizing power if the work is treated as exemplary in some register. Invoking any conceptual structure would transform the particular into a mere instance of a rule or a type. But example allows the particular itself to have scope: Hamlet becomes a type because of what he does not because he instantiates some principle.

Exemplification then is the means by which we can connect how our responsiveness engages us in imaginative work relating to the practical world. Critics still for the most part talk of a cognitive dimension to art by which we come to know something through the particular. I will try to show how the concept of exemplification is richer and less problematic than the concept of conveying any kind of "truth." Exemplification is oriented toward action rather than the simple recognition of underlying conditions. And exemplification points toward future uses rather than ideas of capturing some abiding core of wisdom. It is we who adapt the text to the world by showing how it helps us sort experiences and specify how they matter as means of determining values. Think, for example, of how one could argue that Ashbery's "Instruction Manual" has consequences for our appreciating what is involved in imaginatively dwelling in any given place.

We could simply use the concepts of example and exemplar without any supportive contexts. In a moment I will argue that the critics now turning to this concept do exactly that. But I think that the best way to approach any concept is to see its place among other concepts and other practices, so we recognize what cooperates in its functioning and what might be affected by its functioning well.

So I will turn once again to the overall framework provided by Wittgenstein's later philosophical thinking. My version of that framework will now be quite familiar. On the most practical levels we learn from Wittgenstein how grammar works by exploring examples and by adapting them in order to examine what understandings are plausible for given speech situations. Therefore exemplification is inseparable from the work of display. We do not refer avowals and expressions to rules, but we adjust to them by comparing similar instances and testing which contexts best apply. More generally, we must rely on examples to learn what is appropriate as we learn the language, even when we are learning grammatical rules. (I am now trying to toilet train a puppy by moving the waste products she produces inside the house to the outside and leading her to join them, in the hope this example takes.)

Examples also have enormous consequences for how we determine values. We have to compare examples if we are to clarify which particular expressions are most appropriate for given conditions of speaking. We learn to issue signs of respect and disrespect, and we learn to adjust our terms to avoid confusion by, in part, remembering just what we did to create confusion in the first place. So it becomes very important to build repertoires of examples in order to provide a basis of comparison when one is faced with complicated needs to express oneself or to respond to expressions (or to keep certain odors out of the house). And, on the most general level, it is exemplars and exemplary practices that make it possible for us to see and to shape possibilities for determining paths for our own lives. As Richard Eldridge shows, ultimately *Philosophical Investigations* stages Wittgenstein's philosophical practices as exemplary for their habits of questioning and their unrelenting scrutiny to stay within the boundaries of the observable without reducing the observable to what can be tested empirically.

Some Uses of the Concept of Example in Literary Criticism

The concept of example was rarely deployed in the age of New Critical close reading and rarely adapted for aesthetic purposes during the reign of cultural studies. Ironically, these almost antithetical approaches to literature both idealized the kinds of knowledge texts could produce, so the particularity that exemplification tries to preserve simply did not matter. For the New Critics the imaginative labor of breaking through to genuine expressive particularity directly produced nondiscursive knowledge. Cultural and historical inquiry, on the other hand, resisted particularity by trying to subsume it into types and general projects that had significance for public life. So cultural and historical inquiry develop often brilliant ways of treating literary works as examples *of* how social structures take hold. But they very rarely speculate on how the work *as* example or as exemplar might provide significant experience in its own right.

As the emphasis on the cognitive in literary studies has waned slightly, and the need for visions of the worldliness of literature intensified, we find several critics making interesting use of the concept of exemplarity for literary experience. There is Joshua Landy's important idea of "formative fictions," by which particular fictional acts bid for authority by dramatizing the power of a given perspective. David Nowell Smith brings out a similar concern for the power of poetry by invoking "what Heidegger calls poetry's projective saying." By virtue of this mode of saying, "beings enter the open in a singular and transformative manner." In both cases the work of art stands as a particular in the world; it does partially depend on concepts but becomes a site with the power to modify how the conceptual interacts with the actual.

And there is Richard Eldridge's treating Wittgenstein's use of example and desire to be exemplary as themselves romantic examples of how the ineffable might be engaged.[1]

Anthony Cascardi and Tyrus Miller take more historical routes to clarifying the value of this concept. Cascardi reminds us that the idea of example has been around at least since Aristotle to map a route between text and world that emphasizes the work of the particular "to move its readers emotionally to recognize what is true, rather than simply *to know that* it is true."[2] Philip Sidney's "Apology for Poetry," for example, contrasts the power of the exemplary image to move the soul in a way that philosophical discourse does not. And Miller invokes the history of rhetoric to argue that "the avant-garde after World War II . . . reinvented exemplarity in a new form." Instead of seeking a representative function for the particular. the "experimental presentation of examples" would "actively reverse the temporal direction of exemplarity, making the work exemplify not something already given in the past and in history, but rather something that the present has yet to bring forth fully and that will be realized only in the future" (*SE*, 8).[3] Such examples are "proleptic" (ibid., 9).

These theorists provide important reminders and dynamic possibilities for exploring what power particular works of imagination can take on in the world of their audiences. But Miller's claims can serve as an example of why we need somewhat different perspectives before we can use the concept of exemplarity to cover a wide variety of literary experiences. Miller seems to me wrong in his version of how authorial uses of exemplarity changed after World War II. Claudius's speech is as free from being subsumed under concepts as work by Jackson Mac Low. And Keats's "This Living Hand" is as compelling in its uncanny particularity as any contemporary poem.

Yet there is also something to the idea of the proleptic exemplar offering a distinctive perspective on contemporary "experimental" work in all the arts. Shakespeare and Keats complete the example; then ask audiences to test whether they can adapt it into their imaginative repertoire. Mac Low and John Cage require an audience to complete the work: there is indeed no example until specific audience members try to reconstruct the work as a distinct work, with all the ambient features provisionally ordered.

I dwell on Miller because it seems apparent that he ran with a very productive idea without sufficiently worrying about the history of that idea for writers or its significance for twentieth-century philosophy. And without these concerns, one cannot sufficiently relate how the arts seek the status of exemplar to the uses of exemplification in other basic social practices. I want to stress how exemplification is a basic feature in many language games. The arts invoke some of the practices and complicate others—all by soliciting the same kind of self-consciousness that pervades Wittgenstein's late philosophy.

This chapter concentrates on two contexts for specifying how such embedding works. For the first, we will have to depend again on Wittgenstein's analyses of exemplification as serving a variety of grammatical roles. Then my second context helps specify how exemplification actually serves as an instrument for adapting particulars to more general concerns while bypassing the authority of concepts. Finally I will introduce my own theory of the demonstrative speech act as fundamental to how most lyric poetry uses exemplification. For poetry does not just provide the interest and the capacity to use its materials as examples. It aggressively asserts itself as exemplary because its basic function is not to report on the world but to position speakers within the world as bringing to bear powers to test the implications of affect-laden language.

The Grammar of Example in Wittgenstein

We do not need more explication of Wittgenstein. But we do need to see how Wittgenstein's clarifying the roles of example in our language illuminates how imaginative objects can seek real-world consequences without relying on explanation or argument. Examples are purposive deployments of display. The self-conscious deployment of display is best captured by how the concept of "perspicuous representations" operates in Wittgenstein's own thinking.[4] As we have seen, Wittgenstein's practice is largely built on illustrating by example distinctions basic to the grammar that make possible certain ways of formulating what the world can become in language. Examples orient us to the powers inherent in our ways of making sense—both as general conditions of language use and as defining particular ways of addressing situations.

A striking example of the first case occurs early in *Philosophical Investigations,* when Wittgenstein insists on a sharp contrast between a language game that concentrates on descriptions of color and a language game that focuses on "a means of representation" rather than on something represented (*PI,* 50). Color can be invoked in a description. But also many of our assertions about color refer instead to aspects of color charts, hence to what enables us to recognize specific colors in the first place.

An emphasis on doing in language rather than knowing through language requires careful attention to the grammatical features that underlie cultural competence. Displaying these grammatical relations entails showing that many sentences occupy "a shifting border between logic and the empirical, so that their meaning changes back and forth and they count now as expressions of norms, now as expressions of experience" (*Remarks on Colour*, pt. 1, 32).[5] We have to learn by example what the rules are. But we also have to realize that in many cases we use examples to indicate how situations might be more manageable if we proceed without the rigidity of rule: "What one acquires here is not a technique; one learns correct judgments. There are also rules, but they do not form a system, and only experienced people can apply them rightly. Unlike calculating rules" (*PPF*, 355). What is most difficult here is to express this indefiniteness correctly and without distortion (ibid., 356).

Now we can turn to the question of how typical literary works fit this Wittgensteinian context. I think literary works can be said to exemplify what they display to the degree that they explore why it might matter to stay with the particular formulations the work elaborates. Readers typically adjust to such displays by concentrating on what features of the agent's behavior directly make manifest the work's emotional concerns. Once we realize how Yeats uses the interrogative mood, the affinity of questioning and exclaiming becomes a constant possibility for reflection on situations that invite very different imaginative frameworks from what "Leda and the Swan" poses as basic human needs. And because of the emphasis on what is embedded in concrete situations, we do not have to treat the expressive register as offering signs or symbols of a distinctive inner life. The inner life is lived as a dimension of what is outwardly visible.

Even more important, the use of examples seems to me a basic form of aspect-seeing that has a significant place in literary experience and in literary education. We use the example to get others (or other states of ourselves) to look at a phenomenon in a different way and test how the path implicit in the example helps us go on to satisfy our interests in particular situations. When we see into the amazing power of Claudius's intelligence to fill the room, we understand better why Hamlet has to see other imaginary worlds in which to flourish. And then this model of generational conflict becomes something we can use to fine-tune our awareness of different but related situations that we might encounter. Analogously, Eliot's Causabon has become an example for me of life at the opposite end of the spectrum, defining typical fears of age-driven intellectual impotence.

In many of these uses there is possible a very important distinction for literary theory that I have already invoked several times in talking about display. We can treat the example as an instance of something for which we can provide a concept. Or we can treat the example as having to take the place of a concept because we have available only the particular case by which to generate considerations of its possible uses or implication.[6]

In relation to the first category, we might say the example is an illustrative instance of something known: red is an example of a color, an expression of greed is an example of ugly behavior or of healthy capitalist practice, and the case of hatred can be clarified by an analogy to Iago. The second category has no such relation of standing in for a more general mode of articulation. So we have to speak not about "examples of" but about "examples as" because the particular chosen functions as a guide to possible employments and emplotments where rules might be too blunt to apply or difficult to formulate. For example (now a loaded phrase), we show someone how to ride a bike by building a picture of particular behaviors to imitate. Or, agents try various examples in order to understand better what someone is feeling, with the hope of making adjustments rather than developing an accurate concept for that feeling.

This context helps explain the significance of treating imaginative works as "one-place predicates." Such predicates call attention to their own particularity: Hamlet as character does not refer to any conceptual model but in itself takes on the status of model. The particular itself becomes our guide for how we might employ the images and the actions constituted by the text. In fact, we might even take all significant expressive activity as seeking to establish the kind of specificity that invites being treated as an alternative to having a real-world referent for each specific name in a work of fiction.[7] Speech acts become examples of aspects of character. And descriptions, such as Toomer's "Face," become exercises in testing the imagination's capacity to engage the kinds of details that resist conceptualization. The expressions resist being explained so that they can become the features by which we characterize their relation to other actions by the agents or provide interpretive frameworks for other unrelated actions.

Nelson Goodman on Example

Wittgenstein is obviously very good on the general roles examples play. But for the actual grammar by which we put examples to work I want to turn to the more patient and more extensive analyses of exemplification offered in the work of Nelson Goodman. Goodman's treatment often lacks Wittgenstein's subtlety. Yet it establishes a more systematic sense of how examples do not picture the world in a Tractarian fashion but refer us to our frameworks for making sense of that world. This project also shows how works of art utilize and extend those frameworks.

Goodman treats exemplification as one of three tightly connected basic modes of symbolic functioning that each selects from and organizes its universe, therefore becoming "itself in turn informed and transformed":

> Representation and description relate a symbol to things it applies to. Exemplification relates a symbol to a label that denotes it, and hence indirectly to the things (including the symbol itself) in the range of that label. Expression relates the symbol to the label that metaphorically denotes it, and hence indirectly not only to the given metaphorical but also to the literal range of that label. (*LA*, 92)

This is difficult material to process. But it helps that Goodman's primary examples are works of art because it is crucial in that domain to keep what a picture describes or represents distinct from what kind of a picture or an act of picturing the work demonstrates. And the history of art provides clear examples of how taste shifts among the three modes of symbolization.

Denotation is stressed when art is prized for what it represents or describes. Exemplification displays what can be manifest in stylistic choices or stylistic modes, as in the display of formal or decorative properties for which the work provides an instance. These provide clear instances of relating a symbol to the label that denotes it because we have to refer to the kind of style in order to characterize the particular. And expression stages the symbol as a figure of psychological states (*LA*, 93) by the metaphoric extension of those formal properties. Style becomes motivated when we imagine its attributes bearing psychological properties, such as the play of line in a Pollock.

All three modes of symbolization line up in this way. A shade of red in a painting might describe what the artist sees or might exemplify a possible

138   Chapter 5

shade of red capable of achieving certain contrasts with other colors or might express anger or vengeance as the artist brings to bear traditional metaphoric associations that the color red can come to denote. Or we can see the functions as all available within one symbol or work. A painting such as Munch's *The Scream* can denote a specific state of torment. It can rely on distorted shapes and intense color for their direct power to exemplify for the viewer a mode of art that offers states of heightened intensity inviting participation in the direct force of the extreme gestures comprising how the work signifies. And the painting can reach out metaphorically to suggest how the pictured pain might be seen as dramatizing the effects of the cultural alienation making the individual so painfully alone.[8]

The Roles Sorting Can Play in How We Use Examples

Goodman calls the work texts do in the world an enhancing of our capacities to sort experiences and compose worlds (hence his title, *Ways of Worldmaking*). Sorting is the use of labels that identify properties that they are denoted by and so make it possible to define classes into which particulars can fit. This definition is so abstract that it is hard to see its utility. Yet Goodman's striking ability to find the appropriate example helps immensely to see how useful this concept can be. He points out that there are two ways to make a red color swatch refer to the world (*LA*, 53–56). We can ask others to check whether this color matches another object such as a sweater. This would be a clear instance of establishing the truth or falsity of a description. But one can also use the colored swatch to ask someone to find in a pile of sweaters all those that match its shade of red. This is reference by using a model that enables us to sort particulars.

  I think this sorting by example is absolutely crucial to anyone concerned with the worldliness of the arts. Works and elements in works can be used in the construction of repertoires by which we identify and often deepen our capacity to handle distinctions we need in the world beyond the text. My formula is that by learning to see into works we make it possible to use them for the activity of seeing as. The more fully we see into Claudius's speech or Yeats's use of questions in "Leda and the Swan," the better we can use these texts to recognize or adapt to other aspects of experience not in the fictive world produced by the text. We might become wary of someone with a brilliant command of qualifiers, and we might be more conscious of the roles we can assign interrogative statements.

The beauty of the concept of sorting is the range of uses it sponsors—for example, the distinction Gibson makes between "semantic descent" and semantic ascent" (see note 40, chapter 1). These versions of "seeing as" take place by trying to engage particulars in terms of complex processes of identification and disidentification. We need not imitate these works that prove the source of our examples (as classical epics hoped to inspire). We can be quite general. We can be satisfied envisioning the figure of Hamlet as a type for suicidal adolescence or frustrated revenge. Or we can focus on the precise qualities his speeches give the actions. We might say that the text of *Hamlet* makes us appreciate the specific weighing of being against not being or the movement from frustration in one's efforts to make effective judgments to the sheer acceptance called for by the statement "ripeness is all."

Other examples of sortings sponsored by literary texts range from seemingly every educated male in Europe comparing himself to Werther, to an African American grandmother in a friend's class who proclaimed "I am Isabel Archer." And in Chinese culture, so often in advance of the West, restaurant menus are usually presentations of pictures or accompanied by elaborate images. The idea is that every sense should be enhanced while weighing the possible delights of the food.

Finally, we can sort by deciding that certain examples do not apply, especially those that seem possibly relevant. Prufrock's "I am not Prince Hamlet" provides a perfect example of something like identification by disidentification because no one would have thought him like Hamlet had he not drawn the comparison in the first place. This case is also an example of identification by virtue of what one refuses to use as projections of identity.

Exemplification of Intentional States

The example of Prufrock introduces what I think is a serious problem with Goodman's analysis, at least if one wants to talk about the range of exemplifications available in literary experience. For Goodman, expression is a matter of what properties the symbol literally or metaphorically possesses as a material object. He is a nominalist. So in his view we sort properties, not acts. Characters are there in their words, but are not available as imaginary constructs, especially imaginary constructs that we see into in terms of psychological needs and desires for which we provide figures of intentionality. All literature becomes versions of red swatches of cloth labeling what we can look for in experience.

The problem is how we get to establish richer versions of expressive activity as our ways of populating possible worlds that become extensions from the texts we read.[9] It all depends on what can be displayed and what can be said to be symbols for what is denoted by a label. Is the label always essentially a third-person objective property? Or can we treat expressive acts as making present aspects of an alternative mode of understanding that puts the self into the world without turning the self into an object. Then we could capture Richard Moran's concern for how expressive activity preserves "an asymmetry between first-person and third-person" positions without tempting us to propose an inner life that one can come to know and to describe.[10]

Within Goodman's nominalism, there is no mystery about being denoted by: when we select red sweaters of a certain shade from a pile of variously colored sweaters, we are using what the swatch is denoted by—namely its place on a color chart. Now imagine a fully expressive act. It would be difficult to sort those sweaters by what Don Juan thinks when he imagines red. Thinking of properties is not possessing them, except perhaps metaphorically.

Perhaps the only way of making some intentional states have the property of being denoted by what they refer to is to distinguish sharply between imagining something to be the case and expressing how for this character something is the case because he or she composes it that way. More generally, we might say that while lyric poetry can employ examples *of* various properties defining the relation of its parts to the world beyond the text, these labels do not capture the poem as a distinctive act. To capture this distinctive act we have to distinguish between serving as an example of something and being an example as this particular conjunction of properties. This is how we can treat the expression as an act that "tells me itself" and nonetheless manages to make humanly significant how it possesses the properties to which it refers.

The case for the power of our sentences consists also of a much less abstract point or a point so concrete that it can be made only abstractly. Once we see the work as a whole, we can treat it as not just a series of perceptions and names but a complex, self-reflexive event that models this event for a corresponding level of self-reflection on the part of the audience. The ordering force of sentences need not be something we just recognize as a fact about our experiences. The ordering itself can be a profound experience because we dwell imaginatively at the very core of putting relations together and experiencing the effect and the affects composed by those synthetic acts. The one thing held in common by most of our experiences is that they explore the capacities of our sentences to make sense of what we focus on as our interface with the world. What can be a more important form of sorting than to place an emotional life in the very conditions that make manifest the qualities of our activities? Because poems offer self-reflexive sentences, they demonstrate myriad possibilities for recovering the lives sentences can help us live.

Consider again a passage from Wittgenstein that I have already employed for other purposes. Wittgenstein has just defined description (in a language reminiscent of the *Tractatus*) as "a representation of a distribution in space" (*PPF*, 70). Then Wittgenstein invents this way of dramatizing what cannot be included within such distributions but can be displayed: "If I let my gaze wander round a room and suddenly it lights on an object of striking red colour, and I say 'Red!'—I haven't thereby given a description" (ibid., 71). The exclamation "Red!" cannot be treated as label in the same way "Red" can. We cannot look up the exclamation on a color chart because attention is not focused primarily on the referent. Rather, the statement illustrates "the dawning of an aspect" and so calls attention to a state the subject experiences in relation to changes in the object's appearance. "Red" still denotes the label for a color. Yet its primary function is no longer to denote the color it names. As Geoffrey Hellman puts it, the exemplified red "has been transferred from a domain of literal application to a different domain."[11] The role of the exclamation point is closely analogous to the role of "this feels so," with the emphasis on a "so" whose significance we can only guess. What is being expressed can only be exhibited—largely because it establishes in public something that is not observable except through the speaker's utterance.

Yet such guesses can be more or less appropriate and suggestive depending on what else is displayed that gives the utterance a context and a framework. And to give such contexts is the role of the maker. Expression here does not invite description of the person but exemplifies an aspect of the person acting. So the exclamation becomes a means of making the speaker's state a distinctive feature of the scene that cannot be explained simply by an objective description. This label possesses the property of testifying to the speaker's willingness to make an affective investment in what he or she sees. The subject still occupies the boundary marking the limit of the world of fact, as in the *Tractatus*. But now the subject need not silence her exclamatory impulses because the grammar of our language includes the means for making these expressive possibilities intelligible.

Here the agent's exclamation need not depend on any narrative that would risk turning the subject back into an object of the forces that the narrative recounts. The subject recording the perception "Red" is primarily acted upon. But "Red!" is not just the active presentation of a feeling. It seems to me that the exclamation point has the force of a second activity, an affirmation of what it has become possible to see. Once the exclamation point contextualizes how the label is being used, this way of adapting the label invites further accounts that may clarify why this particular agent is so moved by this red. Now the assertion of the color provides both an invitation to look again at the object and a label for an avowal by the subject. And this state is not simply recognized; it is asserted as if the subject were affirming this capacity for recognition as fundamental to its concrete sense of agency.

Sorting Metaphoric Expressions

If I understand Goodman correctly, we need another set of three functions if we are to establish the distinctive roles played by the specific category of metaphoric expression, which is basic to our understanding of how we can sort individual works of art in order to understand the force they are capable of exercising in cultural life. And if I understand Wollheim correctly, we need to extend each of these three categories of metaphoric expressions to include not just powers that properties can take on, such as color samples, but also powers that actions can take on, such as efforts to identify with what Leda must feel in the claws of Zeus. (If I do not understand Goodman or Wollheim correctly, I am happy to claim what follows as my own proposal.)

Let me list the metaphoric functions in descending order of generality and perhaps ascending order of intensity. First, the metaphoric level of expression brings into play the possible cultural forces that expression can make articulate. For the artwork not only represents how it is situated in its culture but also interprets those conditions, so that we continually process the details as having metaphoric force building patterns of significance. The work articulates norms of what is entailed in social practices as it simultaneously displays possibilities for changing those entailments.

One good example of the metaphoric use of cultural context is Ashbery's cross between the repressions of his own culture and the small resonances of generosity and curiosity in what he dreams of as life in Guadalajara. A second example maps a very different terrain. The fiction of Jane Austen is tightly bound to specific cultural settings so that she can give compelling critiques of its characteristic forms of behavior without actually making overt critical statements. She shows that there is little in human life more paralyzing than the pathos of versions of pride exercised in small communities. Yet as she criticizes these traits she manages to have her heroines eventually identify with the authorial consciousness, adding to that consciousness a capacity to act in terms that expand the culture's frameworks for thinking about what women want and what they need. If Austen's heroines did not begin by being proud and taking themselves far too seriously, they might not be capable of showing the moral courage eventually to alter those cultural conditions.

Second, the arts provide many of our specific models for how psychological attitudes are formed and influence behavior. As we will see, expressive activity tests and extends the demands on capacities to interpret the world. Simple expressions are denoted by the language at its most direct and most accessible. Think, for example, of "I am sorry" or "I am angry." What we take as self is here primarily a matter of how the person attaches agency to standard affective predicates (or avowals). But when we build complex acts of apology or the intricately mastered angers driving Swift's work, we need all the resources of a complex grammar, and we need related models from the culture that help us refine our sense of what can be denoted by that level of displaying apology and anger. Our repertoire of examples makes a huge difference in our capacity to interpret what expressions ask of us or provide for us.

Where would Western culture be without Hamlet to provide models of melancholy? And where would modernist American poetry be without the attitudes defined by T. S. Eliot to kick around? Literature is especially important in this regard because it builds models of complex personal concerns and investments by sheerly verbal means: inner life is not hidden but is in the manner by which writers and characters establish articulate identities.

Learning to close-read character can be very close to learning how to adapt intricate grammatical structures to establish meaningfulness in practical situations.

The third metaphoric role played by expression in the arts is for me the most suggestive and the most intimate. I have argued that expressions possess metaphorically the properties they assert: a sad painting will have some basic features that read as not just referring to sadness but providing an experience of sadness. The expression also possesses the metaphoric implications of the qualities the making brings to it. Toomer's "Faces" is not content to describe faces. It brings one face alive by virtue of foregrounding the poet's effort to lodge the metaphoric within the physical. So there emerges the great and constant paradox of art—that by intensifying specific physical traits the work also gains in possible imaginative scope because the precision of the physical features provides a distinctive anchor for metaphorical implication. In the case of Toomer's poem, faces all become particular emblems of everything that focusing on the material properties of skulls can elicit. Metaphoric properties build up a range of implicit dimensions for the words on the page. And the specificity of the text expands as we attach these dimensions to it. The work takes on substance in the same way that self-consciousness comes to recognize how its objective attributes both limit its powers and intensify our realizing what had been inchoate can make available for the will.

These metaphoric projections occur on two levels. The first, concrete level consists in possibilities of drawing out identifications with the dramatic situations in the work. The metaphoric possession of properties such as Madame Bovary's desperate neediness invites our identifying with the passions the work produces so as to establish an understanding of why the work might offer compelling experience. Participation, then, is how we respond to what we read by "realizing" its metaphoric potential for intensifying what would otherwise be states of ordinary picture-thinking.

The second level orients us in the opposite direction—not toward involvement in the world of the work but toward speculations about our sense of how the work might matter for other experiences—in life and in art. Technically, our reading produces examples proleptically denoted by the work we can envision them performing. As we "see into" the elaborate models writers construct, we perforce develop opportunities to "see as" what these models as examples can afford. The very activity required to interpret expressions produces resources to be adapted to other contexts.

An Erotic Interlude: Playing with Levels of Exemplification

The interests in appropriation in all the contemporary arts make the work of dealing with examples a central vehicle for aesthetic experience. Acts of appropriation, or the suggestively named procedure of sampling, explicitly test the imaginative utility of what tend to become in our culture little more than ineffective labels, or labels whose use is to signify cultural capital. So these works aggressively foreground self-consciousness at work dealing with how examples can be resources for artists—in part by both creating complex problems of labeling and reference and helping to solve them.

Consider what Dodie Bellamy's *Cunt Norton* has accomplished by writing over passages from thirty-two poets taken from the 1975 edition of the *Norton Anthology of Poetry* so as to bring various aspects of sorting into the foreground of art practice.[12] There emerge at least thirty-two ways of seeing vaginas and penises. And Bellamy makes her audience come to think that they possess the capacity to internalize all thirty-two ways of putting sexual pineapples together. In Bellamy's text the erotic imagination at its wildest depends for its permissions and intensities on the multiple stances afforded by examples drawn from a quite traditional canon, some of whose basic powers are gloriously made visible. The range of poetic imaginings honors writing's capacities to establish a wide range for appreciating and intensifying possible states of self-consciousness.

This, for example, is Chaucer's rendering of the innocence, directness, and mutual easy adaptiveness possible in erotic experience:

> So have I blis, of oo thing God hath sente me
> thee. So generous, really. Is it okay that I touche
> thy face? Thou art so scarlet reed aboute thy clit,
> still burning away al that maketh the ozone dien.
> Thou art siker as I holde thee and want thee for
> womman is mannes joye and his font. My cock, it
> groweth beanshoot harde against thy softe side that
> I may on thee ride til sonne rise morning harde. It
> is exciting, allas—I am so ful of joye and of solas
> hot for thee in thy rental car. Oon word, and I wol
> fleigh down fro the beem onto thy ravenous wet
> pussy. (*CN*, 8)

146   *Chapter 5*

Then there is the expansiveness of Wordsworth, where there is explicitly a synthesis of immediate pleasure with a sense of belonging to a greater force of eros available only to self-reflection:

> I touch my body and pretend it's thy hands deeply
> infusing my dwelling, lightly squeezing my breasts,
> sliding through ocean and the living air, and the
> blue sky, and tapestries. I love feeling thy head
> for its spirit impels all my thinking. All objects
> become thy mouth, open and dribbling, and
> therefore am I still a lover of thy meadows. I love
> it when thou art "meta," telling of all that thou
> behold'st from this green earth with thy mouth.
> We are both more than what each half creates, this
> is what I perceive with thy tits on my lips. I love
> the language of the senses—thus anchored, I love
> smelling thee, especially thy asshole, the guardian
> of my heart and soul and all my moral being. Thy
> voice aroused makes me grow taut with longing
> for thy genial breasts, that I may come upon the
> banks of thy fair river, my dearest. (*CN*, 23)

The rhetoric of E. E. Cummings is so good at demystifying this "meta" beloved by Wordsworth's speaker that his language can still bring the 1920s alive as a frame for the unbridled simplicity of mutual sexual pleasure (yet with an abstraction of joy foreign to Chaucer):

> Girl, let's have fun. (Here, dab my tears that float
> many bells down.) Spring on your hands and
> knees—let's pluck and dance as woman and man,
> both fingered. Hey Pumpkin Fuck, what my eyes
> sow isn't what they reap. Help me go from total
> abjection to a few and down (shower me with
> forgetting). How I long to love you more by more,
> to drown inside you, crying until my grief bird
> snows and stirs. . . .
> When we fuck like demons, joyful is our song, joy
> so pure I'd never give my heart to anybody else.
> Would you?

> ... Only you can pomp
> my must and shall, can move my father through
> me uncircumcised. With your nipples rain pity on
> me till I turn green as grain. (*CN*, 50–51)

But the darker sides of eros cannot be put off entirely. This is William Carlos Williams, whose modernist imagination seems committed to subordinating the pleasures of eros to the construction of meaning. Bellamy captures with painful precision his aggressive and desperate bid for masculine power in plain language:

> These are the desolate, dark weeks—but when I
> move my hand across your body I feel like a man.
> The year plunges into night and my cock feels like
> one of those small water pistols in a windswept
> place without sun, stars or moon—just dripping
> instead of shooting. You spin a dark fire—whirling
> my stomach, penis, and balls—and I fuck you,
> aware of nothing, knowing not loneliness,
> coming to life. Fucking you, my reason embraces
> emptiness ...
> When I come your cunt is comfortable and your tits
> make the sweetest music. The source of poetry is
> seeing orgasm after orgasm, shaking you until you've
> stopped ticking. Yesterday went so well I want to
> plant myself inside you like a fucking stone. My snake
> waits for your hips that spread across the chair,
> my snake is quick and sharp and ready to strike,
> quietly waiting for your invite to sleep over.
>   ... All is permitted,
> as long as we come—and in our chests, for the
> first time, understand that we are only mortal,
> and being mortal we can't defy our fate: savage
> sexual energy is enjoyable. When you're among the
> jonquils and the violets, coming is everything, and
> all you can do is shake your tits. (*CN*, 46–47)

Much of the specifically pornographic content here is deliberately bad (or "Flarfed"), written in inflated and clichéd language with only raw statement rather than intricate plotting as the ground for emotion. But in emptying these human voices on the level of dramatic content, Bellamy oddly gives a powerful presence to something like the voice behind the voice or, better, to the voice of desire underlying the inarticulate flesh-bound utterances of the speakers. So the individual style remains, or is even more pronounced, as the content gets simplified.

The stunning feature of Bellamy's invention is how this raw, insistently revolutionary violence on authorial intentions turns out to realize perhaps the most conservative aspects of the modernists' humanist imaginings: ultimately sexuality seems to depend for its richness on the variety of exemplary textures and tones literary traditions establish as conditions of self-reflexive experience. And Bellamy's text realizes, on many levels, the possibility that the richest presence of eros in language can be realized only if one does not claim ownership of sexual pleasure or even of sex organs because the various positions and the various pleasures simply extend beyond the boundaries of person or specific gender. In sex, as in poetry, it must be abstract, and it must change for it to give the maximum pleasure.

The power here also ultimately depends on Bellamy's mastery of the logic of sortings. Her revolutionary gesture is to realize how ever since romanticism, and probably well before, literary work has been distinguished from argument and practical discourse by the way it establishes possibilities of reference. As I have been arguing, the discursive in all of its forms tries to subsume individual details into generalizations or categories that can be tested and so have probative value. Literary work has to make its manner link to its matter, so it has to preserve its particularity as an action: the presence of Chaucerian eros must be possessed by the text and not just referred to.

But this is only one aspect of the problem facing writers. For they also have to maintain this commitment to particularity while still having their renderings of experience play a role in the values basic to social exchange. So this particularity must become representative by stressing its exemplary force. The text matters in social exchange less for what it can claim as truth than for what it can specify as captured by the properties it exemplifies. In our four samples, the language functions by presenting an example that functions *as* a way of speaking, without relying on a concept *of* anything. Bellamy can stage the manners of thirty-two writers because she is concerned not with the truth of what they claim or with the truth criticism might find in why they claim it. Rather, all of her textual energies are devoted to making it possible for an audience to participate affectively and self-reflexively in what the manner of the writing establishes as possible states of being.

Yet Bellamy's choices would probably infuriate the targeted writers because these decisions treat exemplification in such general terms. There is care to individualize the voice but not to specify a speech situation or highlight any particular and surprising mode of attention to the world or to language. Bellamy's theoretical achievement is to recognize how general an example can be yet have the capacity still to carry effective power over from an original text. Exemplification seems to be anything that brings to bear what might be considered distinctive of attitudes characteristic of certain authors or works.

However, it is conceptually dangerous to end by praising Bellamy for her understanding of the role of generalized example. We have to recognize that we lose something as well as gain something when we loosely adapt examples. One might say that insofar as the strategies of appropriation deal on this generalized level of example, they cannot capture the modes of responsiveness to life made possible by the richest artworks. One measure of richness might be just that while the text is open to generalized exemplification, it also makes manifest what one misses when one only relies on these aspects of the exemplifying process. Think of the difference between how Bellamy's generalized Williams performs the work eros can do and the quite specific imaginings of his "Queen Anne's Lace" and "Asphodel, That Greeny Flower."

Yet my tone of ultimately justified aesthetic conservatism here falls into a trap Bellamy prepares for pompous academic voices. For I have yet to ask how Bellamy's text might also provide a specific concrete example of a distinctive sensibility that could be useful in the world—precisely because of how it treats the relation between generality and particularity. So now I have to turn to how her ironies about the culture transmitted by the *Norton Anthology* are quite particular and quite devastating. More important, her text offers a serious specific set of actions exploring how stressing generalized examples can perform social roles impossible if we insist on more precise aspects of singularity. Especially in the domain of eros, it matters that we cultivate quite general forms of both joy and wariness and guilt because these involve the possibility of fully participating in a variety of situations. Greater refinement may produce more exotic or refined feelings. But there are situations, important situations in our lives, for which this level of refinement may be a liability rather than a virtue.

In fact, Bellamy's generalized voices produce their own distinctive, particular affective intensities and possibilities for intricate versions of sorting experiences. Her versions of emotion allow complete provisional identification with the speaking voices and the informing presence governing those voices. At that level of appropriation there need not be any defensiveness, no worries that one is not getting the point and so must don a protective shell for one's inadequacies as a reader. All the emotions are on the surface, aggressively on the surface, in a way that expressively challenges any claims that erotic emotion ought to be deeper or more precise.

To be deeper or more precise would involve the audience distrusting what we might call generic feelings and so imposing a hierarchy of emotions that in turn will produce endless anxiety about whether one is feeling correctly or with sufficient depth. It is on such questions that academics thrive but also may do real harm by denying rights to simple and powerful pleasures. So Bellamy joins pop artists such as Roy Lichtenstein and those that embrace the commodity status of their creations in celebrating the importance of surfaces. In what arena can this be more important than an erotic one?

The Demonstrative as a Lyric Mode

In my view theory sets the stage by clarifying how example is open to different degrees of generalization and specification. Theory probably cannot make determinations for what is appropriate in specific cases. It can only call for flexibility and establish the possible values involved in the stances we choose. So in order to bring this chapter to a conclusion I am going to turn to another aspect of Bellamy's text that has significant theoretical implications. I want to argue that there is a fairly large class of texts, mostly lyric poems, that call attention to how their own expressive activity imaginatively deploys the status of exemplar. Such texts call attention to how they perform the function of display, and they stage as their import their sense of the possible uses to which such displays can be adapted. So I think the best way to approach such writing is to imagine it performing a speech act I will elaborate as "the demonstrative."

The concept of demonstrative speech act will help us respond to three concerns that have been underlying my arguments in this chapter. Is it plausible to think of a single kind of speech act as capable of linking expression and exemplification as I have been elaborating them? How can we honor in practical terms the efforts to identify authors' interests in keeping display distinct from epistemic practices? And how can we in the process recuperate much of what literary critics have wanted from the concept of the "performative" as the source of our sortings while still preserving the core of what Austin accomplished in his characterization of the social functions of performative utterances?

We can address these questions because the concept of a demonstrative speech act allows us to bring Austin's work on the performative to bear while also distinguishing literary production from us the social contexts basic to Austin's analysis. Both my demonstrative and Austin's performative involve doing something within the language uttered so that it has effects beyond illocutionary assertions.[13] But Austin saw the performative as covering only those speech acts that accomplish something through language by invoking social ritual. He rightly banished from his account all fictional expressions and all discourse that is not expressly bound to social conventions beyond the conventions of language. However many philosophers and literary critics think Austin made a serious mistake in refusing any psychological dimension for his performatives. So they propose a Nietzschean view of the performative that honors precisely what Austin tried to avoid—that is, the subjective dimension of doing things in language for expressive effects, either deliberately or symptomatically.[14] This view then developed substantial critical force when Judith Butler turned the deconstructionist idealizations of the performative located primarily in works of art into a mode of engaging gender identifications and the modes of subjection that they have involved.[15]

I find these adaptions of Austin's performative embarrassing because they do not honor the immense importance of what he accomplished by narrowing the concept to social rituals, where intention does not matter and there is no role for the individual performer beyond performing a rigid script. Austin's exclusions do nothing for our aesthetic interests. But these exclusions help him secure a strong, concrete demonstration of ways in which our activity in language is not regulated by modes of knowing. There is a social aspect to grammar by which performing certain activities counts as having successfully produced social consequences. So we have to figure out how we can both honor Austin's achievement and find ways of also honoring the interests critics and philosophers have in what they call the performative features of literary composition? There is not a perfect match, yet I will argue that my concept of the demonstrative provides a strong account of literary performance and also clarifies what kind of reception such performance anticipates.

Negatively we can distinguish demonstrative speech acts because they invite attention to what the specific agent is doing in linguistic modes that are not intended to work within the boundaries of epistemic protocols. Demonstrative acts do not try to make language a transparent picture of the world. They emphasize how an agent performs, and they dramatize the relation to an audience established by that performance.

I choose the term "demonstrative" for three basic reasons. It carries a motive: demonstration desires to change what audiences understand by virtue of qualities embedded in the act itself. So it is an appropriate figure for what can be accomplished by expressive, performative activity. In fact, the term reminds us that demonstration can be a mode of teaching in its own right by emphasizing the power of example, as in teaching someone to fly-fish or to develop manners. Second, I want to pick up the associations the term has with demonstrative people, people eager to articulate their feelings and develop intimate bonds with audiences. Finally, "demonstrative" evokes the kinds of indexical operators such as "this" and even "as" that call attention to the work examples do. Wittgenstein's "This is so" offers a powerful abstract model for an assertion that depends on the agent's relation to the contents and context rather than depending on its descriptive adequacy in relation to the world.

There are also three basic kinds of demonstrative speech acts. The first is closest to the Nietzschean performative. It occurs when speakers try to make the speaking a display of various stylistic or psychological traits with which they want to be identified by an audience. Here we can locate the emphasis on ethos central to classical rhetoric. The second type is also fundamentally expressive, but with a very different valence. These speech acts call attention to affective states intended to solicit or engage the affective engagements of others. We try to find verbal equivalents for what we seem to be feeling or attending to in order to invite an audience into our own intimate spaces. At times our exclamations of pain or joy go so far as to utter onomatopoeic grunts or sighs or laughs that are clear indices of our affective states. So one must be aware that these indices at times are under the control of the agent, whereas at other times, like all expressive activity, they betray forces working on subjects which the subjects repress or of which they are not aware.

Finally there is the pedagogical demonstrative, with a refreshing disinterest in subjective states but no less central for characterizing what we do with language. I refer to our efforts to use models in order to show concretely how something can be done even though it is difficult or impossible to describe the principles involved. The most basic example is teaching someone how to ride a bicycle—very difficult to explain but fairly simple to show, especially if the showing fully intervenes in how the tutee feels his or her body and develops ways of maintaining balance. I think it evident that there is a wide range of such cases—from the intimate processes by which a spouse teaches the partner to pick up cues by exhibiting behaviors, to learning to wield the now current art form of the public apology.

Demonstrative Sentences and Metaphoric Roles They Play

Let me begin by listing a range of representative general sentences that I think indicate kinds of demonstrative speech acts:

> "The task can be done like this."
> "Try to recite the poem by emphasizing these variations in pacing."
> "Why do you want to make me as worried as I am evidently becoming?"
> "This is what I can do when I get a chance to speak in public."
> "This is how a good husband would deal with my anger."
> "It hurts here, not there."
> "This bemused face is a good indication of how I feel."[16]

All of these sentences reflect the fact that in appropriate cases we often find ourselves relying on modes of display because what we feel or what we want to accomplish is much easier to show than to characterize in discursive terms. And that showing is not merely a pointing to some factor or force that can be said to shape the situation. Affectively one demonstrates what one is feeling; semantically one provides a model for how some aspect of the language can operate; and stylistically one exemplifies possible powers of a medium for intensifying how the agent can participate in the object of his or her attention. And hovering on the margin of these sentences is the possibility of further discourse where the speaker might take degrees of responsibility for choosing this particular mode of display. Display in general presents second-order possibilities of fleshing out one's investments by contextualizing them, if not by offering explanations for them. One asks of the agents what place the displays have in the lives from which they issue.[17]

Works of art and rhetorical performances use these elemental demonstratives. But to characterize the overall speech act involved in such work one has to shift to the notion of "metaphoric demonstratives." First, they display an attitude that the work can try to contextualize, qualify, justify, and test by elaborating how it possesses (or fails to possess) various capacities for interpreting the situation presented. Here the metaphoric register consists in the work's interest in overwriting the details presented so that they will carry an intended interpretation. How can we speak of the seeing of a face?

Second, metaphoric demonstratives call attention to how the performing presence is at every moment taking responsibility for constructing an imaginary world (usually as a possible real world) that has its primary appeal directly because of this constructive activity. Here performance is necessarily self-reflexive. But that does not necessarily entail irony or endless self-referentiality. Rather, the self-reflexiveness can be focused simply on the effort to share with the audience an explicitness about the possible values in the constructive activity shaping how the work unfolds. This self-referentiality is no different in kind from the self-referentiality that allows the exclamation "Red!" to serve also as a taking of responsibility for one's enthusiasms.

I have written two essays elaborating how we might apply the notion of demonstrative speech act to literary works.[18] So I need say here only that this concept matters because in most accounts of literary art there is insufficient attention to the ways authors insist on their presence in the form of a constant purposiveness at work in making the choices that shape what kind of world the fiction establishes. This lack of attention is not surprising when philosophers talk about writing because philosophers almost always choose representational fiction or drama, where one can easily concentrate on the world presented rather than the author presenting. But we have seen that literary studies is also now reluctant to stake anything on authorial agency. And we have seen the price of that reluctance: criticism has failed to attend the imaginative resources by which works establish agency and make thick descriptions available for the worlds that such agency must engage.

Finally, criticism attentive to this demonstrative dimension can ultimately test the powers of example to make alternative worlds available and so to effect large-scale change even though the examples bypass the route of description and argument. As late Wittgenstein often reminded us, the concreteness of example affords the best means of bringing people to "look at the world in a different way" (*OC*, 92). Examples address not just our attitudes but also our understanding of how the attitudes fit into larger practices and frameworks. Because these examples emphasize how needs and desires lead us to develop stances toward the world, they can have the power to articulate how change might be both possible and necessary.

Two Poems by Robert Creeley as Exemplary Demonstratives

I cannot resist trying to demonstrate the possible values of reading poetry in terms of what the demonstrative highlights. One could turn to Shakespeare's *Sonnets,* those masterpieces of instruction in the powers and pains of love, or one could attend carefully to Yeats's sense of how poems establish character and responsibility. But I choose to concentrate on two poems by Robert Creeley because he wields the demonstrative force of poetry so explicitly and yet so subtly that he exemplifies a mode of writing that I think has widespread contemporary significance.[19]

Consider, for example, what we might call one of Creeley's "signature" texts from *For Love* (1962), "A Song":

> I had wanted a quiet testament
> and I had wanted, among other things,
> a song.
>   That was to be
> of a like monotony.
>   (A grace
>
> Simply. Very very quiet.
>   A murmur of some lost
> Thrush, though I have never seen one.
> Which was you then. Sitting
> and so, at peace, so very much this same quiet.
>
> A song.
>
> And of you the sign now, surely, of a gross
> Perpetuity

>   (which is not reluctant, or if it is,
> It is no longer important.
>
> A song
> Which one sings, if he sings it,
> with care.[20]

Here Creeley manages an homage to traditional "song" while wresting its elemental structuring devices away from what Charles Bernstein calls the "official verse culture."[21] To this homage Creeley binds an intricate psychological drama. The poem seems nervous, moving out of a past into an uncertain present which affords a possibility of quiet but is haunted by a self-conscious disgust at his own efforts to provide a name for that quiet which would inevitably displace it. The effect of this self-consciousness is to turn typical formal devices such as rhyme into figures of dissatisfaction, such as parenthesis. And when these formal devices grow problematic, the poem has to compensate by demonstrating the force of another kind of formal structure—the capacity of the speaker's breath units to become the driving force of the lineation.

The poem's drama centers on this relation between unhappy self-consciousness and fundamental bodily energies, where rest and quiet become active possibilities. As we attend to these rhythms of breathing we also recognize how much we become caught up in other temporal factors that all establish attention to the poem's pacing. Every element emphasizes movement, except for the repetition of "A song" because that repetition figuratively becomes the space demanding to be mobilized. It is as if the poem had to find through repetition a version of song that could carry or possess the fullness of care—not a minor resource for the mind to have when it sorts for possible attitudes that might honor the complexity of psychological life.

If we are to become articulate about that fullness, we must attend to another aspect of the demonstrative—the expressive working out or realizing of an attitude reconciling the competing pulls in the poem. In a typical practical scenario we could assume that the attitude would be named and could be put to immediate practical work. But poets tend to want their attitudes more complex and more perspicuous than that. They want a sense that the poem realizes something by having its naming process produce a fresh twist on our standard cultural repertoire.

Here Creeley composes an attitude displaying a synthetic capacity to reconcile three states of mind—an uneasy care not to embarrass the self by trusting language, the wary care not to expose too much vulnerability ("if he sings it"), and the invested care that allows one to sing the song and participate in the desires it offers for the quiet she can bring. The desire for quiet inspires the song, and the song can celebrate the quiet if one can also take responsibility for the interference that is self-consciousness. Ultimately that taking of responsibility requires simultaneously acknowledging desire and accepting warily the fact that one often has little control over one's feelings. If he sings it, it had better be with the multiple forms of care that the poem comes to exemplify.

There seem to be two levels of demonstration taking place here—one as the presentation of a complex state of mind and another presenting the satisfaction possible when one can envision and will this successful demonstration. I raise this issue of willing because I suspect this is what we engage when we talk about aesthetic emotion in literature. It is not a primary emotion but a reflective one concerning the state of satisfaction in our engagement with the affects displayed in the work.

And I indulge in this speculation because of the degree of self-reflection, explicit and implicit, that occurs in my second example from Creeley. Notice how his "Something" crosses expressive and pedagogical aspects of the demonstrative:

> I approach with such
> a careful tremor, always
> I feel the finally foolish
>
> question of how it is,
> then, supposed to be felt,
> and by whom. I remember
>
> once in a rented room on
> 27th street, the woman I loved,
> then, literally, after we
>
> had made love on the large
> bed sitting across from
> a basin with two faucets, she

> had to pee but was nervous,
> embarrassed I suppose I
> would watch her who had but
>
> a moment ago been completely
> open to me, naked, on
> the same bed. Squatting, her
>
> head reflected in the mirror,
> the hair dark there, the
> full of her face, the shoulders,
>
> sat spread-legged, turned on
> one faucet and shyly pissed. What
> love might learn from such a sight. (*RC*, 281)

Criticism might learn from such a sight to tread lightly and honor the primacy of the narrated scene. But the poet's demonstration of skills that complement and deepen the "lesson" compels me to offer a critical supplement. It is probably too simple to speak of enjambment in Creeley because that suggests a distanced, controlling intelligence rather than what seems the sheer wary care of a breathing that does not want to rest, even in this sexual scene, until the mind can be satisfied that there is learning taking place. For most of the poem there is an expression of tenderness that seems inseparable from a strange sense of instability. Notice the momentary confusion in interpreting the sense of the two instances of "I" in the fifth stanza. "I suppose" renders the narrator's need to explain "embarrassed," and the second "I" is the object of the embarrassment.

Then most readers would expect the "who" clause that follows to refer to that "I." But Creeley shifts perspective to move from watching the woman to attributing to her a subjective sense of complete openness. This shift in perspective then entirely erases the "me" to focus marvelously on the act and the surrounding details—her using only one faucet is especially touching. Logically it is by erasing the "me" and so attending to detail that there can be a final perspective shift to love itself as potential agent capable of taking all the internal "I" rhymes into something that extends far beyond the scene. How we learn from this sight to appreciate intimacy is inseparable from this way of telling.

Chapter 6

WHAT LITERARY THEORY CAN LEARN FROM WITTGENSTEIN'S SILENCE ABOUT ETHICS

> Man, a manifold, mendacious, artificial, and opaque animal, uncanny to the other animals less because of his strength than because of his cunning and shrewdness, has invented the good consciousness to enjoy his soul for once as simple; and the whole of morality is a long undismayed forgery which alone makes it possible to enjoy the sight of the soul. From this point of view much more may belong in the concept of "art" than is generally believed.
> —FRIEDRICH NIETZSCHE, *Beyond Good and Evil*

> That value is inescapable in human experience and conduct is one of the facts of life, and of art, which modern art lays bare.
> —STANLEY CAVELL, *Must We Mean What We Say?*

If one were to read a good deal of literary theory's recent speculations on ethics and the ethical, one might be convinced that the smartest thing Wittgenstein did was keep relatively silent on ethics after his "Lecture on Ethics" (1931). Wittgenstein was not silent because he thought ethics unimportant. Rather, he probably thought ethics was too important to be left to philosophers, let alone literary critics. Many of the questions ethics must address prove very difficult to answer in cogent arguments, largely because ethics must involve both expressive and judgmental features. At one pole, individuals must testify to how they determine particular commitments to pursuing a good life according to their own lights. The ethical domain is a matter of establishing and pursing a specific orientation of self-consciousness. At the other pole, ethics must place that expressive dimension in relation to forms of reasoning that provide publically defensible justifications for actions in such a way as to address basic social concerns for mutual respect, for objectivity, and for justice.

More problematic yet for Wittgenstein was the ease with which both the needy ego and frustrated social interests could leap in to fill the Tractarian silence about ethics. Terry Eagleton reminds us that Marx said no one had written more about money than he who had so little of it.[1] But writing about ethics is not like writing about money: to write about ethics is at the least to have to struggle with the temptation to identify the writing self with the projection of possible ethical values. Righteousness haunts this writing because people want to claim the right path for themselves even when their arguments are somewhat shaky. Yet they use their commitments to assess the arguments. So it should not be surprising that Wittgenstein explored the possibility that the only available escape from the righteousness of making the self exemplary was to idealize confession as individual appeal for understanding and for forgiveness, without recourse to principle at all.[2]

This chapter then cannot be devoted to Wittgensteinian arguments about ethics. It can only honor his sensibility by scrutinizing those who do claim ethical value for literature and then developing an account of literary valuing that seeks multiple possibilities of attunement and provisional identification. Anything involving generalization I will treat suspiciously; almost anything involving careful attention to particular acts of phenomenological valuing will be praised and emulated. I will even claim that in so doing I am following the model of Wittgenstein's *Culture* and *Value* because of how that book approaches artists and works of art.

This discussion of value will focus on two basic concerns: what is the place of valuing in the phenomenology of reading literary works, and how can we recast criticism to concentrate on these particular events rather than on the two schema now prevailing in the field—the concern for moral judgment of actions and characters and the post-structural emphasis on replacing moral concerns with what they see as the core of "ethics"? This poststructural ideal calls for adjusting one's sensibility to the demands of the other made visible through the event qualities specific to careful reading. Obviously I will use my version of a phenomenological perspective to claim instead that few readers actually ignore the variety of acts of valuing involved in reading literature.[3] But fewer still, alas, seem to want to accept this diversity as a sufficient condition for criticism to celebrate. So I will have to work toward the possibility of freeing literature from ethics so that the often intimate and intricate values accessible to reading and teaching literature can stand and be counted.

The need to deal with these issues has become quite pressing because literary criticism's emphasis on ethics seems a rather desperate bid for another version of worldliness capable of addressing an increasing marginality for verbal art. The hope is that claims about the force of criticism's capacities to enact ethical judgments will give literature clear social uses and so justify the place of literary criticism in our educational structures. But even if this need is compelling, the dominant modes of drawing out ethical implications in literary experience simply do not give an adequate account of the kinds of valuation that take place in what Nietzsche called "slow reading," nor of the treating of reading as an art in its own right, demanding care in the application of techniques and ways of composing experience. And without a decent account of where valuing enters reading, it proves difficult to provide an adequate general picture of the place of ethics in human experience.

I will not try to counter these claims with proposals for a better account of ethics. Instead, I want to show how to avoid ethics entirely as a topic for literary theory so that we can focus on different kinds of valuation that are central to literary experience.[4] Perhaps then we will see that my epigraph from Nietzsche for this chapter is at least half-right: the spectacle of our floundering to adapt moral languages to experience allows us to see, or least to hope, that "more might belong in the concept of art than is generally believed." More was certainly involved in our reading of texts such as "The Instruction Manual" and Creeley's "Something" than a moral perspective might engage, precisely because valuing was so intensely intimate a process of directly feeling the mind's pleasure in its own work at attunement.

Derek Attridge: The Ethical Ideal of Reading as Responsibility for the Other

I promise not to dwell on the negative. But I have to begin there because criticism of dominant attitudes seems the only way now to combat the almost ubiquitous tendency in literary theory to make talk of values equivalent to hypotheses about the ethical qualities of literary experience. We need to see how there are internal problems in the prevailing calls for attention to possible ethical consequences of reading. And we need to see to how these theories blind us to the possible significance in other ways of talking about values that have real but indirect social consequences.

There seem to be four general positions on the ethical qualities literature brings into play that seem still to inspire lively practices. But I will focus on only two because the other two seem somewhat outdated. It is also the case that important aspects of the general positions fold into what I consider the two more capacious and vital positions. For example, I think new directions in poststructural versions of ethics largely subsume J. Hillis Miller's *Ethics of Reading* while taking Derrida and Levinas in somewhat different directions: the otherness basic to Derrida's concept of writing now takes on more political and practical versions of challenges to unified and rational self-consciousness. (One might even say that poststructuralist ethics has taken over the idealizing role of virtue ethics by calling for heroic attacks on concepts such as virtue. For there remains in this new critique of the conceptual a strong but unacknowledged influence of the concept of "authenticity," perhaps inevitably so long as we dismiss efforts to submit our differences to social negotiation.)[5] The other two perspectives adapt a completely different orientation. Virtue theory derived from Aristotle (with a significant boost from Alasdair MacIntyre) still influences how many critics read because of powerful work by Wayne Booth and many other critics. But much of its energy is now subsumed in the ideal knower postulated by cognitive theorists such as Martha Nussbaum and Alice Crary because this ideal figure internalizes goals of moral understanding.

One of the two perspectives I will discuss identifies literature with an experience of concrete power by which we can distinguish the ethical from the moral; the other tries to revitalize the moral because of the powers of literary experience to focus situations and render fully human responses that challenge our conventional modes of judgment. Both have a great deal of trouble dealing with the various kinds of attunement, participation, and exemplification on which I have been concentrating. So studying them should prove a very useful way to indicate the need for ways of talking about the values sought and provided by writers that need not be mediated by the models ethics provides for reflection.

I have chosen Derek Attridge as my example of poststructural ideals of ethical reading largely because he is a concise and extremely eloquent proponent of how poststructuralist ethics is intimately connected to how one reads literature. Here is Attridge's basic version of the contrast between ethics and morality, which is central to poststructural thinking:

> We can only continue to use terms with ethical implications like "responsibility" and "obligation"—indeed "ethics" itself—if we are prepared to make some kind of distinction between the most fundamental ethical demands, which always involve unpredictability and risk, and specific obligations governing concrete situations in a given social context, which require the greatest possible control of outcomes. To the latter, the name morality is often given ... Moral codes [are] embodied in social norms, religious institutions, the laws of my country, and, probably, my own superego. (*SI*, 126–27)

This contrast systematizes Levinas's basic concern for how otherness has priority over sameness because it makes the ego aware of its dependencies and its lack of mastery.[6] We come in the world not as its designated masters but as creatures doomed to what seems already given and independent of our purposes.[7] Yet we do not have to suffer this situation passively. We can actively embrace what otherness involves and so turn fear into affirming the "ought," which defines our ethical responsibility for this other precisely because it makes me aware of my own lack of mastery (ibid., 126). This ethical responsibility is very different from moral responsibility, which derives from the various positive systems and codes that provide humanity's arrogant means for escaping that otherness in fictions of mutual self-mastery.

Why should we believe that risk and unpredictability play a fundamental role in distinguishing the ethical from the moral? Attridge thinks that literary traditions enable him to provide a strong answer to this question because they offer a range of texts all responding to two kinds of unpredictability and risk—the direct otherness of particular situations that challenge our understanding and something such as an ontological or a metaphysical otherness that reminds us of the limitations of mind and of ego when confronted with the concrete singularity of striking particular events.[8] Attridge sees that "there is no necessary correlation between being a good reader" or a good artist and "being a good person; nevertheless some of the same values are at work in both spheres":

> To respond to the demand of the literary work as the demand of the other is to attend to it as a unique event whose happening is a call, a challenge, an obligation: understand how little you understand me, translate my untranslatability, learn me by heart and thus learn the otherness that inhabits the heart. (*SI*, 131)

The same imperatives that drive readers to respect this otherness hold for ethical experience: ethical experience just is the sense of demand for modes of response that can take a kind of responsibility for what is other to the comfortable ego. Responsibility consists in actively embracing what we cannot control or easily understand. And responsibility demands that we care for what so challenges us because the challenge provides possible paths for both growth as a self and care as a condition of witnessing to what we cannot master. The "call coming from the work itself . . . as singular staging of otherness" (ibid., 124) makes "my responsibility for the other . . . more demanding" than "certain kinds of support and succor for other persons . . . enjoined by conventional moral codes":

> My obligation is to refashion what I think and what I am in order to take the fullest possible account of, to respect, safeguard, and learn from, the otherness and singularity of the other. . . . The other cannot come into existence unless it is affirmed, welcomed, trusted, nurtured. (ibid., 125)

By basing responsibility on something utterly different from the terms of morality, Attridge can develop two important challenges to traditional views of ethics. The first is the residue of Levinas's training in existentialism, now filtered through what I have been calling the display features of literary expression. Where Wittgenstein argues that there can be no description of logic because logic is necessary for all description, Attridge argues that it is the ethical act "that is prior to all possible grounds" (ibid., 127). One cannot give reasons for one's ethical decisions because the "ought" of responsibility brings the other into existence as a kind of primordial act: "We find ourselves already responsible for the other—and this fact constitutes the artistic sphere as much as it does the ethical" (ibid.). Think, for example, of reading a writer such as Beckett. We confront an enterprise that is less an imitation of the world than the working out of terms by which the very existence of the work can issue a demand in the present tense to take seriously all that refuses to produce a world that the ego can find comforting.

Second, Attridge claims that responsibility for the other as other is the only ground of possibility for ethics (ibid.). The embodiments of otherness in event and in the sense of limitation of the subject's powers of self-definition simply are aspects of what it means to be a subject. The idea of responsibility for the other is not derived from ethics. Rather, the "ought" of responsibility comes into existence as inseparable from there being an ethics at all:

> To act morally toward other persons entails . . . as full an attempt at understanding them and their situation as one is capable of; yet both the primary claim of another person upon one and the final measure of one's behavior lies in the response to, and affirmation of, the otherness which resists that understanding. (ibid., 129)

Some Problems with Attridge's Position

Attridge is so eloquent on literature that when I cite him I almost come to believe him on ethics. But when I recover my better judgment, I suspect that Attridge's claims about ethics actually blind us to what are significant values distinctive to literary experience. The achievement of Levinas, indistinguishable from the danger of Levinasian thinking, is his managing to make claims for ethics on the basis of what have traditionally been reasons for separating the literary from the ethical. Ethics gains in dramatic intensity when it can invoke qualities of singularity, eventfulness, distrust of conceptual clarity in favor of affective complexity, and the capacity to dwell in contradiction. But this conception of ethics also loses the space of normative reasoning that ethics has traditionally tried to occupy in various ways. And that is a major loss because then neither Aristotle's nor Kant's nor Hume's nor Rawls's questions shape its practices.

We see this clearly if we ask whether being a good person correlates with an ability to treat an event as a call to understand how little you understand? I think the judgment that we are dealing with an ethically good person does not depend on the person's sensibility to the unfolding of singularities but on that person's becoming trusted to reflect carefully on how he or she can correlate individual interests with public answerability. Several of the persons I most trust in their characterizations of singularities score considerably less well on any scale measuring reliability and thoughtfulness toward others. Ethics as well as morality seem impossible to base on event qualities because ethics loses all of its focus on reflective action and judgment, especially judgment about what is to be done, when it is tied too closely to single moments of responsiveness.

Conversely, good reading depends entirely on being open to specific and surprising event qualities. Reading is haptic: we prepare for a variety of events. Only a Horatio can remain a friend to Hamlet, and only by separating what makes a good friend from any kind of generalized ethical concern. Living eudaimonically, on the other hand, is a matter of durations: we prepare to allow ourselves and other people to expect certain behaviors and social attitudes when we encounter various events.

My comments can be dismissed as mere ideology. Yet I would claim for them at least the possibility that they represent widely held understandings of the nature of ethical and moral thinking that need at least to be addressed by Levinasian ethics.[9] But that claim, too, will not prove persuasive without the backing of specific arguments challenging Attridge's basic efforts to correlate good reading with the good person. Let us begin by questioning the role Attridge asks the concept of "otherness" to play. As I have already discussed in my appendix to chapter 1, a respect for otherness has some use in describing how the experience of reading can challenge previously held ideals. However, "otherness" or the "other" are terribly abstract terms that do not correlate well with any analysis of actual human behavior, even in relation only to texts.

For, as Attridge admits, no practical situation ever presents itself as a matter of sheer otherness or sheer sameness. But then Attridge goes on to treat "otherness" as a workable theoretical concept even though pure otherness is not even imaginable, and pure sameness is also pure tautology about which nothing can be predicated. How much otherness must a text or situation have before it can be covered by Attridge's idealizations? The question does not admit any cogent answer. Instead it indicates how problematic such ontological terms are when we ask practical questions of them. We are always negotiating degrees of otherness and of sameness: think of Shylock's "Does not a Jew bleed?" speech. We can make no predications about the pure "other" because by definition it is beyond language, which serves as the negotiation of identity and difference.

And yet Attridge seems confident that otherness is a sufficiently clear and powerful concept that it can produce an "ought" that can shape behavior. Here Attridge has to rely on his argument that ethics is primordial: its claims are based on the forms of experience rather than on the forms of logic. But while Wittgenstein poses good reasons to believe that logic must precede descriptions because it is the precondition for that activity, I see no cause to accept the similar claim about ethics because historically at least it has been treated as a mode of inquiry that involves the weighing of reasons and the understanding that human dignity depends on responsibility for the reasons one gives. Only Levinas's religious beliefs will give ethics the foundational place logic assumed for the young Wittgenstein. But if we assess this claim in secular terms there seem to be good reasons not to grant any ethical imperative to the presence or absence of otherness.

Paul de Man offers the best reasoning I know for denying this claim. In "Theory of Metaphor in Rousseau's Second Discourse," he imagines the first human seeing a disturbing "other" approaching that nonetheless has significant similarities in appearance.[10] Even if this scene could provide a model for why language had to develop so that these two could communicate, one has to ask what traces the language will carry of their mutual suspicion and fear and fantasized violence toward this being who challenges my control over what had a world for me alone. This other need not be benevolent at all. And attempts to assume a shareable world could prove very dangerous. What fascination we have with this other is no more likely to elicit an ethical "ought" than it is to produce an ethics of wariness and fear, as it has in capitalism. At best the imperative might be to negotiate this otherness of the other rather than embrace it as somehow being required of my ethical authenticity. (Fear has a better evolutionary claim than does ethics to be prior to logic—historically and ontologically.)

This difficulty of getting from otherness in literature to otherness as shaping ethical ideals seems to me crucial for appreciating one potential value of literary experience. Ethics ultimately must deal with actual situations and determine single courses of action in relation to each situation. In contrast, most imaginative writing ultimately deals with possible worlds, where fascination with otherness can generate, and can sanction, a wide variety of responses—from identification to violent repudiation. Think again of Hamlet's hearing the terrifying otherness in Claudius's opening speech. And when literary works put otherness at the center of attention, they are interested not in the otherness per se but in the ways a sense of otherness might shape particular stances toward experience. The emphasis is not on authenticity but on exemplifying what it may be like to undergo certain experiences. If there is an "ought" in relation to imaginative life, it is the imperative to put imagination to work to transform objects and persons into intricate and rich sources of experience.

Alice Crary as Exemplary Moral Interpreter of Literary Experience

When we turn to Anglo-American philosophy's influence on attributions of ethical value to literary works, we find exactly the opposite approach from Attridge's. This critical work adapts the language of morality to what disciplinary philosophy would like literature to be, while largely ignoring the traits which theorists have cited to proclaim literary experience as different from any practical orientation. So the proponents of this mode of inquiry risk blinding themselves to the sense of complexity, the power of imagination, and the force of strangeness that tempts critics such as Attridge to challenge any claims smacking of traditional morality. The cult of the "other" and "otherness" proclaims the dangers of any kind of conceptual order because such an order is committed to generalization and repeatability, while literature presents singularity, the event, and a persistent challenge to any conceptual ordering principles. Yet the moral cognitivists would insist that this ordering is what literary texts explore, in ways that invite the distribution of praise and blame. So these critics also have reasons to honor the various forms of concreteness and complexity that literature offers: such conditions are what challenge us to develop adult moral awareness. But then theorists have to provide a language for what is valuable about that complexity and concreteness. And in my view that language turns out to impose an ultimately philosophical vocabulary producing conditions within which literature cannot know itself.

One could talk here about Cora Diamond or Martha Nussbaum or the more intricate psychoanalytically tinted analyses of Stanley Cavell. But I want something more recent and more directly connected to a reading of Wittgenstein, so I have chosen Alice Crary's Beyond Moral Judgment.[11] Crary builds an ethics for literary criticism largely based on treating Wittgenstein as a pragmatist concerned with the affective, interpersonal dimensions of our language use. The result is a scrupulously clear and intelligent set of arguments for how philosophy can clarify and foster moral values by the study of literary works.

Crary begins by insisting on an Aristotelian definition of morality (not too unlike Attridge's concern for what makes a person ethical): "I speak of a person's moral outlook in reference to her view of how best to live, or of what matters most in life" (*BMJ*, 9n1). Then she can build in from the start a basic opposition between how we make moral judgments and how we shape ethical character (although she does not explicitly use the contrast between ethics and morality). So there is a pluralism about values at the core of her enterprise. But there is also a concern that to be philosophical at all one has to defeat any subjective and relativist model that might allow individual agents to develop different constructions of what the moral involves. Therefore she argues that there are some objective dimensions to the question of how best to live because there are shareable moral evaluations of the choices we make that shape character.

Here Crary needs some fancy philosophical footwork. She recognizes that she cannot rely on any traditional model of objectivity because that excludes everything "merely subjective." An emphasis on the objectivity of the text cannot even talk about the mental responses the object elicits (*BMJ*, 15). However, this limitation does not entail simply embracing what Crary calls "the merely subjective," which refers to responses that depend on subjective states—for example, appearing red or seeming funny. There is also a category of the "problematically subjective" (ibid.), which Crary argues comprises "properties an object can be said to possess insofar as it is the kind of thing that would elicit subjective responses in appropriate circumstances" (ibid.). In this category the subject is not bound by the object or objective laws but by conditions of cultural understanding. When we can invoke "appropriate circumstances," we are expected to correlate the internal aspect of individual moral judgment by which "we have reason" to do something with "how things really—or objectively—are in the world" (ibid., 11–12). For example, there are common cases when the object does not merely appear red to one subject but the red seems the case for all the competent observers despite the fact that they all must align their subjective stances to that particular appearance.

Finally Crary invokes a third category consisting of cases where affective properties seem aspects of the actual situation rather than elements shaped by the imaginations of discrete subjects. Here we get close to what typical novels and lyric poems offer: the writers establish conditions within which the affects seem to be embedded within the action rather than subject to an individual's response. We do not so much construct those situations as recognize what is called for by the mode of expression. Hence we can see responses as appropriate when there is an "internal relation to sensibility or affective propensities that allow it [sensibility] to be essentially practical" (ibid., 16). Later in Crary's book she elaborates how this kind of objectivity is "accessible only in terms of particular evaluative perspectives" (ibid., 176) or "intelligible only in terms of certain evaluative perspectives" (ibid., 165). Judgments about sexual harassment need not be merely subjective interpretations of events but can specify an objective condition in which our evaluative frameworks for such encounters seem violated.

Crary bases her case for this expanded notion of objectivity on the claim that there is no way to stabilize any "abstraction requirement" (ibid., 21) that will give us a discrete moral world without subjective elements. We have no idea of what regularities would be on view "independently of sensitivities that we acquire in mastering the concept" (ibid., 24). Our eyes being opened to the world requires developing certain practical sensitivities (ibid., 25). Sensitivity to moral values plays a similar role to "the role played by our perceptual apparatus in a reasonable conception of what it is to be sensitive to color" (ibid., 31). Then she can make the positive case that once we acknowledge the public role of these sensitivities, the moral question becomes, is this "the kind of thing that, in appropriate circumstances, merits certain attitudes of approval and disapproval"? (ibid.). We can treat the resulting moral judgments as "standing in the sort of immediate relation to affect that allows them to be internally related to action and choice" (ibid.).

Crary's ultimate aim is to show how subjects can act in accord with rationality without committing themselves to sheer objectivity. And then attention to how writers carefully construct scenarios can be said to deepen our appreciation of what rationality involves because in such writing the subjective takes on qualities that everyone can both identify with and assess. Insofar as moral decisions emerge from those sensitivities, there is warrant for treating them as "rational" because they invoke what become properties "intrinsic" (ibid., 41) to the acquisition of moral concepts: moral thinking is a matter of "discerning regularities in . . . a version of the world that is already itself moral" (ibid., 38). We articulate or adapt "an already moralized image of the world" (ibid., 39). And because this moralized image is inseparable from our entire sense of how our own affective lives ground us in this practical order, we find ourselves capable of realizing how thoroughly this view "expands the concerns of ethics so that . . . they encompass . . . [a person's] entire personality" (ibid., 47).

This reference to the entire personality as an aspect of ethical rationality enables Crary to see herself as both defining and extending a "set of remarks scattered" through Wittgenstein's later writings "that it seems natural to describe as bearing on ethical topics" (ibid., 120). Then she offers several versions of this "bearing on"—that Wittgenstein's On Certainty "takes for granted a pragmatic account of language . . . on which certain acquired sensitivities are internal to our linguistic capacities" (ibid.), that in his later works "Wittgenstein insists that his own philosophical practice is properly characterized in ethical terms" (ibid., 121), that these works criticize "approaches to language that presuppose we can survey and assess judgments . . . without relying on sensitivities we acquired in learning to judge" (ibid.), and that one can treat as "ethical" Wittgenstein's statements about responsibility involving " 'a kind of work on oneself' " because this statement "involves a peculiarly ethical type of 'difficulty having to do with the will rather than the intellect' " (ibid., 122).[12]

Such attention to the "already moral" built into the fabric of our language allows Crary a quite subtle account of the ethical capacities of literary works. For they "can teach us about the moral life" (ibid., 132) by involving us directly in the exercise of moral sensibility without demanding that we make abstract moral judgments. She shows beautifully how novels can articulate "patterns in our practical lives that only come into view from the perspective of the particular emotional responses elicited from us" (ibid., 142). So the novel both develops and trades on an expanded sense of an objective moral field of concern. For example, Jane Austen's Persuasion seeks emotional "responses internal to an appreciation of 'proper persuadability' " that "are intended to contribute directly to a genuine, fully rational understanding of these features" (ibid., 149). Our educated response exemplifies "possible changes in moral outlook" that realize "the novel's primary moral lesson" (ibid.).

Yet to speak of a "moral lesson" runs the risk of invoking a moralistic attitude where valuing the work relies on concepts that "subject feelings to the governance of prior moral judgments" (ibid., 206). Here Crary seems to echo Attridge's fear that a moral discourse will subsume the concrete otherness that makes for distinctive literary experience. But by insisting on the perspective of concerns for how best to live, Crary allows considerable room for attuning to the text's concrete sense of drama: moral life involves aspects of identification and sympathy sadly absent from our ways of invoking moral judgments. In fact, as Crary shows in her engaging account of Effi Briest, moral judgments can even become modes of self-protection that justify agents in turning away from engagements with the world that might complicate or challenge their moral beliefs.

Some Problems with Crary's Position

Obviously Crary is right about the dangers of moralism. But do these dangers consist only in the simplifications of abstract judgment? I fear that extending the discourse of moral values to virtually all of our concerns with valuing is at least as dangerous. It does not take Foucault to point out that the person who relies primarily on moral assessments without specific moral judgments risks developing a quite narrow and somewhat obtuse overall sensibility.

If Crary's theory were to prevail, educating a literary sensibility would require also producing a more refined, but also more dedicated moral sensibility. Literary training would be relegated to equating sensibility with capacities for moral intelligence. This would be quite different from a situation where we could distinguish what called for moral judgment from texts that encourage the development of other modes of seeing and of feeling. Crary's vision would regulate every aspect of sensibility in order to impose moral frameworks on how we register the possible significance of an action. (We would turn New York City into Berkeley.) So the best of intentions regarding education of "the whole personality" seems likely to produce something close to the worst of worlds. What seems to honor differences among subjectivities in fact threatens to establish an overall conformity—not just of judgments but of modes of being.

With this threat in mind, it seems prudent to examine Crary's moves very carefully. Granted that Crary echoes Aristotle in her argument that the primary concern of ethics is "what matters most in life" or "how best to live," we still have to ask whether Aristotle was right or whether his culture's understanding of what "ethics" implied can be mapped on our own, after the intervention of Christian values. In my view the equation of morality with questions of living well presents two basic problems.[13]

First, defining ethics in terms of living well has the tautological force of treating all significant values as ultimately moral values or at least as values compatible with moral judgment. But is it right that what might seem valued for aesthetic or affective or social or political reasons be treated in moral terms or even be statable in terms that allow moral judgment? Does it matter that in Crary's way of thinking we could not even assign significance to Nietzsche's discourse about the "extramoral"? And must Blake's sense of contraries or Pound's investments in Dionysius or even Henry James's wariness of love be treated in accord with moral frameworks? There seems to be no room in Crary's house for Attridge's "other" or even any literary resistance to moral judgment that does not turn out in the end to be in the interest of moral values.

Second, Crary seems to offer a choice of reductive attitudes when she claims that her view "expands the concerns of ethics so that, far from being limited to a person's moral judgments, they encompass her entire personality—her interests, fears, and ambitions, her characteristic gestures and attitudes and her sense of what is humorous, what is offensive, and what is profound" (*BMJ*, 47; see also ibid., 195, 208). Either this reduces the personality to moral identity or it reduces morality to something resembling psychology. These are unacceptable options. In my view the moral domain cannot just consist of ever-expanding states of sensibility but must include demands that subjects make decisions and take responsibility for certain aspects of identity.

The moral agent cannot think just in terms of inclusiveness but has to offer reasoned exclusions in relation to certain areas of self-definition. Some aspects of the psyche have to be encouraged and some denied, just as some actions have to be affirmed and some denied (unlike the aesthetic state, where all the details can be affirmed). Once morality loses demands for the practical justifying of actions it becomes almost entirely a rhetorical construct aimed at self-regard with no clear practical task to perform. Here again Attridge and Crary join in their almost complete aligning of ethics with speculative attitudes rather than with an emphasis on actions and decisions. And they thus miss the affections and identifications that in literature tie us to the concrete world.

I think Crary's resistance to the aspects of moral thinking that involve practical judgment also makes it much easier for her to be seduced by the authority of philosophy within her account of literary experience, even as she also attempts to reorient that authority to the domain of moral personality. The key here is her subjugating subjectivity to objectivity in relation to what governs moral sensibility. Crary seems importantly right to distinguish different modes of subjectivity that can come into play in any kind of judgment. (Hegel would have been pleased.) But she is importantly wrong that one can stabilize two poles of what I think we have to take as a continuum between "the merely subjective" and "the problematically subjective." As John McDowell puts it, "Understanding the genesis of the 'new creation' may be understanding an interlocking complex of subjective and objective, of response and feature responded to."[14] In fact, it is precisely because we have that continuum between what we might call "the internal life" and "the epistemically sanctioned life" that it can be so difficult to specify the kinds of values at stake in situations that elicit different kinds of judgments ranging from practical to moral to aesthetic.

Treating "judgment" as a single abstract noun or a faculty compounds the problems because this interpretation of judgment too readily collapses differences among a range of situations. I think judgment has to be a process term specifying how we determine values. Then we can acknowledge that the nature of subjective involvement changes with changing contexts, so applying terms such as "objective" and "rational" seems a strangely imperialistic gesture.[15] Theorizing literary experience, for example, depends in part on our being able to place that experience within at least three different procedures of judgment, with accompanying differences in how we conceive the roles of subject and object.

Let us first take a specific argument about a policy question such as what to do about global warming. This question seems to admit of objective answers or at least objective constraints on what counts as an answer, in part because it addresses clear common interests. So this is clearly a case of Crary's "problematic subjectivity." A person's overall political commitments, on the other hand, are less shaped by the problems and more by the distinctive desires and experiences of the subject. If we turn to accounts of "how best to live," it is even more difficult to bind the agent to what one thinks of as the rational options. That does not mean the agent is irrational or that there is no public dimension to the preferences. But it is very difficult to state that public dimension or characterize "rationality" in terms of principles because this is a domain where the subject is primary: rather than judge the person's reasons by public standards, there is cause to try to understand what the subject has at stake in his or her particular version of what counts as obligations to public standards of rationality. So while we are not dealing with mere subjectivity, we are dealing with something such as an inevitable, foregrounded, subjective responsibility for deciding what facts count and what tradition one will use to read the facts.

In many of my moods, I want to agree with Nietzsche's argument that a life which has something left over for its heirs is essentially a wasted one. And I have no firm view at all of when it seems acceptable to give way to passion and when the wiser course is self-control. In such situations our practices usually will not determine which value is most "appropriate" without circular repetition of one's own categories for what is appropriate. While reasoning is important at least for gaining the respect of an audience, I would hate to think that the subject making choices about trusting passion or self-control would seek out abstract reasons as objective determinants of what should be done.

Reasons can play significant roles in decision making even about literary materials, but not as arbitrating principles. Rather, the effort at reasoning provides a clear context in which what remains subjective choice can make sense to others. If rationality could determine our sense of how best to live, there would be no role for confession and "truthfulness" except as a litany of failure.[16] But because these phenomena do play central roles in how we approach subjects, we can see that there are needs to exercise imaginative compassion that simply cannot be satisfied within the disciplinary boundaries of philosophy devoted to the analysis of concepts.[17] There are aspects of our lives—as agents and as responders to the acts of others—where the theater changes from what can be judged discursively to what has to be judged imaginatively for the density and attitudinal subtlety and sensitivity of the rendering. In these cases questions about right and wrong at best become contexts for finding ways to appreciate what agents manage to accomplish.

A Critique of Both Attridge and Crary for Their Relying on the Authority of Philosophy

One way to get a sense of the stakes involved in my critique of these ethical models is to modify Stanley Cavell's closing remark in his *Claim of Reason*: "But can philosophy become literature and still know itself."[18] My concern is whether literature can concede to philosophical modes of characterizing value and still know itself as a distinctive activity.

Attridge would take the path of congratulating the philosopher who in responding to literary work can recognize the values of not knowing oneself. Attridge praises literature in large part because it unmoors all traditional philosophical practices by producing a residue or trace or event that cannot be discursively accounted for. Yet he persists in an unqualified fealty to Levinas's claims about the centrality of the other as giving shape to ethics. So while

Attridge would obviously reject every effort Crary makes to project judgments of moral sensibilities, I think he needs the authority of philosophy to bring the encounter with the other into the foreground as the fundamental ethical principle basic to giving literary experience social value. That authority is certainly not intuitive or sustained by Western cultural traditions.

Crary, on the other hand, explicitly embraces the authority of philosophy even as she, like Nussbaum and Diamond, tries to find in literature grounds for developing new, more open, and flexible attitudes toward morality. She makes philosophy appear in a new light, wary of rules and sympathetic to individual struggles in texts to make sense of the relation between what they experience and the moral vocabularies they seem to have to bring to bear on those experiences. There is for her no event brandishing its singularity. Yet she shares with Attridge the need for ethics to dignify and make actionable the power literary works display: philosophy ultimately is the discipline that gets to know itself as the abiding authority establishing the effective worldliness of literature.

For both thinkers literary examples provide means of showing how affects supplement moral judgment—practically by enlarging our models of moral agency and theoretically by attuning us to structures of affects arguably fundamental to our grammatical competence in dealing with the world. So philosophy need not fear that the affinities with literature make it difficult to reassert its traditional identity. Instead, philosophy can teach literature what power its texts have to provide nascent versions of rationality that only philosophy can fully articulate. But then literature cannot know itself because it requires philosophy to tell it what its truth is and what its uses are in the practical world. We lose the force of those literary examples that produce tension between any sense of moral well-being and the ways texts idealize character traits—Swann's commitment to jealousy is one case in point; another is Shakespeare's fascination with giving up reflection to live in accord with principles such as "ripeness is all."

Far better I think to have a conceptual framework capable of reveling in how these literary experiences challenge any sense that the soul is simple enough to live exclusively in relation to those moral values.[19] I imagine this conceptual framework comprising two levels. I hope I have already established the first: we have to align the literary with the many ways our language games resist epistemic practices and stress modes of display involving participation, attunement, and exemplification. This opens the way to participating self-reflexively in experiences that do not simply confirm the judgments of the discursive intellect.

But were we to characterize literary experience only in this somewhat negative way, we would not have a very strong account of why we might be interested in slow reading as involving significant cultural ideals. So we need a second level of analysis that builds a positive model of valuing out of dissatisfaction with efforts to align literary experience with ethics. This model of valuing will be far more diverse in content than what is allowed within any fundamentally cognitive and moral schema. So this model will also have a greater qualitative range precisely because without a primary concern for knowing, it can comprise features such as intensity and precision and complexity and convincingness and balance (or other measures of formal intricacy), as well as capacities to sympathize not only with persons but also with ideas.[20]

The Roles of Valuing in Literary Experience

It is not likely that trying to provide an alternative account of ethics will afford the flexibility and range of values we seek. Any ethics at all will overly bind us to concerns about the represented world rather than the work performed by the representing agent, just because it needs a recognizable set of public issues. And any ethics will at some point rely on generalization, as Attridge does on the "other" and Crary on the authority of philosophy because ethics must distinguish itself from casuistry and invoke principle.

So I will instead revel in the possibility that at least for literary criticism we need not rely on ethical thinking in any form.[21] Therefore I want to develop a roughly phenomenological view of values or, more properly, of valuing because I think this approach to aspects of value will prove more flexible in adapting to a range of literary texts and more supple in characterizing the kinds of investments involved in literary experience than any form of reading sponsored by specifically ethical modes of reading.[22]

This phenomenological approach has the advantages of flexibility and of fluid movement between first-order modes of care about objects of attention and second-order attention to the feelings and willings or endorsings involved in our various modes of engagement with particular literary texts. And a phenomenological stance accords with the many terms that we invoke in specific literary judgments—terms involving enjoyment and qualities of participation, terms celebrating various kinds of sympathies and vivid antagonisms in relation to characters, and terms involving craft such as energy, precision, inventive pacing, and the capacity to organize materials on several levels.

I begin with some crucial distinctions. First, phenomenology lends itself to talking about noninstrumental values, which are crucial to literary experience. "Noninstrumental values" are not necessarily mere moments of fantasy released from the world of instrumental labors. They are simply values that are not specifically dependent on solving a particular problem or gaining some explicitly desired change in one's material situation. Instrumental values are those produced by specific needs in particular situations, and they are achieved by at least partial resolution of a practical problem. Noninstrumental values on the other hand take two basic forms, defined by David Wiggins as "evaluations (typically recorded by such forms as 'x is good,' 'bad,' 'beautiful,' 'ugly' . . .") and "directive or deliberative (or practical) judgements [sic] (e.g. 'I must ψ,' 'I ought to ψ,' 'it would be best . . . for me to ψ,' etc." (*NVT*, 95).

Wiggins shows how each orientation addresses a different philosophical issue: evaluations get their traction from responding to possible correlations between facts and values, while "directives" try to bridge the gap between "is" and "ought" or "must," often by focusing on the power of example rather than statement. Both evaluations and directives matter because they have the capacity to transform our encounters with fact: they indicate the presence of a caring attitude that establishes frames of meaningfulness for individual experience. In effect such meaningfulness must reside in modifying how we take satisfaction in modifying ways of looking and thinking rather than in practical problem solving.[23]

Here, for example, is Wiggins's inimitable characterization of what difference the "phenomenological account he advocates" can make in our sense of "life's having a point":

> Having tamed non-cognitivism and made of it a doctrine of cognitive undeterminism, which allows the world to impinge upon but not determine the point possessed by individual lives, and which sees value properties not as created but as lit up by the focus that the one who lives the life brings to the world, . . . it will not be for the theorist as such to insist on intruding himself further. (*NVT*, 137)

In my view this lighting up of properties provides a brilliant picture of valuation, or the particular process by which we come to dwell on what flourishes under our attention. Ultimately valuing is the experience of helping something emerge by our imaginative endorsement of what is involved in our acts of participation.

I need a second distinction in order to elaborate what can be involved in these elemental fusings of value and fact. Many of these fusings do not issue in any long-standing values or commitments. So I distinguish between valuings that refer to specific acts of focusing on what agents can bring to the world and values that result from repeated reflection on these events. Valuation is a process term for the specific ways in which we try to "realize" possibilities for fixing on what the light of attention can produce. Establishing "values" on the other hand is a more complex process by which repeated valuations come to establish investments in aspects of our experiences that become constitutive features of our personal and social identities.[24]

I define values as those standards and expectations of ourselves and other people and indeed of certain kinds of objects that we refer to when we explain our commitments and justify our actions. We develop values over time so that they can produce equilibrium and direction for us as we try to shape the overall priorities in individual lives. And while values are not necessarily constructed by reasoning, they are responsive to at least certain kinds of reasoning about relations of ends to means and about what a person wants to make of his or her life. Many factors shape what we take our values to be—including both our absorption in ideology and our struggles against this absorption, as well as our pictures of our needs and projected satisfactions.

Valuings need not issue in commitments the way values do because we need not refer specifically to previous acts of judgment or to the kinds of beliefs that carry conditions for identify formation or to the kinds of reasons that involve weighing this moment against other moments and other orientations that might govern courses of action. Instead, valuing serves as a prelude to what, after repeated occasions, might take shape as values that govern what a person pursues. (These previous judgments will be in the background even if not referred to because valuing occurs within a personal history.)

Specifically, literary valuations take place as the reader tries to engage how texts may be "lit up by the focus that the one . . . brings to the world" (*NVT*, 137). These lights shine on how the text involves our participation in the various ways by which it makes discriminations and on how we might find ourselves endorsing the satisfactions it elicits. When we are caught up in aesthetic experience, we have to renounce the direct route, which might provide discursive understanding, in favor of the slow time established by attention to the manner of the presentation. We thereby create a situation in which we can reflect on our orientations and thematize how the manner establishes significance for the subject matter. And because valuation is an orientation, not a mode of imposition, there are no guarantees that efforts at valuation will be rewarded on any given occasion. Even beloved texts or writers sometimes just seem incapable of singing.

This way of thinking puts us in proximity to Kant's distinction between reflective judgments and the determinative judgments that "subsume particulars under concepts."[25] Phenomenologically reflective judgment concentrates on seeing into why and how the author's purposiveness comes to life as a series of fulfilled choices: readers understand and identify provisionally with the working of the work as a means of anchoring the imagination in a vital and demanding world. And historically the readers find themselves recognizing why the work has been valued, so reading takes on a strange and powerful process of identifying with, and sometimes struggling against, a history of charged encounters. In this respect it is crucial to recognize that this self-consciousness in reading need not be restricted to what the individual does. When we read, we enter a history of readings, so our "actions become meaningful . . . by being incorporated in some larger totality, even if in many cases that totality exists primarily in the actor's imagination."[26]

Reflective Judgment Reconsidered

Why distinguish valuing from simply careful, attentive reading? There is obviously considerable overlap. Indeed I would say that any careful reading is at least prereflexive valuing. But the degree of reflection on what the self is doing as it reads is crucial for how we develop the possible worldliness of texts. Full valuing requires a roughly phenomenological mode of self-reflection. That is, we engage not only the text but also this sense of who we become by virtue of the qualities of our attention to the text and to what the text mediates as possible worlds. Valuing is a mode of focusing on how the self can attune to what is at stake in imagined situations so that it feels its own capacities to realize dimensions of experience that would otherwise simply be given as aspects of objective situations. This attunement becomes a process of letting the emerging world tilt the scales by which novelty seems to add weight and habit becomes less oppressive.[27] Think of the sheer delight produced by our attuning to the results of Ashbery's inventiveness in our reading of "The Instruction Manual."

Kant's concept of reflective judgment is the traditional concept that provides our most important resource for characterizing how valuing takes place. Reflective judgment is not based on concepts but on something very close to attunement. In that sense it is a perfect counterpart to imagination: such judgments depend on capacities for seeing into the dynamics of particular situations. And reflective judgment is oriented not just toward objects but also to the person the self becomes by virtue of how he or she engages with an object. In fact, Kant recognizes that such acts of self-reflection are capable of kinds of identification that can make beauty a symbol of the moral good because of the ways it entices us to generalize our most compelling experiences of valuing.

But while I am immensely indebted to Kant on this topic, I cannot proceed by his way of analyzing concepts. I will deal with reflective judgment only by attempting to show how that concept makes sense for what we can observe as the powers writers count on readers bringing to texts. My own model for a phenomenological approach will combine a method defined by Wolfgang Köhler's Place of Value in a World of Fact with characterizations of valuing proposed in nonphenomenological contexts by Samuel Scheffler and Aaron Ridley.[28] Köhler matters a great deal to me because he shows how an elemental phenomenological perspective can be developed without having to rely on Husserl's torturously intricate frameworks.[29] But Köhler has a somewhat limited sense of how phenomenological attention performs valuations, so I supplement my picture of what reading can become with terms borrowed from Scheffler and Ridley.

Köhler's great achievement is his insistence on how intimate valuing can be. Valuing is both immediate and potentially self-reflexive; it is not the product of rational calculation. In Köhler's view rational calculation has to proceed by separating fact and value, then trying to accommodate facts to values. So he focuses instead on demonstrating how we can locate values within various manifolds of experience. All his attention is on how consciousness feels itself deployed as mediating between absorption within experience and reflection on how that manifold might be characterized.

The valuing subject then has no need for the practical will, which is responsible for our sense that we have to be ready to defend our interests even if preparing for that reduces our capacities to invest in what we are actually experiencing. The practical obeys the law of zero-sum games: if not one, then the other. But in the cases stressed by Köhler, subjectivity is shaped by direct conditions of response and responsiveness that contour to what we experience. These conditions are still self-interested, but not in terms of acquiring or directing what had been the objects of attention.

That orientation of consciousness then makes possible certain conditions of satisfaction for subjects simply in how things and states of mind appear in a present tense divorced for the moment from questions about the future. The boundaries framing subjective participation are not strict ones, so it becomes possible to imagine that the subject itself is part of the objective field rather than simply its observer. Subjects can even feel that the thinking responsive to the situation is not the property of distinct individuals but rather a merging with other subjects responsive to similar traits in the object of attention.

Consider what it means to recognize how a structure informs a simple moment of perception so that facts seem to "belong together" (*PV*, 73). By focusing on this sense of belonging Köhler can characterize certain ways of experiencing values as neither a matter of fact nor a construction dependent simply on our own interests. We often find agreements that do not seem to depend on conscious negotiations among subjective stances but rather on recognizing properties of the world we share. So we need to honor how a sense of "requiredness" or organizational structure emerges within experience even though that sense will not be visible in typical modes of scientific analysis. Think, for example, of proportion in a scene (ibid., 18) or the sense of rightness in relation to phenomena that seem to fit together because they form an intricate pattern or solicit common interests (ibid., 29). In such cases phenomenology can dramatize properties by which "I value" emerges as involving modes of social relations that are different from statements formulated around "I desire" or "this interests me."

Valuing in Samuel Scheffler and in Aaron Ridley

Obviously Köhler's observations have substantial resonance for literary criticism. We engage in valuing as we participate self-reflexively in changes in pacing, or modifications in degrees of intimacy, or intensifications of our sense of relatedness and organization within elements focalized by the text, or larger-scale variations in tone and gesture and conditions of affective identification. Within this conceptual framework, participating in the experience a text provides is not just developing subjective satisfactions but finding ourselves caring about how situations engage feelings and open new theaters for involvement. But at the same time Köhler's focus is rather narrow. His intending subject brings very little to the event and is not strongly modified by it except to recognize the ways organizational structures produce the experience of belonging together. For a fuller picture of what valuing entails as a phenomenological state I want to turn to descriptions by analytic philosophers that are not specifically in the service of phenomenology but are nonetheless significantly useful to it.

Samuel Scheffler's chapter "Valuing" in Equality and Tradition: Questions of Value in Moral and Political Theory (2010) tries to distinguish valuing from other basic subjective states with which it is easily confused, especially by those too impatient for explanation to take the time to attend to the specific textures of experience. So he makes it possible for us to see how the activity of valuing differs from other related ways of attributing significance to experience. Scheffler argues that noninstrumental valuing combines aspects of four distinct behavioral modes. First, value has to be connected with acts of deliberation because we find in the result of our valuings a basic source of reasons for acting in one way rather than another. But deliberation alone will not produce valuings. We need to add specific modes of desire that we can envision the values satisfying. Again, though, while desire is clearly involved in what we value, we also desire what we do not in fact value—as any roué knows. So we have to add a third feature. We must introduce the issue of belief because belief is what allows desire to be a desire involving values rather than some other mode of satisfaction, such as the pleasure of pure consumption without worrying about deliberation or what the satisfaction produces for the agent (*ET*, 27). One must believe that the desire is oriented toward a particular kind of good.

Finally, Scheffler offers the suggestive and perhaps original notion that valuing makes us vulnerable in ways that do not typically attend the exercise of belief and desire. This vulnerability stems from two features of experience—one concerning the object of attention and the other involving the state of the subject. In valuing something we have to face the fear or the risk that what is valued can easily return to being a mere conjunction of facts, making us seem needy fools who have succumbed to illusion or to ideology. And we have to worry that the activity of valuing elicits a sense that one is imposing on others some interest that is fundamentally only one's own. We become exposed to criticism by the degree to which valuing exceeds what is typical to given contexts just because what goes beyond such contexts can be justified only in terms of the person's interests and commitments.

Only by recognizing this complex set of features can we hope to capture how valuings are distinct from purely subjective desires, how they depend on distinctive modes of feeling connected to belief, and how they provide reasons for action without being derived from sheerly practical analyses. Imagine that I am looking at a face but cannot get out of my own self-absorption, so the face remains a sheer object in my visual field. Then I begin to find myself having an intimate sense of participation in what that face seems to be feeling. Valuing begins. Or one could say that there emerges the "dawning of an aspect" by which I can begin to identify with an agent or with a situation and care about that identification. The same transition is possible with landscapes and indeed with texts as I shift from being frustrated or indifferent to feeling I enjoy finding my way about in it and through its guidance. We become vulnerable to loss, but we also have new feelings of intensification and proximity, often generating some of the many affective states grounded in empathy and in sympathy.

Being aware of this combination of traits allows us to elaborate how "I value" affords a distinctive way of being in the world to which the arts appeal. Suppose we ask what distinguishes the self-consciousness within acts of valuation from other modes of consciousness. A plausible answer would begin with the fact that "I value" is not subsumable under "I desire" or "I believe" even though it can be allied with both states. "I value" is closer to a one-place predicate, where the subject is inseparable from the state it makes possible. In "I believe" or "I desire" it is easy to separate the activity of the agent from the object. But in the "I value" of valuation there is no "I" apart from the valuing and no valuing apart from the sense of first-person agency. Subjectivity becomes inseparable from its directions of attention. There is a pull as well as a push fundamental to these ways of experiencing the world because the first person emerges as an aspect of what unfolds as scenes take shape.[30]

The statement "I value" does not provide a picture of an inner event. Valuings are not simply modes of pleasure but ways of willing pleasures as significant because of the person they allow one to think one is becoming. And that becoming can take on a social cast: at times we imagine other people approving what we make of the object, and we imagine ourselves adapting attitudes that need not be limited to our distinctively subjective repertoire. We become agents aware of how social identities can extend our personal intensities. The "for me" effect is situational and embodied: it need not be a matter of overtly stated belief but can involve simply recognizing how one gets absorbed in a particular process that demands attentiveness and a moment-by-moment making visible of one's engagement in the details that emerge from that attentiveness.

So if I am right, the self-reflection that is an aspect of this valuing gives us access to distinctive powers of subjectivity that the arts provide because of where they position the responder—as inseparable from what emerges in the valuing but not the cause of what is valuable in the experience. And then we can attribute another, less psychological reason for the sense of vulnerability that Scheffler points out. "I value" is precarious because it is very easy to reduce it to "I believe" or "I desire" and so eliminate the distinctive sense of subjectivity embedded in the world that the expression can signify. The whole process of valuing itself can be obliterated by an instrumental criticism insensitive to the different routes by which art proposes to engage life.

Scheffler adds psychological complexity to Köhler's account of valuing. But we still need a richer sense of how valuing takes place distinctively in the arts. For this I want to borrow some notions from Aaron Ridley on music, then tilt them toward literary experience.[31] Ridley locates value in the activity it takes to understand music as meaningful or, better, as the motions and timbres of sound saturated with meaningfulness (*MVP*, 56–57): the sense of value within musical experience emerges from the variety and complexity of the responses it invites (ibid., 172). Then he specifies four basic features of our encounters with music in which this meaningfulness not only appears but becomes a condition of our experiencing the work. The categories are cognitive, sympathetic, empathic, and associative. We make recognitions of qualitative and quantitative aspects of the sonic experience we undergo; we locate expressive analogues between the sound and elements of our worldly experience; we identify personal characteristics within the music by seeing it articulate attitudes; and we associate these events with our own personal experience (ibid., 8–19). In all these cases we put the sensuous qualities together so that they echo ways in which we belong to the world and satisfy our interests in participating in that world under a variety of sensuous forms.

These sensuous forms are somewhat different in literary experience because there is not the direct amplitude of structured sound, or, if there is, it is mediated by efforts to contour those sounds to various levels of verbal meaning directed at specific imagined worlds. Perhaps because of these differences, literary experience does not so directly rely on translating sensations into analogues. But it does provide perhaps a greater variety of explicit possibilities for concretely feeling the difference between description and valuation. For the contrast is always present between what is flat and without meaningful labor and what comes alive because of authorial purposiveness.[32]

Few worlds initially seem as flat and merely descriptive as the world of Madame Bovary. Yet that flatness becomes painfully articulate as a constant source of pressure (and pleasure) in the novel, so that we encounter the book as suffused by intelligence, and we find ourselves making constant investments in phenomena such as the way Charles eats or Emma daydreams or Homais brims with self-satisfaction. More generally, the writer's compositional energies continually put pressure on what might be descriptions of a world merely encountered. We are led to feel an intelligence calling to our own, forming potential allies in our constant quest for what can make us care.

The Value of Valuing

Several important considerations merge here, giving us an opportunity to speculate on why a view of texts as valuing might be valuable. On the level of what texts represent, one can say that the major point of narration and setting up scenes is so that readers can forge provisional identifications with what is involved when a character chooses for himself or herself. Some valuings are heroic—Isabelle Archer's decision to return to her husband, or David Lurie's decision to kill the dog that he has befriended, or John Milton's decisions to allow his radical politics to shape much of his effort to compose an epic justifying God to humankind. Others are amazingly quiet—their significance left to the imagination of the reader. Consider, for example, recognizing the work done by Moore's syllabics, or the reappearance of Clarissa Dalloway at the close of her party, or the penultimate chapter of Joyce's Ulysses, with its exhausted dialogue between Stephen and Bloom. In such cases we have virtually to invent models of subjectivity that can explain how so much meaningfulness can be packed into so little action.

In responding to imaginative writing, we value the making and the seeing, the particular inventions and the overall composition, as well as the work of judgment and the sense of liberation produced by imaginative intensities. We enter the space of valuations because we recognize mastery and because we become fascinated by what can shine the kind of light that makes us think states of being get realized rather than simply noticed or suffered. In the process of valuing we adjust to invitations to see in and to see as, to exercise our own capacities for sympathy and for empathy, and ultimately to define the persons we become as readers because we become capable of seeing our imaginative activities as valuable in their own right. Such exercises of our imaginative capacities help make us alive to differences and resemblances. We become sensitive to all manner of shifts in movement and position—of the self and of what the self attends to. And we find life providing details and complex relations to celebrate, although it is often the case that we have to identify with despair as the necessary means for such celebrations.

The Test Case of Yeats's "An Irish Airman Foresees His Death"

I want to conclude with a close reading of Yeats's "An Irish Airman Foresees His Death." The poem is a typical lyric in the sense that it deploys the intricacies of syntax, structure, and rhythm to produce an experience not only to be engaged affectively but to be seen as a process of valuing, hence as something where the manifest compositional intelligence becomes a gift promising to confer new possibilities for participation and for identification—if it is properly appreciated. But the poem is also strange and compelling for the degree of self-consciousness it brings to these processes of valuation. Yeats's speaker seems deliberately to utilize these opportunities for valuation as he self-consciously constructs an identity capable of countering deeply held and widely shared moral values while still commanding our respect. In this dramatic monologue, the speaker models what identification might be like for the reader by foregrounding his own modes of passionate valuing in relation to choices about life and death. He may even reenact Wittgenstein's contrast between religious and moral understandings of subjectivity.

This enactment of purposiveness stages the powers of artifice to challenge ethical reasoning on every level: display invites our valuing what seems unreasonable as still dramatically and existentially plausible. So the poem brings us around again to the limitations of literary ethics. It is not content with singularity because it makes a desperate plea that others understand the unique position it represents. But at the same time it insists on how the imagination can fully entertain and even commit to what seems abhorrent to almost any general moral scheme:

> I know that I shall meet my fate
> Somewhere among the clouds above;
> Those that I fight I do not hate,
> Those that I guard I do not love;
> My country is Kiltartan Cross,
> My countrymen Kiltartan's poor,
> No likely end could bring them loss
> Or leave them happier than before.
> Nor law, nor duty bade me fight,
> Nor public men, nor cheering crowds,
> A lonely impulse of delight
> Drove to this tumult in the clouds;
> I balanced all, brought all to mind,
> The years to come seemed waste of breath,
> A waste of breath the years behind
> In balance with this life, this death. (*WB*, 328)

The compositional activity here gradually takes on a virtual life of its own as it comes to constitute a distinctive power of speaking (and so of making demands on the listener). Helen Vendler characterizes this compositional power as the developing of "a four-square perfect structure," with its tetrameter quatrains, its strong rhymes, and its sixteen-line overall shape.[33] I am tempted to draw analogies between these squares and the stark structural principles of fascist architectural space. But there is also a great deal of subtlety in how the formal details evoke awareness of the valuings that constitute an attentive experience of the poem.

This subtlety is most evident if we track how two-line units eventually form the quatrains by producing and resolving the turbulences involved in a mind trying to catch up with itself. Each quatrain becomes an adventure in foregrounding how it might be valued in terms of the dynamics of making sense that its intricate movements can establish. This dynamic is not evident in the first of the two-line units, which does not manifest any internal tension. It establishes a vague situation so as to stage the mind's subsequent efforts to correlate will and intellect. The second unit is more demanding because it inaugurates two modes of valuing which will be basic to our experience of the action the poem develops. Valuing here is largely a matter of the force of negatives, at this point modestly buried in simple, direct clauses. But there is also a process of building substance for this "I" out of the negatives, as if a pure function of self-possession might be constructed by defining away what a typical "I" might find as motive. This speaker's "I" is not moved by values of hate or of love. So our seeing in to the poem depends for its intensities on the possibility of the airman's having other grounds for his choosing the precarity of battle.

The third pair of lines tries to offer some positive qualities for this "I" as it turns to questions of how it can define itself most fully. But the speaker pushes us off again. We begin to recognize that perhaps no social or material substance can offer a sufficient ground for this act of self-consciousness. So we have to open ourselves to other possibilities for identification, and that task may involve further negations. Yet the negation that arrives has an end-stopped simple clarity that we have to take as intensely held belief because we have so little context to go on:

> No likely end could bring them loss
> Or leave them happier than before.

By the midpoint of the poem we recognize how fully the speaking aligns itself with a set of refusals, oddly combined with tremendously powerful assertiveness on the level of syntax and rhyme.

The last half of the poem will have to develop how we can come to appreciate this conjunction of forces as composing reasons for choosing a life that will certainly entail dying young:

> Nor law nor duty bade me fight,
> Nor public men, nor cheering crowds,
> A lonely impulse of delight
> Drove to this tumult in the clouds;

I cite these lines a second time because the specific forces at play become very intricate. When we first encountered negation in the poem, the negatives modified the verbs in a standard subject-predicate syntax. Now the negatives modify quite general nouns in two beautifully balanced lines. And the balance intensifies the choice to lead with the negatives, as if they had to articulate values that in retrospect seem to have shaped an entire life. Then I find a confusing but exhilarating move to sheer assertion, buttressed by emphatic rhymes. It seems as if all this negation has freed the speaker to a simple state of motivation: he has found his desire in this "lonely impulse of delight." Yet exhilaration here is accompanied by doubt on the part of most careful and caring readers: can this simple mention of delight really justify the monumental choice the speaker is making? Can delight afford sufficient substance for the self that has negated so much of his social being? And can delight provide an adequate name for what solicits the reader's full participation?[34]

Yeats probably invites this questioning so that readers will be prepared to register just how the last quatrain shapes what delight can become for this way of speaking. And because of the focus on delight Yeats insists on how our awareness of formal relations intensifies our capacity to extend form into the shaping of what we experience as worldly content.[35] It is the task of the speaker's final words to bring all this delight under the single figure of this lucid and powerfully balanced chiasmus that at once responsibly summarizes a life and lucidly chooses a death. Against the backdrop of social values that the speaker has to reject because he cannot fully inhabit them, radical delight seems to afford a fullness of expression that leaves no space for doubt or troubled care. The intricacy of the figure articulates a confidence that the self can build an encompassing world out of relations among its own impulses.

Except for my stress on the power of negation (no small matter), my reading so far has simply added a few details to Vendler's account of the speaker's arrival at an intellectually coherent responsibility for himself. Now I want to be more speculative about how value gets defined here. In one sense the speaker faces a challenge that is basic to Hegel's Phenomenology of Spirit: the "I" of self-consciousness must find ways to produce an adequate identification with its own substantial being shaped by history and social relations. But for Hegel that equation develops by mastering the twists and turns of how that relation between subject and substance keeps eliciting names that keep failing until one can look back at oneself as having been formed by the residue of those defeats. For Yeats the triumph of intellect in this poem is not syncretic but instead idealizes purification by the destruction of all values that are not equivalent to this delight in pure self. The speaking must destroy the illusion that the self can fulfill itself by assuming social identities.

Here in the place of "ideas" everything builds to the deictics (or demonstratives) in the final line: "In balance with this life, this death." First, "this" refers to the speaking itself and to the poem as able simply to exhibit the clarity that can justify its radical self-absorption. Only in this way of building to the summarizing pointer, "this," can the poem even hope to provide a figure of speaking that can build on the negations as modes of valuation and not become reduced by these refusals. Second, "this" has an important philosophical role because it mobilizes a crucial distinction between what can be displayed in itself and what seeks further justification by attaching itself to interpretive contexts and moral generalizations. Delight here takes on substance precisely because it does not seek justification or, better, because it tries to clarify an action only in the direct language by which it establishes the particular utterance.

The ultimate role of the negations is to clear the mind sufficiently to allow "this life, this death" to serve as a pure moment of will that is not haunted by doubt or need. The rest of the poem performs a self-characterization that ultimately issues in a taking of responsibility for all its processes. "This" becomes a complete utterance, overwhelming any need to worry about the various "thats" that would perplex a less ambitious realization of how "this" comes to exemplify what display makes possible. In fact, this Yeatsian "this" offers a very powerful figure for a pure valuing capable of aligning the will to the world as it comes to appear.

Hegel's "I = I" Once More

One does not need Hegelian idealism to make the case for valuation. But returning to Hegel's figure of the variable copula may provide the best single image for why valuation can prove so satisfying an endeavor with regard to literary texts. The entire Phenomenology can be seen as the gradual intensifying of the copulative relation "I=I." At one pole the "I" stands for the emerging properties of self-consciousness as one learns to turn the distinctive experiences of the various dramas of sensibility that history produces into the capacity to assert a self as something capable not just of passive reception but of actively willing one's historical identity. At the other pole spirit learns increasingly to recognize and accept the shifting terms of those historical identities. Then "I=I" becomes a formula for the self-conscious relation between spirit and substance at any given time.

I want to reclaim this figure as a shaping fiction for the forms of desire that become articulate in our imaginative valuations. We try to bring our capacities for self-consciousness in accord with an act of affirmation that celebrates our fullest efforts to be responsive to what imaginative experience can afford. In this domain there is no difference between valuing the text and participating in it, and there is no difference between what form invites and our sense of how participation takes on its own substance, its own way of being in the world. In effect, all writing we care about drives us to produce versions of Yeats's "this." We participate in the texts' efforts to criticize illusion so that we can also share something so vital that we cannot not will what our intellect sees, at least for the brief moments when we can sustain this level of identification within what fictions allow as the world.

Everything we see about the work then can be charged with forms of significance that seem to implicate intricate relations with other features bidding for our attention. Everything from shifts in perspective and rhythm, to changing levels of intimacy, to interpreting the interplay between choice and chance, to the satisfactions of empathy and sympathy, provides frameworks by which we can come to appreciate the roles played by the plasticity of our capacities for care. Each of these phenomena make us able to participate in what we encounter without nagging doubts about the possible reality or unreality of what the manner of the work comes to represent.

And all of these phenomena together have the ability to enter into conversation with each other—conversation that is itself exemplary of how expansive a sense of our own powers may become when we extend our orientations toward involvement and appreciation. At the height of such idealizations, we also realize that concretely we are simply imagining reading as engaging the text's efforts to formulate possibilities for its own being valued. I can think of no richer model of social relations because this mode of engaging individuals so fully integrates lived situations with the imaginative possibilities that can be built upon them.

Chapter 7

Appreciating Appreciation

> I recall that my first view of this neat possibility was as the attaching problem of the picture restricted (while yet achieving, as I say, completeness and coherency) to what the child might be conceived to have understood—to have been able to interpret and appreciate.... The passage ... is a signal example of the all but incalculable way in which interest may be constituted. Yet the thing has but to become a part of the child's bewilderment for these small sterilities to drop from it and for the *scene* to emerge and to prevail—vivid, special, wrought hard, to the hardness of the unforgettable; the scene that is exactly what ... [all the characters but Maisie] would never for a moment have succeeded in making their scant unredeemed importances—namely appreciable.
>
> —Henry James, *What Maisie Knew*

> A secret ressentiment underlies every way of thinking which attributes creative power to mere negation and criticism.
>
> —Max Scheler, *Ressentiment*

It should not be surprising that James expresses interest in the phenomenon of appreciation. Perhaps no other term modulates so well between humility and arrogance. And such modulation is basic to how his prefaces construct the ambitions of his novels. But James is also responding to a public rhetorical situation involving the arts, in which "appreciation" was very much a central concern. Witness Walter Pater's collection of essays in 1889 titled *Appreciations*.

This chapter will lament the unfortunately deserved demise of the ideal of appreciation as a foundation for critical study in the arts. And it will try to correct the picture, with the help of Max Scheler's keen criticism of the role resentment plays in modern and contemporary culture, because resentment is arguably what appreciation contests. The model of appreciation in art, which James extends to life, could not survive in part because critics such as Pater were satisfied with exemplifying the concept rather than analyzing its elements. So that model was soon relegated to providing a name for two critical practices, now relegated to the historical dump for failed ideologies.

At one pole, appreciation was narrowed to the domain of connoisseurship, where the primary emphasis on works of art required capacities for extremely detailed attention that mattered primarily for matters of attribution and description. Appreciation seemed to have very little to do with celebrating the power of the overall work or the challenge that it posed for inherited ways of thinking. Instead it became attached to the activities of the leisured classes, who used their interest in art as a barrier against invasion by those who had to worry about making a living.

At the other pole, the concept became an excuse for inattentive generalization as students were forced to sit through courses that offered "art appreciation" or "the appreciation of literary masterpieces" or, more recently, "the appreciation of cultural differences," all in the service of bringing the dream of leisured pleasures to the expanding middle-class audiences entering educational institutions. "Appreciation" in the title became a euphemism for "art history light" or "close reading without historical context" or "pieties about cultural difference without the economics necessary to define the plight of oppressed groups."

I think the concept of appreciation deserves a better fate. In the argument this book has been developing I need this concept to signify our self-awareness as we participate in the variety of valuings discussed in the preceding chapter. Valuing is a gorgeously diverse process. So that activity will not in itself afford a concise or telling picture by which we can address the possible social impact of what is involved in careful attention to how literary texts unfold. To make the social case for why this kind of reading matters we need a master term that incorporates what we do when we perform these diverse valuings. We need a model of valuing capable of including a range of investments without relinquishing claims for the substantial social significance of literary experience.

We also need a model honoring two ideals of reading—that we experience a sense of personal engagement bordering on creativity while also cultivating a sense of recognition bordering on actively belonging to the imagined world made present by the text. And, finally, we need a way of insisting on the importance of cultivating responses by individual subjects even though literary theory has turned to the political romance of developing and addressing constructs we can treat as collective modes of agency. Appreciation involves social transformation agent by agent. It cannot be performed collectively in any substantial way. But appreciation can be performed—effectively, regularly, and with significant diversity, and so in my view it provides much more stable and realistic measures of what the arts can make possible than can these dreams of collective agency. And appreciation has its own form of general agency, but not one built on the rhetoric of community or any other kind of existing social collective.

The task of this chapter will be to establish what appreciation can involve for subjects as they develop modes of self-reflection on what experiences of valuing have produced for them. I will argue that the supreme fiction of literary criticism ought to be that by cultivating appreciation it can provide a counterweight to two forms of deadness that pervade contemporary life—our failures to recognize what might be significantly meaningful for us and our refusals to recognize the immense blindnesses caused by our resentments. The first is a failure of attention, the second a failure of will because the defensiveness accompanying resentment blocks possibilities that experiences can make claims upon us. There are no revolutionary politics at stake here. But neither is there a waste of spirit in a flourish of idealistic fantasy simply unwilling to recognize the limitations of political life in mass society. Calling on the powers of literary appreciation must patiently clarify for each individual, what can be of value to practical life in the whole domain of displays that we sort as particular examples.

The Figure of the Appreciator

I wrote an essay first broaching the concept of appreciation several years ago. I thought I could claim that appreciation is just what readers do as their ways of attributing significance to what engages them.[1] But I had not worked out how valuation takes place in reading and so could not treat appreciation as part of a self-reflexive dialogue with specific features of texts. So in retrospect I have to see myself as pious as was Pater.

However, I think that now I can provide a more concrete and dynamic account of appreciation by tying it closely to how we can respond to expressive activities of all kinds. Appreciation becomes an extension of the concepts of attunement and valuing, but with more attention to the conditions of agency (rather than the qualities of the object) by which we recognize and adapt to the force of expressive activity. So I will argue that the more we flesh out the content of typical expressive acts, the fuller and more intense the demands for something like attitudes of appreciation as models of response to what gets articulated. Appreciation is a state of responsiveness appropriate for almost all of art and much of life.

I have argued elsewhere that practical aesthetics changed immensely with the onset of modernism.[2] Now I need to rely on that argument to clarify what I take to be the typical object for acts of appreciation engaged by literary texts. Writers from Longinus and Sydney to Wordsworth and Arnold did not stress the material object of art but instead focused on the writer's understanding of the powers of imagination and the best ways to make its presence felt in social life. And the aesthetics of both Kant and Hume focus on conditions of audience response such as judgment and taste. Only with protomodernism did the emphasis shift to the distinctive properties by which objects took on the status of works of art—in part because artists and writers thought it awkward and unseemly to praise their own capacities, and in part because the more aesthetics focused on painting and music, the better it could develop significant languages for the value of how the work deployed the material properties involving sight and sound.[3]

Once the emphasis is placed on these physical properties we can separate works of art from other kinds of experiences because of the density of the interrelationships constituting the art object. So this shift helped make possible the fluid mixture of artistic principles that constituted modernist art and writing, along with fantasies of the work as autonomous in relation to the practical world. But that success in turn obscured the ways in which writing is put at a disadvantage when only its material properties are emphasized. Most of the resources of language do not emerge in the sensuous dimension. A full literary aesthetics has to include the uses of rhetoric and not follow modernism's setting itself against rhetoric as socially corrupt.

More important, emphasis on internal relations threatens to narrow the scope of most art objects because the imagination is focused on how the object might be distinct in itself rather than on how it might earn distinction because of its engaging concerns basic to social life in general. This danger is magnified when we try to talk about all of literature within a model that at best fits some lyric poetry and experimental fiction. One simply cannot say very much about most literary works if one talks about the medium in terms of letters or sounds or even internal formal relations. Rather, most texts we take as literary are primarily rhetorical objects: their basic constitutive labor directly engages us in worlds of meaning and the structuring of sense.

It is meanings and not material properties alone that give literary works a distinctive cultural place. And it is our attitudes toward those meanings that give literary works a distinctive cultural force. We must once again stress theories of how audiences are imagined as reacting to imaginative creativity. But we cannot do that if we deal only with empirical readers. Empirical study will deal only with actual reactions. For me the important feature for educators is how artists imagine audiences as having the powers to construct possibilities that alter our assumptions about what is predictable in states of affairs.

The figure of the appreciator then promises to be a worthy counterpart to our intellectual culture's heroizing of the knower—the one quasi superhero seeking to flesh out the power of particulars to engage attention, the other trying to account for the general features allowing the particular what significance it comes to possess. The figure of the appreciator calls our attention to work done within the domain of appearance, without our having to secure knowledge claims about the foundations of those appearances.

Or, to make the same point in another way, appreciation is the elaboration of how we learn to see into expressive behaviors rather than see through them. Appreciation posits the goal of elaborating an individual's capacities to fuse active intelligence with lively affective intensities. It stresses how attention to particulars elicits and even structures feelings; it attunes us to forces and constructive energies shaping complicated experiences; and it engages us in the kinds of energies that shape intense sympathies and aversions, while also setting those particular intensities against the possibility of any kind of moral generalization. And, even more important, appreciation invites second-order reflections on the actions of participating in such sympathies and such judgments. It dramatizes for us how much of our energy is repressed when we confine ourselves to practical judgments and when we ignore the challenge of having to align our wills with what we have come to know.

A Map of My Argument in This Chapter

I can best make clear what appreciation involves by spelling out what I see as its four basic features. The first two largely repeat what I have been saying. Only in theory can we separate our relation to the object from the kinds of self-consciousness the object makes possible. And even in theory it is best to keep those modalities together. So I will deal with the first two aspects of appreciation as corollary conditions of response—one to the object and another to the self-reflexive subject. Appreciation attunes us to the possible significance of the particular powers the work comes to possess when it is carefully read. And appreciation is self-reflexive so that we become aware of how we are modified by our valuing the text because we recognize ourselves as possessing certain powers and as capable of certain gratitudes.

My final two features involve the possible implications of such shifts in attention. I can address one feature by elaborating how appreciation can be an inherently social act, marked by an awareness of how reading puts us in touch with a history of makings and a history of modes of attention to texts. The final feature requires examining how acts of appreciation might matter in adapting this sense of sociality to practical attitudes we take toward our experiences. So the third state finds a productive social dimension through the kind of self-consciousness the object encourages, while the fourth extends the dispositions aesthetic objects create by disposing consciousness to assume certain attitudes toward the world.

Attunement as Self-Aware Quickening of Appreciative Attention

We appreciate acts, objects, and states that we encounter within quotidian experience when we recognize how we attune ourselves to their distinctive characteristics. In the moment of appreciation these characteristics promise to quicken our sensibilities and so intensify our responsiveness to a given natural or social environment. Our responsiveness can be focused on what we immediately perceive or what seems inferred purposiveness that solicits our attention.

This possible purposiveness becomes central when the target of our attention is a literary text. Then we are asked to respond to a particular made object whose particularity is foregrounded—by many of our practices of reading and often by a feeling that any other mode of response would not be adequate to the labor shaping the work. Reading involves recognizing how the work offers a purposive and self-reflexive bid to be fleshed out imaginatively as a specific action. Through our attuning to the activity of the subject shaping the work we recognize its place within what we might call our grammar for engaging experience.

That grammar is self-reflexive. In acts of appreciation we see ourselves identify with Othello's passion, and, at same time, we attempt to project the reading self as a person who can wield that understanding in other contexts. That self can dream of what treating murder as sacrifice can entail or why it matters that Shakespeare plays on the contrast between Moor and Venetian. Then as we reflect on ourselves as consuming subjects, we become open to the dialectic fundamental to art between readerly attention and absorption in what purposiveness can produce.

Technique is the central vehicle by which texts carry purposiveness. How the work displays technical skill intensifies attention to particularity because, as the inner relations grow more intricate, it becomes impossible to relegate the work to any governing concept or type. We have to refer to that intricacy rather than to our ideas about the subject in order to define how the object takes on expressive force. But at the same time we are likely also to focus on the historical dimensions that the technique brings to mind.[4] We understand technique as a resource writers bring to bear, as a comparative ground by means of which they sharpen their own claims to power, and as a means of drawing specific strategies from established modes of enhancing and intensifying what the imagination confronts.

Attridge is right, then, to emphasize the event qualities of these interacting modes of relation intensifying the imaginative concreteness of the work. But these very features impose on us, I think, not a language of truth and of morality but of power and demand and challenge and even fear that one is not quite adequate to what is being asked by that object.

A full demonstration of how various textual objects produce this sense of power and challenge to the imagination is beyond the scope of this chapter. And it is probably unnecessary because anyone reading this is likely to have had the relevant experience. But I do want to indicate how efficiently and how thoroughly an ideal of appreciation can help celebrate significant dimensions of our reading experience by aligning them with the grammar by which we respond to expressive activity in general. So I will attend briefly to two short lyrics by Yeats—elaborating how two quite different paths for evaluation both call on us to engage the purposiveness of the work and so make us attentive to our own resources for various acts of surprising attunements to what is displayed.

My first example, "A Drinking Song," flirts with inconsequentiality, perhaps to establish the importance of modeling how the expressiveness of the poem can be located at a considerable distance from the speaking subject. In fact it is primarily the song form that speaks by creating a virtual space within the syntax and thus asking the reader to complete the poem's suggestiveness:

> Wine comes in at the mouth
> And love comes in at the eye;
> That's all we shall know for truth
> Before we grow old and die.
> I lift the glass to my mouth,
> I look at you, and I sigh. (*WB*, 261)

I read the poem as inviting its readers to correlate three two-line syntactic units. The first consists of the work of the mouth; the second of the eye; and the third of the instrument by which we claim knowledge. The knowledge claim takes twice the lines as do particular body parts, only to whine and give no useful information. So these two lines displace the world of physical actions into an overgeneralized pathos.

The last half of the poem develops three correlations staged by the "I" to the opening three impersonal assertions. The first correlation also takes just one line. The poet matches the truism about wine coming in at the mouth with an action of actually drinking the wine. The second correlation takes only half a line because all one need to say to flesh out "love comes in at the eye" is "I look at you." By making the response a simple action the speaker can make the public wisdom his. And he can avoid the danger of letting the displacing power of mind take over as it did in the two-line unit.

We still have to ask why the bodily correlate for the act of mind is only "I sigh"? Here I think the economy of the poem gets complicated—and thrilling. In one sense the sigh continues the focus on looking at "you": this sigh suggests the immense gulf between the moment of loving and living with that love. But the major force of the sigh is generated by the contrast between it and the two-line unit to which it corresponds. What other bodily parallel might there be to the banal wisdom offered by the reflective mind? How can the poem internalize that action without submitting itself to another version of wisdom? If what the mind says is true, the body can only sigh and act out its desire. Taken dramatically, the sigh is a mark of pathos, a mode of recognizing the truth of the sad generalities of the two-line sentence. But understood in relation to the tripartite structure of the poem, sighing becomes brilliantly active.

Minimally it stages an ironic recognition that more words would create only more pathos. And as an act this sigh counters the mind's tendency toward sad generalization by offering an active bodily response to the verbal sense of pathos: because she elicits this physical response, this desired lady now seems worth all the uncertainty that must follow letting oneself become a hostage to fortune. Style visibly takes on the power to make the responder recalibrate his or her interpretive stance—toward the lovers and perhaps toward the capacity of song itself to invoke its own traditional powers. Singing in this poem celebrates its appreciation of its own powers to embody a positive responsiveness to what can only trouble the mind.

"The Magi" has a very different approach to expressive force and to the syntactic features that model its contours:

> Now as at all times I can see in the mind's eye,
> In their stiff, painted clothes, the pale unsatisfied ones
> Appear and disappear in the blue depth of the sky
> With all their ancient faces like rain-beaten stones,
> And all their helms of silver hovering side by side,
> And all their eyes still fixed, hoping to find once more,
> Being by Cavalry's turbulence unsatisfied,
> The uncontrollable mystery on the bestial floor. (WB, 318)

Again it is attention to the qualities of the act of mind that gives the poem its particular powers as event. The syntax here makes concrete a waiting that cannot long put off the inevitable encounter with terror. Because there is a personalized speaker, the Magi can be taken out of historical context and put into another, more perplexing psychological and mythic state defined in part by intricate links between sound and syntax. The first delay takes place because of a quiet clause that briefly interrupts the movement from subject to object in the opening sentence. The disruption in syntax is countered by the continuity of the long *a*'s that make dissatisfaction pervade the opening. Then there is the much greater series of delays that constitute the middle of the poem—as if the speaker were putting off the very confrontation that the figure of the magi made possible. Fascination shifts momentarily from what the mind's eye has to see to what mediates that seeing.

These hesitations ultimately intensify the sense of horror in two basic ways. "Being by Cavalry's turbulence unsatisfied" presents an absolute clause that complicates the sense of delay. The previous three lines had observed the Magi from the outside; now the poem presents the basis of their significance from inside the speaker's sensibility. And then we see clearly why the speaker makes the identification in the first place. No delay can put off for long this profound dissatisfaction with Cavalry. But these delays do considerably sharpen the force of "uncontrollable"—both in its semantic register as the opposite of an ultimately redemptive scene and in its sonic register setting up the liquid textures of "bestial floor." Ultimately this poem preserves as long as it can details that stress the humanity in both the speaker and the magi so that it can intensify what is involved in the demand to confront humanity's absolute other.

Appreciation as the Valuing of Valuing

Both poems make distinctive contributions to our grammar for dealing with emotions—"Drinking Song" by elaborating song as a mode of concrete action capable of dealing with the pathos of generalized reflection, and "The Magi" by staging ambivalence about our desires to break through cultural frameworks in order to observe the very horror that we also have to sublimate. Appreciation, then, is a matter first of finding ways to value the text and then of finding ways to value that valuing—both as it sharpens some aspect of our attention to possible worlds and as it enriches our sense of our powers to put worlds together, but not with our hands.

Ultimately our aim is not only to understand how the particular offers a significant action but to engage our will in following up how reading stimulates our energies and promises to extend the range and depth of our own structures of concern. We engage most texts in order to exercise our capacities to care about what we encounter even if the satisfaction involves identifying with an ability to unsettle and create discomfort. At the least our engagement can realize how the text may prove exemplary and so help us sort what we care about and why.

Stressing the exercise of our capacities to care may be just to say that appreciation is intimately connected with taking on aesthetic attitudes. But we have to be clear that such attitudes need not be disinterested.[5] Rather, the attitudes afford specific opportunities to satisfy our imaginative interests in fleshing out the existential implications of what we discover in the text. Literary experience proves continuous with the full range of actions that can be valued in terms of what they express—from the sublime skills of athletic performance, to refined versions of cruelty, to what artists do to express how we clumsily try to acknowledge acts of generosity.

Because literary experience need not be disinterested, it has the capacity to modify the interests we have. If we are content with practical judgments, we focus only on our identities in getting and spending. If we focus on how we commit ourselves to exploring what we think of as possible in the valuing of experiences, we set the mind and feelings in quite different orientations—directly concerned with the qualities that we encounter and the implications for our own being of our devotion to those qualities. Literary works have the distinctive trait of inviting attention to two modes or levels of expression that our responses try to bring into conjunction—the modeling of a world we see through our participation in how the text stages expressive activity, and the shape of the modeling activity itself as a process of authorial decision making that tries to articulate an objective shape for how the expression can make a difference in its world. If we stress only the ability to see through texts, we risk missing everything that is involved in the difference between "Red" and "Red!" or in the contrast Yeats draws between empty speech and "I sigh."

Why does it matter that we try to distinguish these two levels of expression? Why not be content to point out how texts imply worlds and how the actions in texts define modes of character and attitude? One reason is that if we choose this more direct route to worldliness, we significantly underplay the pleasures and the implications of identifying with the powers that artists can bring to bear on the world. The short poems by Yeats are great examples of the sheer exhilaration that emerges if we find ways to value the artifice that in these cases gives the existential attitudes precision and bite. But there is also a loosely cognitive reason because we also expand and complicate the nature of what we might find exemplary in the text.

I have argued that we can use our dense engagement with the actions in texts as analogues that help us sort experiences and define significant similarities with and differences from other events. The dramatic content of Yeats's song provides an effective, pointed image for reflecting on how desire exposes us to pain. And "The Magi" is brilliant about stripping away everything but a confrontation with a bleak truth. They are not examples "of" but examples "as."

This kind of exemplarity complicates appreciation in two ways. We are asked to reflect on the possible uses of this concreteness in characterizing other experiences, so that, in effect, they become aspects of our imaginative repertoires. And we are asked to reflect on how the poem unfolds as an expression of the poet's capacities to bring this moment into sharp focus. The poet's mode of activity becomes an aspect of a related repertoire, with analogous roles for appreciation of what imaginative encounters can produce.[6]

The Legislative Aspect of Appreciation

Appreciation is a positive act. It involves taking pleasure in a phenomenon, becoming aware of oneself as having a stake in pursuing that pleasure, and wanting to take all the time necessary for the object or action appreciated to appear as fully articulated as possible. This involvement of the will allows one to suggest a third aspect of appreciation that extends significantly into the social arena. It seems plausible to imagine that the very terms of our engagement in objects of attention tempt us to share Kant's concern to distinguish between judgments about subjective pleasure and judgments that issue in approval inviting the agreement of an audience.

We do not need the full Kantian apparatus that aligns approval with making a universal demand and therefore makes aesthetic judgment a symbol for moral judgment. We need only a phenomenological sense that the very terms of pleasure in an object can produce judgments in which one seeks agreement: in effect the pleasure is too intense or too rich or too attuned to the intricacies of the object for a person not to seek ways of sharing it (and of reassuring ourselves that our intensities do not make us monstrous).

I am proposing that the idea of appreciation fleshes out what is involved in Kantian judgments of beauty and therefore grounds a feasible way of making claims for its social dimension. Once we have that ground we can speculate on how such noncognitive judgments might operate in ways that provide the larger modes of agreement that result in a coherent literary history and practical canon at any given time. The very possibility of a difference between liking and approving gives us a clear interest in finding common terms among different acts of appreciation because we get a fuller picture of how the object might emerge for various people.

Consider a brilliant, concrete phenomenological adaption of Kant by Max Scheler in order to speculate on how an act of appreciation orients the subject. Scheler argues that the values connected to *"material 'goods'* can only be distributed when they are *divided."*[7] The value of cake depends on how its being divided allows consumption by individuals; the value of tax breaks depends on their being used by individuals in different ways. Then there is the work of art:

> In strict contrast to this there stands a "work of art," for example, which is "indivisible" and of which there is no "piece." ... There is no participation in extension and divisibility with these values; nor is there any need to divide their bearers if they are to be felt and experienced by any *number* of beings. (*FKV*, 225)

One can obviously quibble here. People respond differently to art; there is divisibility. Yet Scheler cannot be dismissed because he captures something about even the kind of division in responses we give to works of art. And he reminds us of the strange phenomenon that we share the pleasure of others in aesthetic experiences and that this sharing can increase our own pleasure.

With art the divisions are not absolute. They do not consume the entire object but at the least remain negotiable. Insofar as the object cannot be divided, there is the possibility of imagining plausible ways in which the audience, too, need not divide itself into the tired old empirical subjects by which we all live much of the rest of our lives. The audience need not divide itself because there is an intelligence and a craft to the object that asks to be recognized by all viewers. And there is the constant possibility of our being dissatisfied with the level of our appreciation when we cannot imagine at least some of our differences from other people reconciled by provisionally identifying with the intelligence responsible for the work. The works encourage us to dream of membership not only in a collective audience but also in a collective act of will affirming how the object sustains appreciation by all the members of that audience.

Appreciation has a dialectical aspect: it expands and intensifies when we try to understand how others see differently. Therefore we construct tentative histories and even tentative canons of what matters in literary experience by trying to correlate interests and by negotiating the significance of differences as a central aspect of what constitutes public interest in a work. We need not treat differences as contradictions, but we can try to see in what ways they may be contraries that return us to the object or its historical relations with quickened attention and deepened appreciation of what the object can become for various agents.[8] I am too much a modernist fully to appreciate Whitman's effusiveness. But in reading him I can try to work against my own prejudices and identify with how my friends take pleasure in him. The issue is not moral: there is no manifest imperative to engage others in dialogue. Rather, responsiveness to dialogue may just happen to be the constitutive factor by which texts take on life within a culture.

Appreciation as a Social Force

Finally I want to develop the possible social and perhaps even political significance of the fact that many of our culture's most highly valued literary texts make a specific issue of exemplifying the cultural implications of the possibilities for appreciation that the text affords. The *Odyssey* offers exemplary moments where Odysseus measures his suffering by marveling at what civilized life can offer. Dante must go another way rather than try to overcome the she-wolf released by envy on the world. For to enter into combat with that beast runs the risk of having to adapt her worldview and seek victory for all the wrong reasons. By choosing another path, his *Divine Comedy* can ultimately appreciate and affirm how God's justice and God's love can be one.

Shakespeare's last play is even more striking, especially because many of our more political critics tend to identify with Caliban's righteous resentment against Prospero's imperialist ways. Yet while Shakespeare does give Caliban cause for complaint, he also sees that the complaint only sustains the character in his irresponsible ways and in his willingness to serve any master who promises revenge. There must be another way. I think that other way is best exemplified in the play's epilogue:

> Now my charms are all o'erthrown,
> And what strength I have's mine own,
> Which is most faint. Now 'tis true
> I must be here confined by you,
> Or sent to Naples. Let me not,
> Since I have my dukedom got
> And pardoned the deceiver,
> Dwell in this bare island by your spell;
> But release me from my bands
> With the help of your good hands.
> Gentle breath of yours my sails
> Must fill, or else my project fails,
> Which was to please. Now I want
> Spirits to enforce, art to enchant;
> And my ending is despair
> Unless I be relieved by prayer,
> Which pierces so that it assaults
> Mercy itself and frees all faults.
> As you from crimes would pardoned be,
> Let your indulgences set me free.[9]

The most striking feature of his epilogue is its doubling—not just in rhyming couplets. Exactly halfway through, Prospero states the fundamental plea: applause will release him from the stage world to explore a real world even though he has diminished powers in that world. One might say this is a simple plea to show appreciation and a statement of gratitude for the release from repetition that the applause will provide.

But why then repeat essentially the same message in a parallel ten lines? One answer is that the plea becomes more heartfelt or at least more sensuous and more personal. Now the poetry fleshes out how applause becomes the gentle breath that can fill his sails. More important, now the vocabulary seems to demand our placing this little plea in a context of religious experience. As we hear "despair," "prayer," "mercy," "pardon," and "indulgence," we might think that the play wants us to treat this simple exchange as something close to a primal scene for interpreting the work of grace or how the secular world can learn from religion how to value grace.

The central value here is the plea for freedom, much like the first half of the epilogue. But there seem to be different freedoms at stake in each half of the epilogue. The first ten lines represent the plea of the actor; the second ten lines the plea of the human being playing the part and trying to understand how to value applause. And as the play turns to the human being, freedom seems to take on two attributes that lead well beyond freedom from his role in the play. The first bid for freedom seeks the possibility that there can be no longer the pressure of fear of faults and the kinds of defensiveness imposed by such fear. A person's entire life is figuratively at stake because the audience comes to represent a capacity for response that can either reinforce a monstrosity such as Caliban's or prepare an entirely different way of participating in sociality. The refusal of sharing the possibilities of what pleasure can create is the way of despair.

The second freedom addresses the practical issue of how this alternative to despair and defensiveness can be presented or perhaps exemplified. The crucial need is to refuse to dwell on faults. Then the audience can form a community in which they all recognize that processes of fault finding are as endless as they are unproductive of anything matching what the imagination has learned to desire in this play. And because this is a play, and because there is a possibility of applause, the audience, now also the players in the epilogue, can exercise mercy and generosity. This gets at the core meanings of "indulgence"—socially as forgiveness and theologically as a guarantee of at least minimal grace.

If they can all admit their crimes, the act of mutual appreciation promises a form of freedom that only imagination can foster. They can dwell on what it means to forgive and to have forgiveness itself become the source of a freedom not possible for the Calibans among us. His monstrosity is his being locked into appreciating only what can foster his revenge. Prospero's freedom is his capacity to step out of the play while remembering the possible bonds of mutual appreciation the play can create between the actor and his audience.

I do not intend to browbeat my readers into an ideology of appreciation based on the example of old white men with no other work to do. But I want to try to explain why our best writers often ask us to identify provisionally with the possibility that appreciation is woven into the work of civilization. That explanation is as simple as I hope it is powerful. Appreciation challenges the destructive dynamics of resentment and promises the recognition of individual values rather than the sullen repudiation of what seems different.[10] And the better we understand how widespread resentment is in narrowing human possibilities and sustaining all kinds of violence, the more fully we will appreciate how appreciation can take on social consequences. Therefore I will argue that the cultivating of these aesthetic dispositions is a significant form of social action and probably the best literary experience can do in offering a politics compatible with focusing on the particularity of texts.

I suspect that my audience will not need many reminders of the roles resentment plays in modern political and social life. Just think about how often people seem consumed by (often justified) resentment about race, class, gender, and virtually any privilege given to one group and not to another. It often seems as if resentment were our form of social glue because there we find a strange source of equality and a common vocabulary. But, as Nietzsche showed, this social glue locks individuals into fierce efforts to defend imaginary versions of themselves. Resentment at being denied what we think we are worth only generates oppositional structures between what we resist as oppression and what we often glory in as justifiable domination. When agents enter this condition, they narrow their sense of self-worth to self-defensive abstract identifications much too inflexible to match actual opportunities for exploring new aspects of our experiences.

We can also buttress this commonsense account by turning to Max Scheler's book on the subject—*Ressentiment*. I think his theory is too much bound by a discourse of repression—not surprising in 1912. And his writing this book at this time may be more important than anything its theorizing affords. The book fits into a brilliant and extended critique by German theorists of what was coming to seem an almost totally bourgeois culture. Britain and the United States might be seen to embrace bourgeois modernity, but Germans could consider themselves heirs of a long cultural tradition shaped largely by romantic dreams and the cult of Greek ideals. And now there seemed only this steady quiet desperation of a cultural environment devoted to petty pleasures and persistent envies. How could they come to terms with what had gone wrong and somehow modify what seemed historical necessity? I think of Scheler on the right (much like T. S. Eliot) and Adorno on the left as radical versions of issues defined by a host of great minds such as Weber and Simmel, all devoted to some version of sociology because the shape of society was the pressing problem for intellectuals.

And the shape of society could be defined largely by the resentments governing bourgeois life. Scheler's reading of Nietzsche provides a very useful account of the scope and the cost of resentment. This is Scheler's definition of *ressentiment:* "Ressentiment is a self-poisoning of the mind which has quite definite causes and consequences. It is a lasting mental attitude, caused by a systematic repression of certain emotions and affects which, as such, are normal components of human nature" (*R,* 45). Resentment lies "at the core of bourgeois morality" (ibid., 82) because of widely shared feelings of powerlessness in modern life. How else can the powerless formulate fantasies of power, given the immense distance between the domain of private experience and the possibility of making one's suffering heard in a public theater?

There are two basic routes of repression that give resentment significant power in influencing the moral life of a culture. First, resentment has none of the active quality of expressions of anger. Rather than directly express emotional states, those full of resentment postpone the reactions to a time when it might be safe to express feelings. Postponement also maintains the fantasy that one can take up arms against a sea of troubles—only not now, not when the subject feels painfully connected to a general class of the victimized and the impotent (ibid., 47–48).

Second, this postponement results in a fantasy of power accompanied by a nagging sense of defeat because one has not been able to release one's anger. The sense of impotence can be satisfied only by some form of revenge, and revenge is always intentional, not just emotional because one seeks satisfaction in the idea of getting even. But the agent is aware that actual revenge would be too dangerous, so he or she has to be indirect—which becomes a source of an increasing intensity for the need to attach the self at least indirectly to anything that seems to reduce the power of those who generate the fear in the first place (ibid., 48).

These two factors—inexpressiveness and the reduction of values to fantasies of the power to produce revenge—derive from the ways in which resentment is in large part a fundamentally social emotion. Indeed perhaps resentment has become the ur-social emotion because it originates in comparing what one feels is one's overall value with the value that other people are perceived as achieving (ibid., 53). Then, as one comes to feel impotence, it becomes crucial also to devalue the other person's qualities by denying their particular force and by constructing counterideals that have power only in their negativity (ibid., 58–59). Ressentiment is the opposite of everything Hegel idealized in his figure of "recognition":

> These forces begin by blocking only the active expression of the affects, but continue by removing them from the sphere of consciousness, so that the individual or group ceases to be clearly aware of their existence. . . . At the same time the mass of previously repressed emotions attracts and assimilates the new affect, so that each earlier repression facilitates and accelerates the continuation of the process. (ibid., 69)

Ressentiment reaches its apogee when envy drives the release of the tension between the desire to act and the feeling of impotence by leading us to focus only on events that set in motion negative affects such as vindictiveness. This attitude selects what can reinforce these negative affects, in the process "depreciating or denying the positive value" of primary or noble desires (ibid., 74–75). "The fox does not say that 'sweetness is bad,' but that 'the grapes are sour'" (ibid., 74).

A Concluding Plea

The forces of resentment in bourgeois society are deep and powerful, especially when that society cultivates inequalities in many registers. So appreciation cannot be expected to produce much large-scale change. This alternative to resentment is not even likely to affect very much the ways that the academy has idealized the devaluation of values. Appreciation must find its consequences in each individual case, while resentment seems almost pushed on social agents with their mother's milk, at least for those of us who do not have wealthy mothers.

Nonetheless, the cultivating of appreciation can make substantial differences for individuals, and that possibility can keep alive hope for some significant social change. For there are times when appreciation can provide awareness of more capacious possible grounds of judgment, if only in the vocabulary for human relations that they deploy. And those opportunities may enter into an ideal calculus for judging what we might do in particular circumstances. Reading attentively and affirming the states that result may produce social good beyond the pleasures such states afford, precisely because modern readers continually find themselves participants in the struggle between appreciation and resentment.

The relevance of such observations for political life is not glamorous. These observations do not promise revolution or even modifications in social justice.

Appreciation alone cannot provide concepts that might bring a much-needed flexibility to counter the defensiveness born of the frustrated impotence characteristic of resentment. More important, the proponent of appreciation has to recognize that resentment is sometimes necessary and productive because it martials forces against injustice—nowhere more pointedly than in relation to the privileges held by the richest one percent in American society. But habits of reading for appreciation can help us recognize why self-protection by resentment is so dangerous a social attitude—witness Leontes in *A Winter's Tale*. And these habits of affirmation are not quietist. They offer constant exercises in deploying the will as we try to adapt the attitudes that inform gratitude and respect. These habits introduce us to worlds where we find interests in mobilizing the imagination's capacities for sympathy or cooperation rather than having to negotiate conflicts over entitlements.

On another level, acts of appreciation dramatize self-reflexive paths where we are encouraged to dwell on what we honor rather than suspect or fear. Attention to these paths implicates us in a quotidian politics with no imposing drama and little opportunity for righteousness (unless one writes literary theory). But I suspect that any significant politics is a quotidian politics—either fighting for specific agendas or living out specific commitments to forms of self-regard that have a strong interest in the processes by which one can recognize other people's humanity.

We end this book with the ironic situation that although we can project social values for practices of attuning to a range of imaginative writing, our strongest claim must reside in how depressing the alternatives are. Why value appreciation? The primary reason is that it is much less ugly and much less self-defeating than psychological habits fixated on all that invites feelings of righteous victimage and the accompanying suspicions about positive values that any feeling of impotence is likely to generate. If we can keep our attention on what gives us the kinds of pleasures that an interest in sheer meaningfulness can afford, we might be able to make at least small turns to possible states of mind grounded in gratitude rather than resentment. There will still be enough resentment left over to fuel small-scale envies and large-scale political commitments.

Notes

1. Why Wittgenstein Matters for Literary Theory

1. Heather Dubrow, foreword to *New Formalisms and Literary Theory,* ed. Verena Theile and Linda Tredennick (New York: Palgrave Macmillan, 2013), vii–xviii; cited hereafter as *DF*. I also want to note another collection that is very helpful in teasing out the heritage of close reading from the ideological orientations of many but not all of the New Critics: Miranda Hickman and John D. McIntyre, eds., *Rereading the New Criticism* (Columbus: Ohio State University Press, 2012; cited hereafter as *RNC*), do quite a good job of showing how the heritage of New Critical close reading can be adapted today. I am especially interested in their claims that close reading is ultimately a commitment to aesthetics more than to any political or ethical program—which I like very much—and their equation of close reading with formalism, which this book opposes.

2. Let me list some of the models for reading proposed in the past half century—symptomatic reading, suspicious reading, distant reading, deconstructive reading, the New Formalism, surface reading, and phenomenal reading. The most articulate theory of symptomatic reading is offered by Frederic Jameson, *The Political Unconscious: Narrative as a Socially Symbolic Act* (Ithaca, NY: Cornell University Press, 1981). The best way to understand the force claimed for suspicious reading is the treatment of that topic by Paul Ricoeur in his *Freud and Philosophy: An Essay on Interpretation,* trans. Denis Savage (New Haven, CT: Yale University Press, 1979). On the New Formalism see

Marjorie Levinson, "What Is New Formalism?" *PMLA* 122, no. 2 (2007): 558–690. Franco Moretti, *Distant Reading* (London: Verso, 2013), makes a very lively argument against close reading for its binding us to aesthetic criteria and ignorance about general cultural tendencies. Surface reading, as represented by Stephen Best and Sharon Marcus's founding essay, "Surface Reading: An Introduction," *Representations* 108, no. 1 (2009): 1–21, cited hereafter as *SR,* does honor the aesthetic dimension of texts, but I think in problematic ways that I discuss later in this chapter. Brian Reed, *Phenomenal Reading: Essays on Modern and Contemporary Poetics* (Tuscaloosa: University of Alabama Press, 2012), is also attentive to how texts perform, but he has a tendency to treat texts as addressing social pressures more than I like.

3. Dubrow does engage what she sees as Kant's multiple attitudes to beauty in her "Guess Who's Coming to Dinner? Reevaluating Formalism and the Country House Poem," *Modern Language Quarterly* 61 (2000): 59–77. I should also mention a lively and often brilliant argument for the importance of craft for literary studies, Henry Staten, "The Wrong Turn of Aesthetics," in *Theory after "Theory,"* ed. Jane Elliott and Derek Attridge (London: Routledge, 2011), 223–36.

4. I do not think this project requires engaging Gayatri Spivak, *An Aesthetic Education in the Era of Globalization* (Cambridge: Harvard University Press, 2012) because while she focuses on Schiller she takes his concern for freedom to be realized in cultivating the reader's freedom to project on to the text. This contemporary twist on Idealist versions of freedom is simply not responsive to how Kant and Schiller understood art. But this project obviously requires engaging Robert Kaufman's work *Negative Romanticism: Adornian Aesthetics in Keats, Shelley, and Modern Poetry*, forthcoming from Cornell University Press. Kaufman has heroically been trying to save Kant from the Kantians and the aesthetic from aestheticism. He does so largely by insisting that when Kant separates the aesthetic from the conceptual he empowers it as the protoconceptual. Thus artists' constructions have rich concrete content that still can model ways of valuing experiences, precisely because the protoconceptual can incorporate value concerns more difficult to ground in concepts because concepts involve propositions that have to be objective.

I might not have thought this book necessary if I could agree with Kaufman, a colleague whom I respect very much. But I disagree with his fundamental argument about Kant and therefore with his emphasis on the value for aesthetics of the Adorno he constructs as extending Kant's thinking. So I have to elaborate a very different way of recuperating what I see as the continuing force of idealist aesthetics. I believe Kant wants the experience of beauty to be entirely other than the conceptual because he is dealing with a faculty psychology in which the protoconceptual would make no sense. Kant, after all, does not say that art as Schein is not yet concept (a temporal difference) but is not concept at all (a logical difference). Kaufman develops a capacious and attractive idea, but I suspect there is no way to treat art as ontologically distinctive from the products of understanding and still sneak in the role of a protoconceptual function. The protoconceptual will either cash out as a version of the conceptual and so be an operation of the understanding or depend on a free play of imagination that will be destroyed by taking any kind of conceptual form. Then Kaufman adds a practical problem to his theoretical problem. Because Kaufman can work with the protoconceptual, it is easy to suggest that artworks have political contents because they work out concrete expressions of political ideals. Readers will see that I have to connect texts to the world not by ideas but by the samples and examples they produce, which are capable of providing models for treating particulars as affording some degree of generality. But because examples are not concepts, they depend on individual interests and modes of attention. So the political dimension of art has to be negotiated as a series of individual projections. There is no right story or even room for a single compelling story capable of legislating how we deploy examples. (I should add that I found the lucid arguments of Ayon Maharaj, *The Dialectics of Aesthetic Agency: Revaluating German Aesthetics from Kant* [London: Bloomsbury, 2013] very helpful support in thinking through my objections to Kaufman.)

5. The best guide to Idealist thinking about expression is still "Part I: The Claims of Speculative Reason," in Charles Taylor, *Hegel* (Cambridge: Cambridge University Press, 1977), 3–125.

6. Immanuel Kant, *Critique of the Power of Judgment,* trans. Paul Guyer and Eric Matthews (Cambridge: Cambridge University Press, 2000), section 57, remark 1, 219. Lovers of Kant will understand why I cannot resist quoting the brilliantly concise corollary to his contrast between reason and understanding: "Now since to bring a representation of the imagination to concepts is the same as to expound it, the aesthetic idea can be called an inexponible representation of the imagination (in its free play)" (ibid.). Kant's book will hereafter be cited as *CJ.*

7. I take the phrase "scientific protocols for knowing" from Richard Eldridge's terrific introduction to *The Oxford Handbook of Literature and Philosophy* (New York: Oxford University Press, 2009), 13. Eldridge's book *Wittgenstein, Leading a Human Life: Wittgenstein, Intentionality, and Romanticism* (Chicago: University of Chicago Press, 1997), offers a striking example of how his resistance to the general application of these protocols might help shape various humanistic practices. That I owe Eldridge an immense debt is evident if one turns to passages such as these:

> In going down dead ends in philosophy and then in coming back to himself still in the grip of philosophical problems, Wittgenstein, as David G. Stern puts it, "acts out the tension [between essentialism and conventionalism] in dialogues" in ways that display to use who we are.... This showing ... is ... achieved dramatically and critically rather than through the characterization of processes or substances that are independent of this course of reflection.... Impersonal mindedness in a particular reflecting individual is here both the object of the investigation and the power that conducts it. (2–3)

I also very much admire the editors' introductory essay and P. M. S. Hacker, "Wittgenstein and the Autonomy of Humanistic Understanding," in *Wittgenstein, Theory, and the Arts,* ed. Richard Allen and Malcolm Turvey (New York: Routledge, 2001), 1–36, 39–74. (The essay by Hacker provides a superb summary of how these "scientific protocols for knowing" came to dominate the philosophical culture in which Wittgenstein wrote his *Philosophical Investigations.*) But among philosophers only Eldridge, Garry Hagberg, Danièle Moyal-Sharrock, and Anthony Ross seem concerned with my basic theme: that Wittgenstein is also interested in developing a sense of display, example, and expression that challenges any idea of understanding based only on epistemic evidence.

I should also note other approaches to Wittgenstein's critique of philosophical tendencies to idealize the knowledge possible from propositions and descriptions. For example, one cannot avoid the much more "resolute" attribution to Wittgenstein of deep suspicion of all philosophical claims developed by Cora Diamond and James Conant. See especially their initial arguments in "On Reading the Tractatus Resolutely," in *Wittgenstein's Lasting Significance*, ed. Max Kölbel and Bernhard Weiss (London: Routledge, 2004), 42–97. The passage of time has also made it possible for me to appreciate how prescient Henry Staten was in aligning Wittgenstein with Derrida's critique of knowledge in his *Wittgenstein and Derrida* (Lincoln: University of Nebraska Press, 1986). Finally, I have to acknowledge how Stanley Cavell has led us to what are now called "therapeutic readings" of Wittgenstein. See especially Cavell's *Claim of Reason: Wittgenstein, Skepticism, Morality, and Tragedy* (Oxford: Clarendon, 1982). Much as I admire Cavell, I am resolutely opposed to his emphasis on therapy and ask the role of display to establish a very different, positive, antiepistemic function for Wittgenstein's arguments.

8. I have chosen the epigraph to this chapter in order to bring out the possibility that Schiller lies in the not too remote background of everything Wittgenstein says about the values at play when we turn from the epistemic realm to avowals and to works of art.

9. Wittgenstein's critique of empiricist models of knowing has been taken into the mainstream of contemporary philosophy largely through the concept of how culture develops a space of reasons elaborated by Wilfrid Sellars, *Empiricism and the Philosophy of Mind* (Cambridge, MA: Harvard University Press, 1997), and by John McDowell, *Mind and World* (Cambridge, MA: Harvard University Press, 1996). McDowell is especially interesting because he wants to make broader use of the space of reasons than does Sellars, as if the space of reasons could include much of what Wittgenstein believes grammar allows us to determine. Yet McDowell might not go far enough. In an important essay, published in *Mind, Reason, and Being-in-the-World: The McDowell-Dreyfus Debate*, ed. Joseph K. Schear (London: Routledge, 2013, 15–39), Bert Dreyfus complains that the space of reasoning does not account for the ways that we process the world, which are embedded in social practices that have rules and coherent expectations but are not based on anything quite like timeless reasoning.

10. Ludwig Wittgenstein, *Philosophical Investigations,* trans. G. E. M. Anscombe, P. M. S. Hacker, and J. Schulte, ed. P. M. S. Hacker and J. Schulte (London: Blackwell, 2009), item 236. Cited in the text as *PI.*

11. There are four very good books published in the last ten years that pursue roughly similar strategies to treat reading as an activity that brings the world alive. But three of them are somewhat undertheorized because they trust in a common sense so masterfully wielded that it almost suffices. The fourth is certainly well fortified by theory, but in this case the theory leads in directions that I criticize later in this book. The first three are Terry Eagleton, *How to Read Literature* (New Haven, CT: Yale University Press, 2013); Rita Felski, *Uses of Literature* (Oxford: Blackwell, 2009); and Joshua Landy, *How to Do Things with Fictions* (New York: Oxford University Press, 2012). The fourth is Derek Attridge, *The Singularity of Literature* (London: Taylor and Francis, 2004), hereafter cited as *SI.*

For the most part Felski and Eagleton do not indulge themselves in philosophical language at all. They trust to their considerable powers of description to establish a sense of the various ways the art of writing can engage our deepest reflective interests in what we can experience and why that experience might matter. So Landy's is the book I would most like to have written because it absorbs all kinds of philosophy and theory in its efforts "to reclaim fiction from the 'meaning-mongers'" (8). Landy gives a powerful critique of claims that literary texts provide significant knowledge, and he is terrific on how what matters is not "informative fictions" so much as "formative fictions," which model ways of disposing the self toward the world. In addition, Landy is simply marvelous at turning very wide reading in theory into prose that reads like common sense.

These three books all want to trust in the effective force of quite intelligent and timely remarks on specific values basic to literary experience. But I fear that those ambitious for theory will then continue to construct instrumental accounts unless they are directly challenged by consistent frameworks for reflecting on how literary experience engages and strengthens modes of sensibility and reflection that are quite different from most scholarly efforts to contextualize specific works. Because close reading relies on a range of claims addressed in aesthetics, one has to bring to its articulation all of the philosophical resources it can sustain.

12. John McDowell's *Mind and Nature* helps us characterize two features of display. First he uses the concept of disquotation beautifully in order to clarify his frustration with Richard Rorty's historicism, which wants to put everything in quotation marks and so limit it to conditions of utterance (151). I think the New Critics were right to see the core of display as the desire to resist disquotation or paraphrase into generalized truth claims. For me the prime instance of resistance to disquotation in philosophy is Wittgenstein's own painfully self-conscious style. (See Wittgenstein's *Culture and Value*, ed. Peter Winch [Chicago: University of Chicago Press, 1984], 57 and 68, for Wittgenstein's self-consciousness about the goal of display.) Second, McDowell makes a powerful case for how display can have a role in the space of human reasoning. But display reverses the usual process of empirical reasoning: rather than sponsoring efforts to test the general power of a statement or a description, display asks for reasoning about what might be solicited by the particular so that we might better respond to its powers.

13. G. W. F. Hegel, *Phenomenology of Spirit*, trans. A. V. Miller (Oxford: Oxford University Press, 1976), 105. Hereafter cited as *PS*.

14. See also in Kant's *CJ*, 19, 215–24.

15. Richard Wollheim, *Painting as an Art* (Princeton, NJ: Princeton University Press, 1987), chapter 3; hereafter cited as *PA*. Wollheim insists that he is talking only about painting because that art creates distinctive problems for its audiences. Classical painting at least seems to adhere to the logic of copy, so tightly is the image linked to its referent. Yet at the same time it is emphatically an artifact bound to the world more by models of craft than by models of mimesis.

16. I want to defend reading for a specific kind of intention, which I call "aesthetic intention," at this point in my exposition, but it would disrupt the flow of my introductory claims, so I make my case in an appendix to this chapter.

17. William Shakespeare, *Hamlet*, ed. Barbara A. Mowat and Paul Werstine (New York: Simon & Schuster, 2003), I.ii.1–15.

18. As Claudius speaks, the patterns in his syntax make purposiveness visible because the intentionality is visible but not governed by any kind of rule or law: the reader is not constructing patterns but discovering them.

19. Hegel's richest characterization of the powers art can confer in life is in his section on "The religion of art" in his *PS*.

20. I am grateful to Stanley Cavell, *Must We Mean What We Say?* (Cambridge: Cambridge University Press, 2002), for making clear that for Wittgenstein "behavior is expressive of mind; and this is not something we know, but a way we treat behavior" (262). Yet Cavell's basic model for adapting to that behavior seems problematic to me. He emphasizes that we must "acknowledge" the actions the other performs and the needs driving those actions. I prefer the family of terms around attunement for several reasons, especially the fact that attunement keeps the other person's actions and needs in the foreground. Acknowledgement, on the other hand, reintroduces the dramas of self-positioning because it ultimately becomes another kind of knowledge where the other's activity virtually drops out as the self meditates on its powers of repositioning. Cavell puts his case this way in *The Claim of Reason* (Oxford: Clarendon Press, 1979), 312; herafter cited as *CR*: we honor the knowledge at the core of acknowledgment when we follow "the methods which lead to a knowledge of our own position, of where we stand, in short to a knowledge and definition of ourselves." This stress on one's own position is of a piece with the self-congratulatory tendency to praise the auditor's overcoming of skepticism, with the other person at risk of becoming a mere cipher in a story of the philosopher's heroic triumph: "Acknowledgment is not an alternative to knowing but an interpretation of it.... The concept of acknowledgment is meant, in my use, to declare that what is to be known philosophically remains unknown not through ignorance ... but through a refusal of knowledge, a denial, or a repression of knowledge." See his *In Quest of the Ordinary: Lines of Skepticism and Romanticism* (Chicago: University of Chicago Press, 1988), 51.

21. However, one can resent the person who produces the object one appreciates just because the appreciation makes one realize the poverty of one's art. This is the case of Soleri's relation to Mozart. I think we can live with a political order that cannot overcome this form of resentment.

22. See the first chapter of Derek Attridge, *The Singularity of Literature* (London: Taylor and Francis, 2004).

23. In my chapter on ethics and values I make a similar critique of ideals of knowledge that posit themselves as alternatives to any kind of empiricist standard of demonstrably accurate representation. Such ideals posited in relation to literature come closer to "knowing how" than to "knowing that." But "knowing how" is not something sufficiently reliable or identifiable on which to build theoretical claims about knowledge tout court. In fact, Wittgenstein shows that what we mean by "knowing how" is best treated in terms of familiarity with practices rather than any sense that we are developing discrete observations capable of anchoring generalizations. It is certainly true that we learn something about human behavior when we read Jane Austen or George Eliot or Leo Tolstoy. Yet, rather than treating these senses of moral wisdom as specifiable instances of stable concepts, I will argue that the texts become discrete examples that we use by trying to match them to how people act. We save the particularity of the example

by not generalizing to principle but simply by using the sample as a means of sorting out how the images and reflections do and do not fit particular situations we encounter outside of art. It matters that Emma is blinded by pride and impatience, but what we learn about those traits remains embedded in the deeds and in the consequences of those deeds. We can generalize, but then we are stuck with banal abstractions rather than the possibility of bringing to bear intricate examples that suggest parallels rather than principles.

24. Michael Clune, *American Literature and the Free Market, 1945–2000* (New York: Cambridge University Press, 2010), 7; hereafter cited as *ALF*.

25. John Gibson, "The Question of Poetic Meaning," *Nonsite* 4 (2011), http://nonsite.org/article/the-question-of-poetic-meaning, offers the best way of formulating the text-work distinction, although it takes some modification to adapt it to "instrumental" literary criticism. He separates "sentence meaning," where we process meaning as a chain of connections built by sentences, from "work meaning," where relations are developed across the implications of sentences. Most lyric poetry involves a mode of meaningfulness that requires us to talk about the suggestiveness of situations rather than the pointedness of discreet assertion. And then meaning is not so much given as an endless receding destination where one can reconcile "the communicative force of poetry . . . with the unconventionality and sheer inventiveness of its language." Gibson argues that with this distinction we can honor what critics call the materiality of poetry—but as means and not end, as invitation to experience but not yet the judgment of how it attaches to meaningfulness. He does not extend "work meaning" to utterances that take place in non-art contexts. But I think he could use his analysis to characterize most expressive acts and thereby situate poetry in relation to a broader class of human practices that have the same needs to go beyond sentence meaning. If someone is characterizing how he suffers pain or has a strong feeling, we do not stop with the individual sentences but read their relation to each other as indices of the nature and the quality and degree of urgency in the feeling.

26. I cannot resist bringing up an extreme version of the tendency to find politics everywhere, in part because it also indicates how Adorno is now characteristically used. Consider these two statements from Stephen Ross's introduction to his edited collection, *Modernism and Theory: A Critical Debate* (London: Routledge, 2008), 1–18:

> Critique—particularly the critique of modernity—is essential to those continuities and remains the core of the affinities between modernism and theory. (12)

> Theory's recognition and embrace of critique as a fundamentally negative energy, a process of disruption and challenge rather than synthesis, allowed it to avoid for the most part the modernist mistake of proffering concrete alternatives to what was being critiqued. (10)

When negativity is all we think our discipline can offer, perhaps it is a good thing to be sufficiently blind to treat the negativity itself as a positive state. But then what does one do with the massive evidence that modernist authors frequently do not share this view of its affinities with theory? In fact, modernist writers virtually invented the practice of the essay on poetics in order to clarify the positive roles they saw their work playing in their culture. Not to worry. One can deny that the modernists were sufficiently negative. And then one can praise oneself and one's allies for finding the proper attitude.

27. See Best and Marcus, "Surface Reading." Hickman and McIntyre are very shrewd about the relation of surface reading to close reading: "in our view it is somewhat of a misnomer to call such New Critical Reading 'surface reading,' since . . . it often does move from the more to the less evident, the apparent to the hidden—if not always in the spirit of 'unmasking,' at least to uncover what is not initially apparent" (*RNC*, 237–38).

28. Best and Marcus see surface reading as sponsoring six possible emphases: "surface as materiality," "surface as the intricate verbal structure of literary language," "embrace of the surface as an affective and ethical stance," attention to surface as a practice of critical description," "surface as the location of patterns that exist within and across texts," and "surface as literal meaning." I cannot resist the suggestion that it is symptomatic of the commitment to surfaces that the essay must talk about the location of patterns rather than what they might establish for the reader. And it may be symptomatic that they talk of "embrace of the surface as an affective and ethical stance" in the hope that freedom for the reader maps onto the pursuit of significant freedoms in the existential realm.

29. After I had made a considerable imaginative investment in the concept of attunement I discovered that it provides an important figure for the poetics of "object-oriented ontology," where it can be taken much more literally than in my work. See Timothy Morton, "An Object-Oriented Defense of Poetry," *New Literary History* 43 (2012): 205–24.

30. I should note here that Rita Felski has the same concern I do with the worldliness of the text. But she seems content to establish this worldliness by a fine theoretical introduction followed by chapters on specific categories of literary representation—recognition, enchantment, knowledge, and shock. I am more interested in a worldliness that derives not from identifying literary situations with emotional states but by identifying authors and characters as having and responding to certain kinds of interests that they develop modes of expressing. These expressions cover a wide variety of states and yet require different languages of response than can be provided by the apparatuses we use to establish knowledge.

31. Danièle Moyal-Sharrock, *Understanding Wittgenstein's* On Certainty (London: Palgrave Macmillan, 2004).

32. See Ludwig Wittgenstein, *Philosophy of Psychology—A Fragment,* ed. P. M. S. Hacker and J. Schulte, trans. G. E. M. Anscombe, P. M. S. Hacker, and J. Schulte (Oxford: Wiley-Blackwell, 2009), §254–78; hereafter cited as *PPF;* and John Verdi, *Fat Wednesday: Wittgenstein on Aspects* (Philadelphia: Paul Dry Books, 2010).

33. Clearly, ethical criticism and object-oriented ontology have considerably more respect for the manifest qualities of the work itself than does cultural historicism. So I take the easy way out in now focusing only on what is after all the still dominant mode of criticism in the United States. And even object-oriented ontology pays strange fealty to the rhetoric of knowledge in its strange claims about knowing the object in its unrepresentability. Contemporary ethical criticism, on the other hand, may have all too much faith in representability because it tends to rely on a version of the space of reasons, which I criticize in my penultimate chapter.

34. See chapter 4 of this book, note 6, for the entire passage. See also my "Ponderation in Cézanne and Williams," *Poetics Today* 10 (1989): 373–400.

35. See my "Wonder in *The Winter's Tale*: A Cautionary Account of Epistemic Criticism," in *A Sense of the World: Essays on Fiction, Narrative, and Knowledge*, ed. John Gibson, Wolfgang Heumer, and Luca Pocci (London: Routledge, 2007), 266–86.

36. Wittgenstein explicitly connects exclamation to seeing an aspect in *PPF* (138–39).

37. See also the following remark, which seems to seek alternatives to explanation as a mode of responsiveness: "Our mistake is to look for an explanation where we ought to regard the facts as 'proto-phenomena.' That is, where we ought to say: this is the language game that is being played" (*PI*, 654). I would make a bigger deal of this statement if I could be sure that "explanation" here does not refer primarily to scientific explanation.

38. The closest parallel in contemporary criticism that I know is Joshua Landy's very suggestive work on the concept of "formative fictions," which "bring a restricted audience to a new way of hearing and speaking, and thus a new way of looking at the world." See his *How to Do Things with Fictions,* 10. See also Tyrus Miller, *Singular Examples: Artistic Politics and the Neo-Avant-Garde* (Evanston, IL: Northwestern University Press, 2009), for a very interesting use of the concept of exemplar to characterize distinctive qualities in late twentieth-century art. I should also note that while Wittgenstein has an idiosyncratic concept of "model," since it is limited to clarifying what seeing an aspect involves for a person, we need to see that concern against the backdrop of a rich discourse in the twentieth century on the use of models. For literary criticism the best work on models that I know is Daniel Tiffany, *Toy Medium: Materialism, and Modern Lyric* (Berkeley: University of California Press, 2000).

39. I take some liberty with Gibson's argument in "The Question of Poetic Meaning" (see note 26). For him "semantic descent" is a series of steps in which each provides a little more of the world that language implicates and a little less of language about language. Thus "Juliet is the sun" becomes not just an example of the logic of metaphor but a statement asking us to imagine what Juliet and the sun might have in common: in interpreting the metaphor we ask how the sun can bear "a kind of meaning for us" that is other than simply "linguistic in nature." This level of meaning consists in the set of associations, connotations, resonances, values, and so on that any object that matters in our form of life will have. "Semantic ascent" would be the opposite—referring less to language about language and more to the work's overall sense of its project.

40. Because I occasionally refer to Nietzsche's idea of slow reading, it seems to me worth citing his description from paragraph 5 of the preface to Friedrich Nietzsche, *Daybreak: Thoughts on the Prejudices of Morality* (Cambridge: Cambridge University Press, 1997).

> A book like this, a problem like this, is in no hurry; we both, I just as much as my book, are friends of lento. It is not for nothing that I have been a philologist, perhaps I am a philologist still, that is to say, A TEACHER OF SLOW READING:—in the end I also write slowly. Nowadays it is not only my habit, it is also to my taste—a malicious taste, perhaps?—no longer to write anything which does not reduce to despair every sort of man who is 'in a hurry.' For philology is that venerable art which demands of its votaries one thing above all: to go aside, to take time, to

become still, to become slow—it is a goldsmith's art and connoisseurship of the WORD which has nothing but delicate, cautious work to do and achieves nothing if it does not achieve it lento. But precisely for this reason it is more necessary than ever today, by precisely this means does it entice and enchant us the most, in the midst of an age of 'work,' that is to say, of hurry, of indecent and perspiring haste, which wants to 'get everything done' at once, including every old or new book:— this art does not so easily get anything done, it teaches to read WELL, that is to say, to read slowly, deeply, looking cautiously before and aft, with reservations, with doors left open, with delicate eyes and fingers... My patient friends, this book desires for itself only perfect readers and philologists: LEARN to read me well!

41. I think versions of this perspective dominate the most ambitious contemporary American poetry. I conceive of the account I am giving as a part of an imaginary conversation with Lisa Robertson's essays in *Nilling: Prose* (Toronto: Bookthug, 2012). I try to formulate terms for this conversation in my essay in a forthcoming issue of *Affirmations* edited by Peter Nichols and Sascha Bru.

42. See Steven Knapp and Walter Benn Michaels, "Against Theory," *Critical Inquiry* 8, no. 4 (1982): 723–42.

43. See G. E. M. Anscombe, *Intention* (Cambridge, MA: Harvard University Press, 2000).

2. The Work Texts Do

1. My first point addresses core values in the poetry of Wordsworth, Coleridge, and Shelley. The second point is more compatible with Keats's negative capability. But it is important to see that the two modes are linked by the focus on the energy of the making as a thematic center. And that focus came about, I think, because the romantic poets recognized the power of what was involved in their freeing the imagination from the overt control of rhetoric so that it could become a heuristic and affective instrument in its own right. But when they theorized, they imposed their philosophical anxieties on the activities of imagination and tried problematically to show how they might contribute to philosophical contexts largely shaped by idealist responses to empiricism. Jonathan Culler implies the same critique I am making in his argument that literary studies has retained a very strong component of theological thinking even after the society it addresses has pretty much abandoned such concerns. See Jonathan Culler, "The Future of Criticism," in *The Current in Criticism: Essays on the Present and Future of Literary Theory,* ed. Clayton Koelb and Virgil L. Lokke (West Lafayette, IN: Purdue University Press, 1987), 27–42, and "A Critic against the Christians," review of *Using Biography,* by William Empson, (November 23, 1984): 1327–28.

2. Paul de Man, "Form and Intent in the American New Criticism," in *Blindness and Insight: Essays in the Rhetoric of Contemporary Criticism* (New York: Oxford University Press, 1971), 32; cited hereafter as *FI*.

3. One reason for my choice of adapting phenomenology is that we thereby gain a way of separating literary criticism from the domain of neural science, at least in most

of its current operations. Neural science wants to know what parts of the brain are activated as particular agents respond to different kinds of situations. Because the situations are usually simple, one can elicit measurable responses and pursue standard, publically significant patterns of reaction. The imagination at work in neural science goes into the design of the experiment: the respondents have to be directed into common theaters. This is no way to elicit what is imaginatively interesting about the object or what holds out appeals to be valued well beyond the time of imagining. So until neural science develops new directions of inquiry, one can say that concern for what is imaginative in the potential life a constructed object can sustain for attention will remain a distinctive concern for the humanities.

4. This last question and much of this chapter are the result of continuing lively discussion with my colleague Geoffrey O'Brien.

5. Edward Casey, *Imagining: A Phenomenological Study* (Bloomington: Indiana University Press, 1976). I will take only what I need from this book without really engaging its argument because its basic concern is to account for all forms of imagining. I want only what is useful for characterizing how imaginative acts make claims on us to be valued.

6. I do not claim that Ashbery cares about a phenomenology of the imagination (although this poem has affinities with the work of Raymond Roussel, who did care a great deal about phenomenology).

7. I thank Virginia Jackson for bringing this remarkable poem of Bryant's to my attention.

8. My case for the importance of keeping imaginative activity at the center of criticism shares a poststructuralist resistance to the authority of the conceptual order. But my case does not stress as its alternative to the conceptual order a domain of sheer event (with Eagleton) or singularity (with Attridge) that extends the play of differences and calls for an idealization of the other (either as the other to language or to the demands of the ego). Rather, it seeks to restore a sense of the capacities of images to carry distinctive modes of agency. The purposiveness in these texts then resides neither in the subject nor in the object but in the awareness of their constant interaction. Purposiveness is thinkable only in the social space where subjects exist because of what they make manifest in their relation to objects. Reading for these modes of production honors the labor of the writing and anchors the reading process in something other than the reader's needs and desires, something that resists the authority of the individual consumer. See Derek Attridge, *The Singularity of Literature* (London: Taylor and Francis, 2004), and Terry Eagleton, *The Event of Literature* (New Haven, CT: Yale University Press, 2012).

9. Belinda Luscombe, "10 Questions with William Kentridge," *Time* (December 2, 2013), 68.

10. The affinities with the Kantian tradition of talking about imagination are worth noting here even though Casey derives what he says about "self-evidence" from very different sources. The important parallel is the way both thinkers align with many poets in insisting that products of imagination are always concrete and not visibly organized by governing ideas. Abstraction in imagination is in fact a somewhat extreme claim for the product to set its own agenda by forging structures that resist the conceptual. More important, the romantics were also right about expressions of the imagination having

this power of establishing conditions of self-evidence where the practical interpretive intelligence is always a belated interloper. However, the romantics believed that these conditions of self-evidence derived from realizing deep truths about the world rendered. In contrast, when we stress phenomenology and the modeling it can encourage, we have to root our sense of organization solely in the nature of the specific noetic properties of imagination. Because the activity of imagining makes no claim to deeper significance (although we can make claims for it), this phenomenological perspective helps elaborate how imagination can play a significant role in freeing us to see fresh possible arrangements of situations—practically and formally. These arrangements can be deployed for their own sake or as a deliberate means of looking differently at phenomena to which we have become habituated.

Emphasizing these relational traits makes Casey, and my use of Casey, even more hostile toward interpreters than was the Kantian tradition. For self-evidence is not the basis of interpretation, not a direct means of aligning with intention, but a model of how products of imagination emerge that resist all our languages of purpose in order to bring out what is unexpected and cannot be aligned directly with the language of motives, acts, and judgments. Of course, writers and painters can use the imagination in the service of such judgments, but they risk having the imagination subordinated to practical generalizations.

11. John Ashbery, *Collected Poems, 1956–1987*, ed. Mark Ford (New York: Library of America, 2008), 6; cited hereafter as *ACP*.

12. On this third point see Jasper Bernes, "John Ashbery's Free Indirect Labor," *Modern Language Quarterly* 74, no. 4 (2013): 517–40. In conversation Geoffrey O'Brien also stresses the social. And in his own long poem, "People on Sunday," he establishes a dialogue with Ashbery's poem suggesting a much denser sense of social lives impinging on one another. See O'Brien's *People on Sunday* (New York: Wave Books, 2013), 64–74.

13. Were I to make the historical case for a distinctive post–New Critical treatment of imagination, I would emphasize how in "The Instruction Manual" there is no grand drama for imagination; there is only the possibility of keeping some control over one's life by manifesting a sense of autonomy, self-consciously limited to the daydream and existentially to the making of the artwork. So the question of what constitutes the values involved in choosing come to the fore, again without any trust that the authority here has any public sanction at all.

In this respect I think also of Ashbery's friend Frank O'Hara's "I do this; I do that" poems. They seem just the record of interesting events in which the poet plays a part. But if we treat them as also modeling how the imagination works, the poems become a lot more than records of states of sensibility. They become celebrations of sites where there can be immediate decisions capable of engaging the imagination. The poems invite identifying with the activity of becoming interested in what the imagination finds itself wanting to inhabit:

> it seems they were all cheated of some marvelous experience
> which is not going to go wasted on me which is why I'm telling
> you about it.

In *The Collected Poems of Frank O'Hara,* ed. Donald Allen (Berkeley: University of California Press, 1995), 360.) See also pages 202 and 335. In Ashbery's and O'Hara's poems the individual has no content aside from the qualities of the making and the generic needs that underlie this mode of serious play. The poems share the desire for an audience for personal choices, which also motivates confessional poetry, but without any visible deep personal need for a hearing.

14. I gave a version of this chapter to a very lively group at Norwich University in England. Daniel Kane offered a powerful response that I think I must address here. He argued that "Instruction Manual" was not a good poem and not typical of Ashbery's major work, for the very reasons I praise. The poem tells us what it is doing, is light enough to be very sure of itself, does not even introduce the sense of doubt and accident characteristic of major Ashbery, and actually participates in the colonial imagination shaping its sense of the feelings embedded in the scene. Alas, I have to agree with every complaint, although I suspect Ashbery may be challenging the colonial imagination by showing how it can produce sympathy and a sense of a shared world by its very confident totalizing.

So what can I say in my defense? The philosopher in me, or the one who reads philosophy and fantasizes being a philosopher, wants just to point out that I never claim it is a good poem or characteristic of Ashbery. I do think it quite a good poem, even though it may not be a good Ashbery poem, because of how it stages imaginative life. Nothing Kane said contradicts this claim. But I also want to defend my argument from the point of a view of a rather defensive literary critic. For while this very early poem does not present Ashbery's characteristic sponsoring of accident, uncertainty, and doubt, it does define much of the tone by which Ashbery converts the terrors of those states into modes of acceptance. Ashbery carries over the spirit of play from "Instruction Manual" but concentrates on more emotionally complicated and epistemologically fraught processes of enactment. And the sense of freedom deepening into attachment evident in this poem's presentation of details becomes in the later work a freedom of structure as a necessary means of preserving an attachment to the real rather than yielding to the temptation to flee from that unknowable other. "The Instruction Manual" insists on an imagined control of physical geography. Ashbery's later poems turn geography into a domain of constant figural shift and the construction of multiple levels of awareness and of feeling that cannot be mapped. Yet these shifts in focus ultimately retain the sense of meta-imagination finding solace and purpose simply in the imagination's control over its details and its overall reliance on a self-evidence that challenges the authority of the understanding. So considered strictly in terms of an engaging play with, and play on, the nature of the imagination, the early poem seems to me a quite impressive achievement, in part because it led Ashbery eventually to challenge how it stages the work imagination can do.

15. William Butler Yeats, *The Variorum Edition of the Poems of W. B. Yeats,* ed. Peter Allt and Russell K. Alspach (New York: Macmillan, 1957), 441; cited hereafter as *WB*.

16. Needless to say that this opening sense of selectedness is crucial also to how novels can produce a sense of control by the author of the world to come. I think in particular of the openings of *Great Expectations, War and Peace,* and *Mrs. Dalloway,* as if the more a major novel aims to develop a realistic sense of the world, the more it is likely to dwell at its inception on the authorial freedom to select what and how those naturalizing effects are to be deployed.

17. It is interesting to me that Yeats's concern for the structure of two assertions balanced by two different kinds of questions was apparent even in the rather dreadful first version of the poem, as presented in Giorgio Melchiori's remarkable chapter on the role Leda played in Yeats's imagination:

> Now can the swooping godhead have his will
> Yet hovers, though her helpless eyes are pressed
> By the webbed toes; and all that powerful bill
> Has suddenly bowed her face upon his breast.
> How can those terrified vague fingers push
> The feathered glory from her loosening thighs?
> All the stretched body's laid in that white rush
> And feels the strange heart beating where it lies.
> A shudder in the loins engenders there
> The broken wall, the burning roof and Tower
> And Agamemnon dead . . .
>   Being so caught up
> Did nothing pass before her in the air?
> Did she put on his knowledge with his power
> Before the indifferent beak could let her drop? (74)

See Melchiori, *The Whole Mystery of Art* (New York: Macmillan, 1961), 73–163.

18. I am not arguing for "presence" in terms of ontology (pace Derrida) but for it as an aesthetic state of vivid appearance.

19. I elaborate this distinction in the next chapter on exemplification.

3. Where Doubt Has No Purchase

1. Although I take a tack that is somewhat different from John McDowell's in his essay "Wittgenstein on Following a Rule," *Synthèse* 58 (March 1984): 325–63, I am ultimately buoyed by his way of responding to the paradoxes about rule following that Saul Kripke, *Wittgenstein on Rules and Private Language: An Elementary Exposition* (Cambridge, MA: Harvard University Press, 1982), makes basic to his reading of Wittgenstein. Essentially McDowell argues for two claims that sustain my concern for what agents display in what they say. His basic argument is that we cannot assimilate understanding to interpretation because we have other, more direct ways of adapting ourselves to the linguistic behavior of others, given our mutual involvement in various practices. Second, he suggests that this alternative to interpretation is possible because we are not distanced observers of what people say but members of linguistic communities "bound together, not by a match in mere externals (facts available to just anyone) by a capacity for a meeting of minds" (351).

2. For Heidegger on poetry see his *On the Way to Language,* trans. Peter Hertz and Joan Stambaugh (New York: Harper and Row, 1971), and his *Poetry, Language, Thought,* trans. Albert Hofstader (New York: Harper and Row, 1971). The tendency to idealize

art as a distinctive kind of being is already there in Kant and in Schiller, but much less so in Hegel. And the tradition remains in thinkers who pursue routes very different from Heidegger's to deal with how presentation differs from description. Croce's use of intuition is a good example because it fixes the work as a distinctive object completely separate from the give and take of ordinary life in typical marketplaces. I should also note that I much admire David Nowell-Smith, *Sounding/Silence: Martin Heidegger at the Limits of Poetics* (New York: Fordham University Press, 2013), for his attempt to combine patient and sharp explication of Heidegger's claims about poetry as thinking with the concern to bring that discourse back within Anglo-American discourse on poetics.

3. See Richard Moran, *Authority and Estrangement: An Essay on Self-Knowledge* (Princeton, NJ: Princeton University Press, 2001), chapter 4. At the opposite pole I should mention that John Guillory is probably the strongest critical voice who treats as central to his project an Enlightenment faith in explanation. This argument is developed in his *Cultural Capital: The Problem of Literary Canon Formation* (Chicago: University of Chicago Press, 1993), 327–33.

4. I much prefer this translation by Anscombe to the translation of Hacker and Schulte, which renders *übersichtliche Darstellung* as "surveyable representation" (*PI*, 122).

5. On exclamation see especially *PI*, 27, and *PPF*, 138.

6. See my "Chapter One" note xxxiii.

7. For another critique of imposing the language of perception on a language game to which that language is inappropriate see *PI*, 453. Wittgenstein claims that "to perceive an expectation" makes no sense because we see the object of expectation; we do not infer it by perceiving that someone expects the object.

8. I do not know why Wittgenstein adds that the model allows us to see how the exclamation seems "forced from us.—It stands to the experience somewhat as a cry to pain" (*PPF*, 138). I understand why he might want to give this "now" the same immediacy as the cry of pain, but I think that "now" has to be both compelled by the feeling of event and an invitation (not a compulsion) to further development. See, for example, *PPF*, 207, where Wittgenstein claims that the use of "now" amounts to "giving expression to the lighting up of an aspect."

9. Avrum Stroll, "Wittgenstein's Foundational Metaphors," in *The Third Wittgenstein: The Post-Investigations Works*, ed. Danièle Moyal-Sharrock (Hampshire: Ashgate, 2004), 13–24, offers an intelligent version of the argument that in *On Certainty* Wittgenstein rejects the contrast between what can be seen and what can be shown. But I think one can best accommodate Stroll's observations about Wittgenstein's renewed concern for foundations by arguing that Wittgenstein applies the saying-showing distinction in a new way. I find support for my position in Daniel D. Hutto's helpful essay from the same volume, "Two Wittgensteins Too Many: Wittgenstein's Foundationalism," 25–41.

10. *OC*, 90, is an especially powerful summary of Wittgenstein's thinking on the need to ground knowledge claims in some framework that is not a matter of knowing.

11. Being "part of logic" involves two conditions—that there be a rule-like force to the statement's relation to the practice involved and that the statement can function both as something referred to and as an element of what is involved in exemplifying or illustrating how the rules work: "But if someone were to say 'So logic too is an empirical

science' he would be wrong. Yet this is right: the same proposition may get treated at one time as something to test by experience, at another as a rule of testing" (*OC*, 98).

I want again to acknowledge my debt to Danièle Moyal-Sharrock's thesis in *The Third Wittgenstein* that *On Certainty* returns to the Tractarian idea that logic can only be displayed and not argued for, but now as the means to understand the ontological status of forms of life. I find her arguments substantial support for emphasizing the role of display as not just a mode of expression but as means of characterizing the ontological work done by forms of life.

12. Jacques Derrida, *Limited, Inc.*, ed. Gerald Graff, trans. Jeffrey Mehlman and Samuel Weber (Evanston, IL: Northwestern University Press, 1988).

13. Were Wittgenstein to have tried his hand at deconstruction, he would probably have been very successful. And Henry Staten, in *Wittgenstein and Derrida* (Lincoln: University of Nebraska Press, 1986), makes a brilliant case for the parallels between the two thinkers. But almost certainly Wittgenstein did not consider himself a deconstructionist because there is no good reason to treat irony or skepticism as the only feasible alternatives when philosophy cannot meet epistemic criteria. So I think the example of Moore greatly disturbed him by reinforcing his fears that professional philosophy did more harm than good.

14. Elementary manners are good examples. We do not usually reflect on simple manners such as opening doors for people or letting others explain themselves before making judgments about them. These seem built into the practice of walking or talking as the case may be. But at one pole we can become hyperscrupulous: at the other pole there is the temptation of carelessness. Then either we can condemn the scrupulous or careless agent for not honoring common practice, or we can try to recontextualize the agent's actions by attempting to understand particular anxieties or blindness or deliberate perversity at play. The important point is that at no level can we simply take accepting the practice as necessarily a programmed response.

15. I find some confidence to go on in this vein because of the groundbreaking work on Wittgenstein's relationship to literature by Richard Eldridge; Gary Hagberg, *Meaning and Interpretation: Wittgenstein, Henry James, and Literary Knowledge* (Ithaca, NY: Cornell, 1994), and *Describing Ourselves: Wittgenstein and Autobiographical Consciousness* (Oxford: Oxford University Press, 2008); Marjorie Perloff, *Wittgenstein's Ladder: Poetic Language and the Strangeness of the Ordinary* (Chicago: University of Chicago Press, 1996); and, more indirectly, John Verdi.

16. William Carlos Williams, *Imaginations* (New York: New Directions, 1970, originally published in 1921), 138.

17. Marianne Moore, *The Poems of Marianne Moore*, ed. Grace Schulman (New York: Penguin, 2003), 173. Pictures of the image from the Metropolitan Museum of Art are readily available online.

18. Ludwig Wittgenstein, *Tractatus Logicus Philosophicus*, Trans., D.F Pears and B.F Mc Guinness (London: Routledge and Kegan Paul, 1961), 6.54. Hereafter abbreviated *TLP*.

19. Matthew Ostrow, *Wittgenstein's Tractatus: A Dialectical Interpretation* (Cambridge: Cambridge University Press, 2002).

4. The Concept of Expression in the Arts

1. P. M. S. Hacker, "The Autonomy of Humanistic Understanding," in *Wittgenstein, Theory and the Arts,* ed. Richard Allen and Malcolm Turvey (London: Routledge, 2011), 42; cited hereafter as *AHU.*

2. There are myriad references in statements by nineteenth-century and modernist artists about the importance of distinguishing a copy, which tries to picture phenomena, from an expression, where emotion arises "from the representation itself, from forms and coloration" that present emotions of the painter as aspects of ways of fusing with the objective world. I quote from Maurice Denis, "Definition of Neo-Traditionalism," in *Theories of Modern Art,* ed. Herschel Chipp (Berkeley: University of California Press, 1968), 99. See also Henri Matisse, "Four Self-Portraits, October, 1939," in Chipp, *Theories of Modern Art,* 138–39, as he reflects on how the artist penetrates his subject by identifying with it: "the expression of this truth by the elasticity of its line and by its freedom lends itself to the demands of the composition; it takes on light and shade and even life, by the turn of the artist whose expression it is. L'exactitude n'est pas la vérité" (139).

3. Jean Toomer, *The Collected Poems of Jean Toomer,* ed. Robert B. Jones and Margot Toomer Latimer (Chapel Hill: University of North Carolina Press, 1988), 9.

4. Paul Cézanne is superb on the topic of "realization":

> I am able to describe to you again . . . the obstinacy with which I pursue the realization of that part of nature, which, coming into our line of vision, gives the picture. Now the theme to develop is that—whatever our temperament or power in the presence of nature might be—we must render the image of what we see, forgetting everything that existed before us. Which, I believe, must permit the artist to give his entire personality whether great or small.

This passage from a letter to Emile Bernard (October 23, 1905) can be found in John Rewald, ed., *Paul Cézanne Letters* trans. Seymour Hacker (New York: Hacker Art Books, 1985), 251–52.

5. This is F. T. Marinetti in a rare reflective moment on the space expressive objects establish: "We thus create a sort of emotive ambience, seeking by intuition the sympathies and the links which exist between the exterior (concrete) scene and the interior (abstract) emotion." See his "The Exhibitors to the Public" (1912), in Chipp, *Theories of Modern Art,* 295.

6. Bernie Rhie helps clarify the matter by showing how the face for Wittgenstein offers immediate expression in a way that is not thinkable within Cartesian separations of subject from object. See also Garry Hagberg's powerful elaboration of what Rhie is arguing. See Bernie Rhie, "Wittgenstein on the Face of a Work of Art," *Nonsite* 3 (2011), http://nonsite.org/issues/issue-3/wittgenstein-on-the-face-of-a-work-of-art, and Garry Hagberg, "Wittgenstein, the Human Face, and the Expressive Content of Poetry: On Bernard Rhie and Magdalena Ostas," *Nonsite* 4 (2011), http://nonsite.org/issues/issue-4/wittgenstein-the-human-face-and-the-expressive-content-of-poetry-on-bernard-rhie-and-magdalena-ostas.

7. Actually, I have little to say about poststructuralist theory beyond noting my respect for the force given the concept of expression in thinkers such as Deleuze and Rancière

and indirectly in Badiou (because it is something like expressive power that introduces a new regime). Deleuze is very good on features of expression such as its existence as an intensifier so that it cannot be explicated without loss and more generally his sense of how the expression takes the world into itself, where it can be made to shine. See Simon Duffy, *The Logic of Expression: Quality, Quantity and Intensity in Spinoza, Hegel, and Deleuze* (Farnham: Ashgate, 2006). And Jonathan Culler, "Critical Paradigms: Introduction," *Literary Theory for the 21st Century,* special issue of *PMLA* 125, no. 4 (October 2010): 905–15. My complaint here is that poststructuralist thinkers do not anchor the concept of expression sufficiently in standard human practices so that it always constitutes the exception to ordinary life rather than its extension.

8. In order to capture this force of the made object, modernist writers have developed a wide range of related concepts in secular terms—from T. S. Eliot's "objective correlative," to Joseph Conrad's "rendering," to Woolf's sense of the energies of the subject as flowing over what seem to be the boundaries of the empirical ego.

9. One example of rich commentary on expression in music is Aaron Ridley, *Music, Value, and the Passions* (Ithaca, NY: Cornell University Press, 1995). See also two books by Peter Kivy, *The Corded Shell: Reflections on Musical Expression* (Princeton, NJ: Princeton University Press, 1981), and *Sounding Off: Eleven Essays in the Philosophy of Music* (New York: Oxford University Press, 2012).

10. Jenefer Robinson, "Expression and Expressiveness in Art," *Postgraduate Journal of Aesthetics* 4, no. 2 (August 2007): 19–41. Cited in the text as *EE*.

11. Benedetto Croce, *Aesthetic: As Science of Expression and General Linguistic,* rev. ed., trans. Douglas Ainslie (New York: Macmillan, 1922).

12. Guy Sircello, *Mind & Art: An Essay on the Varieties of Expression* (Princeton, NJ: Princeton University Press, 1972).

13. See Charles Taylor, *Hegel* (Cambridge: Cambridge University Press, 1977), 1–36; cited hereafter as *H*. Taylor offers both a sharp summary of the work expressivist ideals performed for Hegel's generation and a telling account of the Enlightenment beliefs they had to combat. I will use "expressivist" in Taylor's sense as a model for how Hegelian thinking differs from those Enlightenment principles that seek to isolate the object of knowledge from the subject trying to know, for only then can a society idealize the work of science. I should also note there that Anthony Rudd, *Expressing the World: Skepticism, Wittgenstein, and Heidegger* (Chicago: Open Court, 2003), offers further developments of Taylor's work by showing how the expressivism pursued by idealist and romantic thinkers has possibilities of offering very useful responses to skepticism about other minds and about the existence of an external world. I love Rudd's idea that Wittgenstein bases his response to skepticism on making the second person the focal point of philosophy so that he can avoid otherwise intransigent oppositions between first- and third-person perspectives (ibid., 138). But Rudd's concerns differ from mine in several ways: he mentions Hegel but is not concerned with his particular formulations; he is not concerned with art but with traditional philosophical questions framed by skepticism; and he, like his Wittgenstein, is concerned primarily with the addressee of expressive behavior rather than the first-person purposiveness, which fascinates me.

14. The whole is only complete when the two propositions are made together, and when the first is asserted and maintained, it must be countered by clinging to the other with invincible stubbornness. Because both are equally right, they are both equally wrong, and the mistake consists in taking such abstract forms as "the same" and "not the same," "identity" and "non-identity," to be something true, fixed, and actual, and in resting on them. Neither the one nor the other has truth; the truth is just their movement. (*PS*, para. 780)

15. The logic here is a variant of how the Holy Spirit is formed as the active willing of the power of the Father mediated through the love of the Son, whose love is simply the realization of the goodness of that power. Analogously, for Hegel the will is not a separate aspect of agency but finds a shape in relation to the intensity and intimacy of how one comes to know substance.

16. Two Hegelian statements will indicate the basis for my generalizations: (1) "The distinct content, as determinate, is in relation, is not in itself"; it is its own restless process of superseding itself.... Spirit, therefore, having won the Notion, displays its existence and movement in this ether of its life" (*PS*, para. 805), and (2) "Nature, the externalized Spirit, is in its existence nothing but this eternal externalization of its continuing existence and the movement which reinstates the Subject" (ibid., para. 807).

17. Yet Richard Eldridge, in *Leading a Human Life: Wittgenstein, Intentionality, and Romanticism* (Chicago: University of Chicago Press, 1997), has elaborated a significant parallel between the two philosophers. Eldridge argues that Wittgenstein accepts a personal version of Hegelian ideals because he pursues a mode of ethical heroism sponsored by Hegel and the romantics. See especially pp. 117 and 277–78 for the core of the argument and the terrific use of the concept of exemplarity basic to that argument. I am indebted to Eldridge for years of discussion on the topic of expression.

18. I am indebted to Nelson Goodman, *Languages of Art* (Indianapolis: Hackett, 1976), for this term. This text will be cited hereafter as *LA*. Goodman points out that locutions such as "picture of" and "represents" "have the appearance" of sponsoring "mannerly two-place predicates," on the model of name and referent." But "'picture of Pickwick' and 'represents a unicorn' are better considered one-place" predicates or class terms, such as 'desk' and 'table'" rather than "a separable series of assertions." Dickens does not offer a picture of Pickwick; Dickens offers a Pickwick-representing picture. We cannot reach "inside" the picture "and quantify over parts" of it (*LA*, 21–22). Or we could say that rather than being asked to see what the picture of Pickwick refers to, the readers of Dickens's novel are asked to treat the picture as referring to all the traits that the picture exemplifies.

19. Becoming a "one-place predicate" does not banish the work to a formal aesthetic domain but only establishes a different model for its working within the public world. In *On Certainty* Wittgenstein is not content to describe Moore's arguments and then respond to them. He wants his audience to interpret the desires that shape these arguments and that probably blind Moore to what is limited in his whole approach to argument. In other words, Moore is given the status of something such as a literary character because he becomes a figure defining a stance that not only fails to establish a refutation of the

skeptic but elicits the very skepticism he is committed to refuting. This Moore has his identity primarily because of how Wittgenstein reconstructs him. Wittgenstein is still obliged to be accurate in summarizing Moore's positions. The philosopher is not free in the ways poets are to invent how agent and world can mutually construct one another. It matters that thinking such as Moore's takes place, and it matters that this thinking has the self-defeating effect of encouraging skepticism. But ultimately it may not matter much in the long run that it is Moore who thinks this way. The text becomes an expressive act displaying Wittgenstein's own investments in assessing what Moore exemplifies. And we see how the writing of philosophy is continually threatened by, and continually exalted by, the possibility that it can be read for what it is denoted by rather than for what it denotes.

20. See also on the notion of theme: "Doesn't the theme point to anything outside itself? Yes, it does. But that means:—it makes an impression on me which is connected with things in its surroundings—e.g., with our language and its intonations, and hence with the whole field of our language games" (Z, 175).

21. David H. Finkelstein, *Expression and the Inner* (Cambridge, MA: Harvard University Press, 2003), 1; cited hereafter as *EI*.

22. I think I understand the narrow context in which Finkelstein argues that Wittgenstein is not an expressivist: we have to keep in view how "psychological self-ascriptions" are both "like winces and smiles and how they are unlike them. The expressivist loses her grip on the latter. As I read Wittgenstein, he does not" (*EI*, 97). I have to agree with the general idea here. But there is a substantial danger that by using "expressivist" as a term that can be equated with the process of avowal, one simply ignores the other contexts for Wittgenstein's use of expression, such as references to an expressive face or reference to the work music and writing accomplish. Ironically, Finkelstein is very good when he addresses those other uses of expression. He stresses how expression contextualizes what it interprets (ibid., 109) and that the relevant self-ascriptions "contextualize the very actions that they are interpretations of" (ibid., 110). Perhaps Hegel could not say it better. Finkelstein is also a perhaps unwilling ally of expressivism when he shows how the unconscious cannot be "expressed" because it is irreducibly passive (ibid., 116–23). Then he argues beautifully in chapter 6 that John McDowell is wrong to claim that "Wittgenstein's philosophy of mind can be encapsulated in the remark that mental life is lived in the space of reasons" (ibid., 127). Finkelstein argues instead that "it is less misleading to say that, according to Wittgenstein, mental life is lived in the logical space of animate life" (ibid.). That seems right to me, but only because then we can treat "logical space" as fundamentally grammatical space, which severely transforms the status of logic.

23. I would like to call attention to this passage from *On Certainty:* "Propositions of the form of empirical propositions, and not only propositions of logic, form the foundation of all operating with thoughts (with language).—This observation is not of the form 'I know . . .' 'I know . . .' states what I know, and that is not of logical interest" (*OC*, 401).

24. I make this remark under the influence of Richard Moran's subtle essay "Cavell on Outsiders and Others," *Revue internationale de philosophie* 256 (2011–2012): 239–54; cited hereafter as *COO*. This essay analyzes what is problematic in Cavell's account of skepticism about other minds. First, Moran cites Cavell's distinguishing two kinds of skepticism—about the existence of a knowable world and about access to other minds.

In both cases Cavell uses the figure of the Outsider to envision the kind of knowledge that would refute the skeptic. But the task of the Outsider is different in each case. In the case of external-world skepticism the Outsider has only to make itself known as a comprehensive position. But for knowledge of other persons the Outsider has not only to make itself known but also to "find oneself in the knowledge that others have claimed to have" achieved, finding oneself in the language framing the descriptions and explanations (ibid., 252). Objects in the world "do not have a view on how they are described" (ibid.). But persons can reject views of their minds because they fail to capture the right emphases or tones by which they hold descriptions. The person would have "to recognize itself in this knowledge and accept that it is in fact understood" (ibid., 253).

Then Moran makes his most important move. He points out that in the second case we may not be dealing primarily with matters of knowledge at all. At stake is not the outsider's knowledge of the world but the outsider's grasp of intentions or decisions to see the world in a certain way: "what we think of as a mind . . . is just that, or that aspect of one's existence, about which the subject claims a say with respect to the terms in which it shall count as understood, or where the phenomenon to be understood . . . includes an understanding of itself as a constitutive element" (ibid., 254). There can be rich responsiveness to other minds, but it will involve not just minds but wills and therefore will take a kind of recognition that is different from knowledge and from generalizations about other minds.

25. The role of display in late Wittgenstein extends to the claim that agents cannot be expected to be argued into changing values but have to be led to "look at the world in a different way" (*OC*, 92). Notice, too, how in 1946 he still echoes the motif that ethics is a matter not of explaining the self but of making determinations about the possibility of changing one's life to accord with the simple fact that the world exists:

> I believe that one of the things Christianity says is that sound doctrines are all useless. That you have to change your life. (Or the direction of your life.)

> It says that wisdom is all cold; and that you can no more use it for setting your life to rights than you can forge iron when it is cold. . . . Wisdom is passionless. But faith by contrast is what Kierkegaard calls a passion. (*CV*, 53)

26. For an elaborate reading of what the self-reflexive operator suggests about style as a model for self-possession see my essay "Style," in *The Oxford Handbook of Philosophy and Literature,* ed. Richard Eldridge (New York: Oxford University Press, 2009), 420–41.

27. This formulation betrays the origin of my argument because I wanted to define the limitations of Stanley Cavell's concepts of acknowledgment and coming to own one's expressions of selfhood. I claim that Cavell ends up treating confession as a mode both of coming to know the self and of seeking recognition, while for me confession displays a concreteness that cannot be translated into other modes of discourse without substantial loss. And confession for Wittgenstein must seek recognition or forgiveness in a distinctive way because it is bound to reveal what cannot be justified in any general moral scheme. Confession simply is an effort at honest self-exposure which can seek only awareness in the other of the effort at honesty. See my "Cavell and Wittgenstein on Morality:

The Limits of Acknowledgement," in *Stanley Cavell and Literary Studies: Consequences of Skepticism*, ed. Richard Eldridge and Bernard Rhie (New York: Continuum 2011), 62–77. This difference between recognition and other possible modes of response to confession is raised beautifully in Elizabeth Beckwith's contribution to the same volume, "William Shakespeare and Stanley Cavell: Acknowledging, Confessing, and Tragedy": 123–35. I also find very useful on the concept of confession Garry Hagberg, *Describing Ourselves: Wittgenstein and Autobiography* (Oxford: Oxford University Press, 2008).

28. I say "crucial" because the two remarks show complete continuity between 1931 and 1945, a period during which Wittgenstein felt the need to reconcile his grammatical approach to philosophy with his concern for the values dealt with by religion. But the remark in *PPF* uses a different German term—the beautifully appropriate "Geständnisses." So I cannot claim any specific term of art here. Rather, the best one can say may be that Wittgenstein reaches for a dramatic notion when he wants to be especially forceful.

29. In this contrast between ethics and forgiveness Wittgenstein is strangely true to the spirit of Hegel.

30. These observations about art lead Wittgenstein to a key expressivist principle—that the work of art aims not so much to give fresh information as to involve the audience differently in its attitude toward information: "Don't take it as a matter of course, but as a remarkable fact, that pictures and fictitious narratives give us pleasure, absorb us" (*PI*, 524). Art invites participation, and participation colors how we process information (see ibid., 543). And then meaning completely shifts valences to emphasize what is displayed in the expression: "If the feeling gives the word its meaning [in this case 'hope'], then here 'meaning' amounts to that which matters" (ibid., 545).

One of Wittgenstein's most interesting discussions of concreteness in art occurs in sections 16–25 of the "brown" book, Ludwig Wittgenstein, *The Blue and Brown Books*, ed. Rush Rhees (New York: Harper, 1965); cited hereafter as *BB*. Here he moves seamlessly from the expression of a face to the kind of meaning we best attribute to art objects. The passage begins with questions about how we recognize a drawing of a face as a particular face (*BB*, 162ff). For Wittgenstein recognition is not a matter of finding a prototype in one's mind. Rather, it is like cutting "a seal from an impression" (ibid., 165). We typically do not rely on a mental comparison but in effect recognize a person coming into a room "by means of what you would say when you recognize him" (ibid.). The impression is completed by the agent's action and does not depend on referring the image to a knowledge bank. Similarly in regarding a tune, nothing need come into one's mind except the tune actually whistled (ibid., 166). In such cases "'Understanding a sentence means getting hold of its content, and the content of the sentence is in the sentence'" (ibid., 167). The hand pointing to what one sees or what one feels is really part of what one sees (ibid., 175). More generally, one can contemplate a "sample" not as an instance of some more general class but as the description of its own color (ibid.). In such cases "you don't wish to make a general statement independent of the particular experience you have had, but rather a statement into which this experience enters" (ibid., 177).

31. See my essay "Exemplification and Expression," in *A Companion to the Philosophy of Literature*, ed. Garry Hagberg and Walter Jost (Oxford: Wiley-Blackwell, 2010), 491–506. I will pay due homage to Nelson Goodman on exemplification in my next chapter.

32. See Stanley Cavell, *Must We Mean What We Say?* (Cambridge: Cambridge University Press, 2002), and Ralph Berry, "Is 'Us' Me? Cultural Studies and the Universality of Aesthetic Judgments," in *Stanley Cavell and Literary Studies: Consequences of Skepticism*, ed. Richard Eldridge and Bernie Rhie (New York: Continuum, 2011), 30–46.

5. Expression and Exemplification

1. See Joshua Landy, *How to Do Things with Fictions* (New York: Oxford University Press, 2012); David Nowell Smith, *Sounding/Silence: Martin Heidegger at the Limits of Poetics* (New York: Fordham University Press, 2013), 188; and Richard Eldridge, *Leading a Human Life: Wittgenstein, Intentionality, and Romanticism* (Chicago: University of Chicago Press, 1997), especially 227–32, in which exemplarity is linked to "expressive performance."

2. Anthony Cascardi, *Cambridge Introduction to Philosophy and Literature* (New York: Cambridge University Press, 2014), 34.

3. I should also mention a dossier of four essays on philosophical example in *boundary 2* 40, no. 2 (Summer 2013) on how moral examples in philosophy complicate its relationship to literary imaginations. None of the essays is concerned with the roles of sorting and modeling, although the authors would probably think they make such idealizing more difficult.

4. Hacker and Schulte translate "Die übersichtliche Darstellung (*PI*, 122) as "surveyable representation." So I use Anscombe's translation here.

5. Ludwig Wittgenstein, *Remarks on Colour*, ed. G. E. M. Anscombe, trans. Linda L. McAlister and Margarete Schattle (Oxford: Wiley-Blackwell, 1991), §1.32.

6. Not distinguishing among kinds of exemplification produces a good deal of deconstructionist angst about the gap between the particular and the conceptual, as in Thomas Keenan, *Fables of Responsibility: Aberrations and Predicaments in Ethics and Politics* (Palo Alto: Stanford University Press, 1997). Arguments such as Keenan's were another reason the concept of exemplification did not take hold even after theorists recognized how difficult it was to sustain truth claims in relation to literary texts.

7. I am obviously interpreting Goodman's concept of one-place predicate to accord with my own argument. "Examples of" become "examples as" when the conjunction of details they display offers an observer a more dynamic connection to the world than what would be established by quantifying over the discrete properties shared by symbol and what it is denoted by. The ending of Ian McEwan's *Atonement* offers a striking account of the pleasures and the pains of dealing with historical matters under conditions that establish one-place predicates.

8. I think that what makes something metaphoric for Goodman is simply that it functions to denote what it is denoted by. A red face denotes a particular picture. To treat the redness as a mark or sign of anger one has to apply a sense of what states of feeling the red can be denoted by. The three modes of metaphoric expression are denoted by first the cultural setting, then our vocabularies for psychology, and finally by our sense of what uses the expressions might serve in practices of sorting (*LA*, 74–95).

9. Richard Wollheim is Goodman's best critic with reference to the limitations of his nominalism with regard to works of art, not surprisingly given Wollheim's interest in "seeing in." See Wollheim's essay "Nelson Goodman's Languages of Art," reprinted in *The Philosophy of Nelson Goodman: Nelson Goodman's Philosophy of Art,* ed. Catherine Z. Elgin (New York: Garland, 1997), 18–42. In a second essay in that volume, "Are the Criteria of Identity That Hold for a Work of Art in the Different Arts Aesthetically Relevant?" 73–92, Wollheim supports this claim with a powerful argument that "disagreement between us begins only when notational requirements are taken as providing not just necessary but also sufficient conditions for identity." From Wollheim's perspective "sufficient conditions for identification occur only when some reference to the history of production is added" (91). Without that supplement, Goodman's account seems too generous in offering possibilities for exemplification because possession of properties is the only criterion (88–92). We need some feature that will actually signify that the property is relevant for the situation—hence the concern to add conditions of production as contexts for works of art (30–31).

I might also point out that there is a similar difference on the topic of example between Goodman and Wittgenstein. Because Wittgenstein embeds the working of symbols within a grammar of practices, he can offer a directionality to exemplification that is not possible in Goodman. By showing how the symbol can vary between expressions of experience and expressions of norms, Wittgenstein suggests that the analysis is incomplete until one can determine how the practice involved best defines what the exemplary qualities are for any given inquiry.

10. Richard Moran, *Authority and Estrangement: An Essay on Self-Knowledge* (Princeton, NJ: Princeton University Press, 2001), 12.

11. Geoffrey Hellman, "Symbol System and Artistic Styles," in *Nelson Goodman's Philosophy of Art,* ed. Elgin, 297.

12. Dodie Bellamy, *Cunt Norton* (Los Angeles: Les Figues Press, 2013); cited hereafter as *CN*. Bellamy characterizes "cuntings up" of thirty-two poets as "a joke," but it is also a fiercely feminist undoing of the bids for authority of these voices:

> The literal cutting of texts forces your mind in new directions, allowing you to transcend the false logic that we live in. The cut-up reveals the truth behind the crap that's being fed to us. The illogic behind the logic. So, I'm appreciating Burroughs more and more.

See Sara Wintz, "From Cut-Up to Cunt Up: Dodie Bellamy in Conversation," *Poetry Foundation: Open Door* (November 21, 2013), http://www.poetryfoundation.org/harriet/2013/11/from-cut-up-to-cunt-up-dodie-bellamy-in-conversation. It is also important to note that the title *Cunt Norton* refers both to Eliot, the subject of the first pornographic piece, and to the 1975 *Norton Anthology,* on which she performed her conceptualist appropriations. That anthology is a classic figure of oppression, resentfully carried around by all sorts of students who took little pleasure from its contents.

13. When I first used the term "demonstrative" for literary speech acts I was unaware of David Kaplan's well-known essay, "Demonstratives: An Essay on the Semantics, Logic, Metaphysics, and Epistemology of Demonstratives and Other Indexi-

cals," in *Themes from Kaplan,* ed. Joseph Almog, John Perry, and Howard Wettstein (New York: Oxford University Press, 1989), 481–564. Now that I am aware of it I can only point out how much I wish I could muster Kaplan's clarity and capacity to generalize with amazing effectiveness. There are significant similarities because I am concerned with the possibility of singular reference, and I could use his contrasts between the content and the character of semantic elements. But I do not have a class like indexicals that I can directly interpret. Instead, I have to proceed with a kind of speech act rather than a specific mode of reference for which there is a specific sense-content. For my demonstrative there is a specific kind of "uptake" but not a specific route of reference unless one can work out a way to use Goodman's version of reference by example. And even then the class of relevant cases would not be limited to a kind of performative.

14. The foundational text here is Jacques Derrida's misguided but humanly persuasive reading of Austin in "Structure, Event, Context," in *Limited Inc,* ed. Gerald Graff, trans. Jeffrey Mehlman and Samuel Weber (Evanston, IL: Northwestern University Press, 1988), 1–25. I also want to mention an essay by J. Hillis Miller, "How to Be 'in Tune with the Right' in *The Golden Bowl,*" in *Mapping the Ethical Turn: A Reader in Ethics, Culture, and Literary Theory,* ed. Todd F. Davis and Kenneth Womack (Charlottesville: University of Virginia Press, 2001), 271–86, which misunderstands Austin even more than Derrida does and treats all actions in speech as speech acts, yet the essay produces a terrific reading of Henry James's novel.

15. Judith Butler, *Gender Trouble: Feminism and the Subversion of Identity* (London: Routledge, 1990), and *Giving an Account of Oneself* (New York: Fordham University Press, 2005). For a more general view of the controversy about the performative see Jonathan Culler's essentially Derridean account of the issues in "Philosophy and Literature: The Fortunes of the Performative," *Poetics Today* 21 (2000): 503–19.

16. When I was writing this, my dean at the time, Janet Broughton, gave me the example of her daughter's complaint that she felt "Blurgh!"

17. Ayon Maharaj pointed out in conversation that I need "this" in my examples because the language is not strictly performing the task. Rather, the language is pointing to the task that is being realized. In Austin's speech act the language does perform the task—that is how he can separate the effects of the performative from any psychological conditions. But I do not think I have to worry about separating the demonstrative from any psychological implications because I am not claiming any efficacy for the demonstrative as meeting certain felicity conditions. I think the demonstrative is simply a frame by which we set off certain uses of language because of their emphasis on display as their means of communication. Yet demonstratives are not coextensive with avowals because demonstratives place the emphasis on exemplification and not just expression.

18. Altieri, "Tractatus Logico-Poeticus," *Critical Inquiry* 33 (2007): 527–42, and "Why Style Still Matters," in *Oxford Companion to the Study of Philosophy and Literature,* ed. Richard Eldridge (Oxford: Oxford University Press, 2009), 420–41.

19. In fact, although I initially chose Creeley simply because his poems are short and widely praised, as I began working with the poems the idea of the demonstrative seemed to work so well for a representative contemporary poet that it makes me more suspicious than I would like to be about its general scope.

20. Robert Creeley, *The Collected Poems of Robert Creeley, 1945–1975*, ed. Penelope Creeley (Berkeley: University of California Press, 2006), 112; cited hereafter as *RC*.

21. Charles Bernstein, *A Poetics* (Chicago: University of Chicago Press, 1992), 6.

6. What Literary Theory Can Learn from Wittgenstein's Silence about Ethics

1. Eagleton, *The Trouble with Strangers: A Study of Ethics* (Oxford: Wiley-Blackwell, 2009), vii.

2. See my treatment of "confession" in chapter 4.

3. I should note my affinities with Allen Grossman, who uses the concept of valuing in one essay in his *True-Love: Essays on Poetry and Valuing*, (Chicago and London: The University of Chicago Press, 2009). And I have to note how attentive Martha Nussbaum is to my concern for this variety of values. See especially Martha Nussbaum, "Exactly and Responsibly: A Defense of Ethical Criticism," in *Mapping the Ethical Turn,* ed. Todd Davis and Kenneth Womack (Charlottesville: University of Virginia Press, 2001), 59–82, and "The Discernment of Perception," in Nussbaum's *Love's Knowledge* (Oxford: Oxford University Press, 1990), 54–105.

4. I feel licensed in using the term "valuation" by its use in works by David Wiggins and Samuel Scheffler. I prefer the term to "evaluation" because "evaluation" suggests holding particulars up against standard models or principles. I want to identify a more immediate sense that one is attuning to what invites reflection on the specific values elicited by the text's specific modes of attending and of composing. For Scheffler, see *Equality and Tradition: Questions of Value in Moral and Political Theory* (Oxford: Oxford University Press, 2010), 15–40; cited hereafter as *ET*. And for David Wiggins, *Needs, Values, Truth: Essays in the Philosophy of Value,* 3rd ed. (Oxford: Clarendon, 1998); cited hereafter as *NVT*.

5. For a good, sympathetic, but sharp critique of Miller see Andrew Gibson, *Toward a Postmodern Theory of Narrative* (Edinburgh: Edinburgh University Press, 1996), 12–13; cited hereafter as *TPT*. Gibson is also quite useful in specifying four ways Levinas becomes central to his own project (ibid., 16ff), thus helping differentiate it from Miller's.

6. Probably the most thorough rendering of Levinas's foundational role in the shaping of poststructural ethics is developed by Simon Critchley in *The Ethics of Deconstruction: Derrida and Levinas* (Oxford: Blackwells, 1992) and in his terrific concise book *Infinitely Demanding: Ethics of Commitment, Politics of Resistance.* (London: Verso, 2007). Critchley reminds us that one of the criteria that poststructural literary critics have for ethics now is its capacity also to sustain models of political thinking. In my essay "Can There Be a Plausible Ethics Developed from Poststructural Ontology?" *boundary* 2 42, no. 2 (May 2015): 231–45, I offer an extensive critical encounter with *Infinitely Demanding.*

7. For Levinas "the other" is primary because our most elemental experience of the call of ethics is based on our sense of our own incompleteness. We need the other even for self-definition—there is no "I" without a "you." But at the same time the "I" cannot fully recognize this dependency in conceptual terms because the concept of the other is inherently infinite—no particular can satisfy as standing for that sense of otherness mak-

ing my hold on being unstable and inadequate. This is why ethics must oppose the concepts of morality and be constructed in relation to a condition carried by events rather than by concepts of the good. One might say there is an eventfulness characterizing the "I"-"you" relationship which is doubly belied by any reliance on concept: the concept needs generalizations that are incompatible with the singularity of the event, and the "you" resides only in the event because no concept can be adequate to what precedes and makes possible the entire domain of self-consciousness. Perhaps Andrew Gibson captures this parallel to resistance to concepts in the aesthetic domain best in his version of the distinction between ethics and morality: "Ethics . . . operates as a kind of play within morality, holds it open, hopes to restrain it from violence or the will to domination, subjects it to 'a kind of auto-deconstruction'" (*TPT*, 15). Neither Attridge nor Gibson even mentions any connection between morality and ideals of fair or careful judgment.

8. Gibson is richer than Attridge and more subtle in his treatment of Levinas. One aspect of the strength of his book is its insistence on the historicity of the ethics it proposes: the ethics addresses postmodern social conditions where "ethics cannot emerge on the basis of a shared world" (*TPT*, 85). Yet what world is ever shared, if you look closely enough? And ethics does not need a shared world; it needs only the possibility of mutually looking at issues that can otherwise divide people absolutely. Ethics is for most contemporary philosophers trained in analytic traditions not a laying down of laws but an enterprise of searching for provisional negotiations about what might be shared. But Gibson is mild in his sense of a desperate postmodern condition when compared to Terry Eagleton in *The Trouble with Strangers* and to Alain Badiou in *Ethics: An Essay on the Understanding of Evil*, trans. Peter Hallward (London: Verso, 2002). Both these thinkers seem to me to offer extreme versions of virtue ethics, where only the hero capable of producing singular events need even aspire to the ethical. And then they will not even grant an interest in morality for us lesser folks because morality is flawed from the start by its dependence on negotiating social norms—no sublimity there. Finally, Gibson, like Critchley, is clear from the start how the possible political utility of the version of ethics elaborated remains the fundamental concern.

9. Let me state my own position on ethics and morality so that the reader can test whether it can provide an adequate framework for making the criticisms I do. I have learned from Kwame Anthony Appiah, *Experiment in Ethics* (Cambridge, MA: Harvard University Press, 2008), that a concern for ethical value places a person in two arenas of discourse. So the only way to avoid confusion is to assign each to a separate domain. For Appiah ethics is shaped by Aristotle's concern for "what traits of character we need to live well" (ibid., 37). Ethics is the domain in which we reflect on human flourishing. In contrast, Appiah sees morality as the domain where we reflect on "the constraints that govern how we should and should not treat other people" (ibid., 203). Appiah's distinctions nicely capture the etymological difference between ethos and mores, the former with its emphasis on character, the latter with its emphasis on social custom. And then we can recognize that morality need not concern itself with "flourishing." It provides an arena for coping with human need and human limitation in such a way as to negotiate considerations about justice and about justification. Contra poststructural ethics, the discourse of morality need not take the form of "codes." It aims at consensus, and one way of gaining consensus is to invoke rules and codes. But

that is not the only or the best way to reach agreement in our assessing the actions that affect interpersonal relations.

More generally I cannot even claim to myself that I have a coherent ethical view capable of determining questions about whether ethics is cognitive or noncognitive or quasi-realist. I lean toward a noncognitivist stance because the space of reasons that involves knowing leads toward what David Wiggins describes as a state where "eventually there will only be one thing to say," (355) while the space of reasons for ethical judgment seems to show no movement toward resolution of people's different views. I explain that lack of movement by the subjective factor that colors our choosings and our reasons for such choosings. So for me there cannot be "truth" in ethics, but there can be "truthfulness" (as Bernard Williams characterizes it in *Ethics and the Limits of Philosophy* (Cambridge, MA: Harvard University Press, 1985).

10. Paul de Man, "Theory of Metaphor in Rousseau's Second Discourse," *Studies in Romanticism* 12, no. 2: 475–98.

11. See Alice Crary, *Beyond Moral Judgment* (Cambridge, MA: Harvard University Press, 2009); cited hereafter as *BMJ*. Another reason I do not write about Nussbaum or Cavell is that I have taken up their work on other occasions. I devote an entire chapter to Nussbaum in my *Particulars of Rapture* (Ithaca, NY: Cornell University Press, 2005). And I take up Cavell's work at length in two essays, in "Cavell and Wittgenstein on Morality: The Limits of Acknowledgement," in *Stanley Cavell and Literary Studies: Consequences of Skepticism,* ed. Richard Eldridge and Bernard Rhie (New York: Continuum, 2011), 62–77, and in "Wonder in *The Winter's Tale:* A Cautionary Account of Epistemic Criticism," in *A Sense of the World: Essays on Fiction, Narrative, and Knowledge,* ed. John Gibson, Wolfgang Heumer, and Luca Pocci (London: Routledge, 2007), 266–86.

12. I think her evidence for Wittgenstein's interest in ethics in his later philosophy is very slim indeed. It consists as far as I can see in one passage in Ludwig Wittgenstein, *Philosophical Occasions 1912–1951,* eds. James Carl Klagge and Alfred Nordmann (Indianapolis: Hackett, 1993), 161, and one in *CV,* 17 (the latter of which is hardly an aspect of his later thinking). Of course she never considers those motifs such as "display" and "expression" and "confession" with its special criteria of "truthfulness" that might make Wittgenstein less than an active defender of philosophical ethics. Finally, I think it is wrong to consider Wittgenstein's ideas about language as constituting a fundamentally pragmatist position. Wittgenstein does believe meaning is determined by the use of something in the language. But the measure of appropriateness is not empirical success in manipulating the world or in reaching practical agreement. The measure of use is "fit," and fit is only in part an empirical matter because agreeing that utterances fit situations does not make it so. Rather, our understanding of use depends on networks of possible meaning that require our reflecting on how language as a whole hangs together. For example, Moore's intended use of "know" is quite clear, and several people have agreed with him. But still Wittgenstein argues that he misuses the term because he confuses a commonsense model with a grammatical one.

13. Crary has support for this expansion of morality to cover issues of living well in the careful reasoning offered by David Wiggins about the importance of questions about the meaning of life. See his "Truth, Invention, and the Meaning of Life," reprinted in *NVT* 87–138. But Wiggins interprets the good life as distinctively a question of mean-

ingfulness rather than the moral quality of one's choices. So he avoids the issue of specific moral attention to actions that Crary calls for. I think there is a huge distinction between the meaning of life, which seems a cognitive question or a "subjectively problematic" one, and the property of meaningfulness for lives, which seems not reducible to the cognitive or the moral. In Wiggins's case the argument equates "meaning" with "inner purpose" (*NVT*, 137), so there is a range of possible choosings that are candidates for producing meaningfulness. Moral considerations do not exhaust how inner purpose can get established and played out.

14. John McDowell, *Mind, Value, and Reality* (Cambridge, MA: Harvard University Press, 1998), 166. The topic is too large to get into, but McDowell's efforts to combine reason and experience seem to me to provide a much richer philosophical framework for the worldliness of literature than talk of direct moral sensibilities.

15. I do not know why Crary insists on preserving a concept of "objectivity" then effectively gutting it by offering measures such as appropriateness, which must admit of degrees rather than providing completely stable grounds for judgment. (To handle degrees of objectivity is one reason the concept of intersubjectivity was invented.) And while there is another possible sense of "rational" based on the interests of particular subjects, that is not one that tempts Crary. And it would not help her in accounting for the moral power of literary works.

16. I think I am arguing in the spirit of Bernard Williams, *Ethics and the Limits of Philosophy*.

17. I am assuming that the versions of studied indifference to the plight of characters in writers such as Flaubert, Beckett, and Coetzee offer a complicated form of compassion: if we could achieve this distance, we might find the only means of allaying the pain of suffering over what we cannot control.

18. Stanley Cavell, *Claim of Reason: Wittgenstein, Skepticism, Morality, and Tragedy* (Oxford: Clarendon, 1982), 496.

19. Crary's resistance to this challenge is most striking when she tries to contain "intensity" within moral sensibility by making it depend primarily on epistemic complexity. For example, intensity becomes a matter of "the quantity and quality of the connections it leads" a reader to make (*BMJ*, 160). Crary evinces no sympathy with the sense that it is the author, and not qualities of the text per se, that places a substantial value on intensity and that this intensity may be a function largely of sheer identification with the imaginative situations a text elaborates. Even with authors as overtly "moral" as Jane Austen, theory can recall us to an awareness of how thoroughly the interest and the vitality in her novels occur in the presentation of characters enacting their delusions and responding freshly and complexly to those moments in which they adapt what one might call the "extramoral path"—as when Emma finally hears Knightley's declaration of love.

20. Several years ago I argued that Anglo-American philosophers were comfortable emphasizing morality in literary criticism because they focused on realist fiction rather than on poetry. See my "Lyrical Ethics and Literary Experience," *Style* 32 (1998): 272–97, reprinted in *Mapping the Ethical Turn,* ed. Todd Davis and Kenneth Womack (Charlottesville: University of Virginia Press, 2001), 30–58. Now I see that such philosophical emphases involve larger questions because these philosophers tend also to reduce fiction to something close to exercises in describing the world rather than producing lively,

particular, imaginative paths through a variety of possible worlds. So at one pole these philosophers tend to ignore utterly the presence of formal values ranging from the sonic to the elaborate patterning of feelings that we find most clearly in poetry; at the other pole they tend to give reductive realist accounts of affective values such as intensity and complexity even in realist fictions that might in fact be capable of challenging the primacy of traditional moral valuations.

21. One of my purposes in setting up this contrast between ethics and other models of valuing is to free myself from the notion that "value" seems something ultimate, something that forces choices between various goods so that one might maintain consistency and loyalty to single, dominating principles. Most of us are responsive to a multiplicity of values, all coexisting. But when we proceed theoretically, we seem to think we have to work out one comprehensive scheme that best suits our interests and our dispositions.

22. I am heartened that two fine books have also made a case for a flexibility of valuings in literary experience, but on very different grounds from mine: Rita Felski, *Uses of Literature* (Oxford: Blackwell, 2009), and Sianne Ngai, *Our Aesthetic Categories* (Cambridge, MA: Harvard University Press, 2012). Rebecca Porte's talk at the 2012 Modernist Studies Association conference, "The Propositions: Modernist Poetry & Aesthetic Logic," also presented a very intelligent call for a plurality of readerly values.

23. The production of meaningfulness comes very close to an instrumental value. But perhaps we can distinguish it from more overtly instrumental values because the production of meaningfulness never quite reaches practical satisfaction and is continually questioned and vulnerable to constant revision. Meaningfulness is a matter of degree and so is impossible to cast as a concrete goal. Instead it is an accompanying condition of our actions. I also think very little hangs on whether values are instrumental or noninstrumental so long as we grasp the difference between needs that can be resolved definitively and those that we accept as ongoing conditions of our lives.

24. On the difficulties of turning from what I call valuations to values one actually lives by, see *NVT,* 267.

25. Let me cite the passage because it has obvious parallels with what I am trying to argue:

> Every determining judgment is logical because its predicate is a given objective concept. A merely reflecting judgment about a given individual object, however, can be aesthetic if (before its comparison with others is seen) the power of judgment, which has no concept ready for the given intuition, holds the imagination (merely in the apprehension of the object) together with the understanding (in the presentation of a concept in general) and perceives a relation of the two faculties of cognition which constitutes the subjective, merely sensitive condition of the objective use of the power of judgment in general (namely the agreement of these faculties with each other). (Kant, *CJ*)

Kant's parentheses make visible how much he is trying to pack into this summary sentence. But for my purposes we need only two features. The most important one is the contrast between determinate judgment and reflective judgment. Determinate judgment serves the understanding by subsuming particulars under concepts until "one reaches the concept that contains the principle of the entire classification" (*CJ,* 18). In contrast, reflective judgment "specifies the general concept by adducing the manifold under it" (ibid.). Determinate judgment attributes purposes by aligning particulars with conditions of use; reflective judgment opens a domain of purposiveness by aligning with a nature that seems to have the power to specify itself. When nature is presented for aesthetic aspects of reflective judgment, the power to specify by adducing the manifold becomes "genius," and the response to how the particulars align with purposiveness becomes the domain of taste. Then as a second feature of Kant's case we need to highlight how the lack of objective determinants in reflexive judgment puts conditions of subjectivity on stage (in ways that may lead beyond monadic individuality). The space of valuing is the site within which subjectivity finds paths for tracing how the object specifies itself.

26. I quote David Graeber, *Toward an Anthropological Theory of Value: The False Coin of Our Own Dreams* (London: Palgrave, 2001), because he makes a strong case for this sense of social meaningfulness as a constant model of value in disparate societies.

27. There is great passage in David Wiggins, my favorite philosopher on questions about value, imagining that an adequate moral phenomenology for interpreting how agents can give a point to their lives would also have to accept the kind of nonbehavioral evidence literature can offer. See *NVT*, 137. Chapters 4, 5, and 7 play a background role here.

28. Wolfgang Köhler, *The Place of Value in a World of Facts* (New York: Liveright, 1976); cited hereafter as *PV*.

29. One might also note that Wittgenstein's interest in doings rather than knowings and his concern for matters of fit invite phenomenological consideration of the small-scale valuings that accompany such states.

30. The concepts of "push" and "pull" are developed in Robert Nozick, *Anarchy, State, and Utopia* (New York: Basic Books, 1974).

31. Aaron Ridley, *Music, Value, and the Passions* (Ithaca, NY: Cornell University Press, 1995); cited hereafter as *MVP*. I wish I could use a literary critic or philosopher on literature, but I see only Ridley making the points I need. This may be because music almost has to be valued to be meaningful in the world, whereas literary texts obviously invite all the forms of meaning that language can provide.

32. I steal this point about labor from a conversation with Keston Sutherland.

33. Helen Vendler, *Our Secret Discipline: Yeats and Lyric Form* (Cambridge, MA: Harvard University Press, 2007), is also terrific on the timing of the poem as it grows through negatives to a "positive explanation of his action, one that arises, it seems, from his placing solitary delight above social considerations and spontaneous 'impulse' before considered reflection" (7).

34. Some readers will not be able to take pleasure in this refusal of social bonds and in this flirtation with what would become the romantic side of absolutist politics. But even they might recognize what it would be like to value the reading of this poem because of the brilliant artifice and, I think, the brilliant rendering of a possible attitude toward contemporary life.

35. I can then argue from this example that a fundamentally aesthetic attitude toward texts need not entail any reliance on formalism. Certainly the poem stressed relationships shaped by formal elements in the verse. But almost all of these relationships also function to develop significant features of the speech act as an existential event in

which we are invited to participate. We are also invited to see these formal relations as aspects of the worldliness of the text because they structure possibilities for establishing intimate connections with how texts and characters make possible ways of valuing particular experiences. Here there are none of the transcendental features of form that Yeats stresses in "Sailing to Byzantium." And even in that poem the urge for the transcendental is itself an activity to be participated in as exhibiting basic human passions.

7. Appreciating Appreciation

1. Charles Altieri, "Why Appreciation Ought to Be Revived as a Model for the Study of the Arts," *Frame* 20, no. 1 (2007): 63–80.

2. See my essays "The Place of Rhetoric in Contemporary American Poetics: Jennifer Moxley and Julianna Spahr," *Chicago Review* 56, no. 2/3 (2011): 127–45; and "What Theory Can Learn from New Directions in Contemporary American Poetry," *New Literary History* 43 (Winter 2012): 65–88.

3. Traditionally the aesthetic was the arena in which theorists explained the possibilities of judgments that were not oriented to practical consequences. Instead, these judgments were based on characterizing responses to how objects could seem significant for the experiences they caused rather than for the use values that they promised. But two basic pressures altered how aesthetic inquiry affected literary study. The first was internal. If philosophers and artists of all kinds were going to idealize states of response that subordinated practical interests to more reflexive ones, they had to demonstrate what it was in the object that warranted such differences in response. The second pressure was more vague and general, but no less powerful. As the "humanities" increasingly came in conflict with science, proponents felt the need to develop concepts such as "nondiscursive truth," which required them to focus on how particular art objects could solicit concrete analyses capable of competing with those sciences.

The history of applying Kant's aesthetic theory provides a useful illustration of these shifts. Kant recognized from the start that he needed both a principle of judgment and an image of the object that enabled him to contrast aesthetic experience with the domains of understanding and of rational morality. Hence his notions of "reflective judgment" and the purposiveness without purpose created by the genius having nature give the rule to art. But while he elaborated the nature of the art object, Kant's main focus was on the conditions of response by which the audience's dispositions toward the world might be modified by experiencing such objects. Concentrating on response allowed him to elaborate a difference between merely liking and approving the work, a distinction that requires the subject to experience capacities for universals contained within the act of judgment. And then he could show how aesthetic experience became symbolic of moral experience because it approached the universals that in moral judgments were determined by practical reason.

But by the late nineteenth century, theorists and artists had abandoned Kant's psychology of judgment. All the emphasis had to be placed on the power of the purposive object to provide distinctive pleasures and open paths for the mind not limited by the constraints of empirical understanding. So where the emphasis on judgment had been, now there was only reliance on formalist accounts of the art object as possible explanations of how art might provide alternatives to practices devoted to economic rationality. In effect, the greater the pressure to specify alternatives to the culture of commodities, the greater the need for concrete models on which the claims to difference might be based.

4. Artists and writers can offer versions of expression without any reference to romantic inwardness—think of Malevich earning the exclamation mark after "red" by how he positions a red square in relation to a larger black one, or of Van Gogh earning it by how his image of a compressed bedroom plays its red against a sickly green, or of the colors cited in Ashbery's "Instruction Manual." Henry Staten is very good on the demands technique makes on readers. See his "The Wrong Turn of Aesthetics," in *Theory after "Theory,"* ed. Jane Elliott and Derek Attridge (London: Routledge, 2011), 223–36.

5. Kant's focus on pleasure rather than on other terms for engaging the object traps him in an unnecessary opposition between interest in the existence of the object and interest only in the state of the subject. If we can be clear about the worldliness of the text, we can speak not about separate worlds for subjects and objects but about a distinctive world where the subject becomes aware of its possible pleasures in the capacity to put objects to certain kinds of uses.

6. I elaborate this argument about "example as" in chapter 4.

7. Max Scheler, *On Feeling, Knowing, and Valuing,* ed. Harold J. Bershady (Chicago: University of Chicago Press, 1992), 225; cited hereafter as *FKV.*

8. In his dissertation, *Knowledge and Experience in the Philosophy of F. H. Bradley* (New York: Farrar, Straus, 1964), T. S. Eliot emphasized how F. H. Bradley allows us to replace talk of fixed objects by imagining degrees of objectivity depending on different levels of reality. Hallucinations involve only the consciousness of individual agents, while matters in our practical world get fixed by the many discourses and uses given them by a variety of agents. Differences in the status of art objects seem to me to follow a similar path: the degree of reality of an imagined world depends on the texture created by multiple ways of appreciating its power and therefore its significance.

9. William Shakespeare, *The Tempest,* ed. Robert Langbaum (New York: Signet, 1990), 87.

10. Marc Ferro, *Resentment in History,* trans. Steven Rendell (Cambridge: Polity, 2010), 132, puts the case well:

> It is certain that on the one hand, the disillusionment regarding the great hopes raised by the idea of progress, whose promises have not been kept, and, on the other hand, the tightening of the constraints imposed by the development of globalization, cannot help but multiply centers of resentment, as the experience of the past century has amply demonstrated. Unless bursts of magnanimity spread, our future does not look bright.

Bibliography

Allen, Richard. "Introduction to Allen and Turvey," *Wittgenstein*, 1–36.
Allen, Richard, and Malcolm Turvey, eds. *Wittgenstein, Theory and the Arts*. London: Routledge, 2011.
Altieri, Charles. *Affirmations: Of the Modern*, vol. 2, issue 2; special issue on "Modernism and Rhetoric," edited by Sascha Bru and Peter Nichols. http://affirmations.arts.unsw.edu.au/index.php?journal=aom&page=index.
———. "Can There Be a Plausible Ethics Developed from Poststructural Ontology?," *boundary 2* 42, no. 2 (May 2015): 231–45.
———. "Cavell and Wittgenstein on Morality: The Limits of Acknowledgement." In Eldridge and Rhie, *Stanley Cavell*, 62–77.
———. "Exemplification and Expression." In *A Companion to the Philosophy of Literature*, edited by Garry Hagberg and Walter Jost, 491–506. Oxford: Wiley-Blackwell, 2010.
———. "Lyrical Ethics and Literary Experience." *Style* 32 (1998): 272–97. Reprinted in Davis and Womack, *Mapping the Ethical Turn*, 30–58.
———. *The Particulars of Rapture*. Ithaca, NY: Cornell University Press, 2005.
———. "The Place of Rhetoric in Contemporary American Poetics: Jennifer Moxley and Julianna Spahr." *Chicago Review* 56, no. 2/3 (2011): 127–45.
———. "Ponderation in Cézanne and Williams." *Poetics Today* 10 (1989): 373–400.
———. "Style." In Eldridge, *Oxford Handbook*, 420–41.

———. "Tractatus Logico-Poeticus." *Critical Inquiry* 33 (2007): 527–42.

———. "What Theory Can Learn from New Directions in Contemporary American Poetry." *New Literary History* 43 (Winter 2012): 65–88.

———. Why Appreciation Ought to Be Revived as a Model for the Study of the Arts." *Frame* 20, no. 1 (2007): 63–80.

———. "Why Style Still Matters." In *Oxford Companion to the Study of Philosophy and Literature,* edited by Richard Eldridge, 420–41. Oxford: Oxford University Press, 2009.

———. "Wonder in *The Winter's Tale:* A Cautionary Account of Epistemic Criticism." In *A Sense of the World: Essays on Fiction, Narrative, and Knowledge,* edited by John Gibson, Wolfgang Heumer, and Luca Pocci, 266–86. London: Routledge, 2007.

Anscombe, G. E. M. *Intention*. Cambridge, MA: Harvard University Press, 2000.

Appiah, Kwame Anthony. *Experiment in Ethics*. Cambridge, MA: Harvard University Press, 2008.

Ashbery, John. *Collected Poems, 1956–1987,* edited by Mark Ford. New York: Library of America, 2008.

Attridge, Derek. *The Singularity of Literature*. London: Taylor and Francis, 2004.

Badiou, Alain. *Ethics: An Essay on the Understanding of Evil,* translated by Peter Hallward. London: Verso, 2002.

Beckwith, Elizabeth. "William Shakespeare and Stanley Cavell: Acknowledging, Confessing, and Tragedy." In Eldridge and Rhie, *Stanley Cavell,* 123–35.

Bellamy, Dodie. *Cunt Norton*. Los Angeles: Les Figues, 2013.

Bernes, Jasper. "John Ashbery's Free Indirect Labor." *Modern Language Quarterly* 74, no. 4 (2013): 517–40.

Bernstein, Charles. *A Poetics*. Chicago: University of Chicago Press, 1992.

Berry, Ralph. "Is 'Us' Me? Cultural Studies and the Universality of Aesthetic Judgments." In Eldridge and Rhie, *Stanley Cavell:* 30–46. Best, Stephen, and Sharon Marcus. "Surface Reading: An Introduction." *Representations* 108, no. 1 (2009): 1–21.

Butler, Judith. *Gender Trouble: Feminism and the Subversion of Identity*. London: Routledge, 1990.

———. *Giving an Account of Oneself*. New York: Fordham University Press, 2005.

Cascardi, Anthony. *Cambridge Introduction to Philosophy and Literature*. New York: Cambridge University Press, 2014.

Casey, Edward. *Imagining: A Phenomenological Study*. Bloomington: Indiana University Press, 1976.

Cavell, Stanley. *The Claim of Reason: Wittgenstein, Skepticism, Morality, and Tragedy*. Oxford: Clarendon Press, 1979.

———. *In Quest of the Ordinary: Lines of Skepticism and Romanticism*. Chicago: University of Chicago Press, 1988.

———. *Must We Mean What We Say?* Cambridge: Cambridge University Press, 2002.

Cézanne, Paul. *Paul Cézanne Letters*. Edited by John Rewald. Translated by Seymour Hacker. New York: Hacker Art Books, 1985.

Chipp, Herschel, ed. *Theories of Modern Art*. Berkeley: University of California Press, 1968.

Clune, Michael. *American Literature and the Free Market, 1945–2000*. New York: Cambridge University Press, 2010.

Crary, Alice. *Beyond Moral Judgment.* Cambridge, MA: Harvard University Press, 2009.
Creeley, Robert. *The Collected Poems of Robert Creeley, 1945–1975.* Edited by Penelope Creeley. Berkeley: University of California Press, 2006.
Critchley, Simon. *Ethics of Deconstruction: Derrida and Levinas.* Oxford: Blackwells, 1992.
———. *Infinitely Demanding: Ethics of Commitment, Politics of Resistance.* London: Verso, 2007.
Croce, Benedetto. *Aesthetic: As Science of Expression and General Linguistic.* Rev. ed. Translated by Douglas Ainslie. New York: Macmillan, 1922.
Culler, Jonathan. "A Critic against the Christians." Review of *Using Biography*, by William Empson, *TLS* (November 23, 1984): 1327–28.
———. "Critical Paradigms: Introduction." Special issue of *PMLA, Literary Theory for the 21st Century* 125, no. 4 (October 2010): 905–15.
———. "The Future of Criticism." In *The Current in Criticism: Essays on the Present and Future of Literary Theory*, edited by Clayton Koelb and Virgil L. Lokke, 27–42. West Lafayette, IN: Purdue University Press, 1987.
———. "Philosophy and Literature: The Fortunes of the Performative." *Poetics Today* 21 (2000): 503–19.
Davis, Todd F., and Kenneth Womack, eds. *Mapping the Ethical Turn: A Reader in Ethics, Culture, and Literary Theory.* Charlottesville: University of Virginia Press, 2001.
de Man, Paul. "Form and Intent in the American New Criticism." In *Blindness and Insight: Essays in the Rhetoric of Contemporary Criticism.* New York: Oxford University Press, 1971, 20–35.
———. "Theory of Metaphor in Rousseau's Second Discourse." *Studies in Romanticism* 12, no. 2, 475–98.
Denis, Maurice. "Definition of Neo-Traditionalism." In Chipp, *Theories*, 94–100.
Derrida, Jacques. *Limited Inc.* Edited by Gerald Graff. Translated by Jeffrey Mehlman and Samuel Weber. Evanston, IL: Northwestern University Press, 1988.
Diamond, Cora, and James Conant. "On Reading the *Tractatus* Resolutely." In *Wittgenstein's Lasting Significance*, edited by Max Kölbel and Bernhard Weiss. London: Routledge, 2004, 42–97.
Dreyfuss, Burt. "The Myth of the Pervasiveness of the Mental." In *Mind, Reason, and Being-in-the-World: The McDowell-Dreyfus Debate*, edited by Joseph K. Schear, 15–39. London: Routledge, 2013.
Dubrow, Heather. Foreword to *New Formalisms and Literary Theory*, edited by Verena Theile and Linda Tredennick, vii–xviii. New York: Palgrave Macmillan, 2013.
———. "Guess Who's Coming to Dinner? Reevaluating Formalism and the Country House Poem." *Modern Language Quarterly* 61 (2000): 59–77.
Duffy, Simon. *The Logic of Expression: Quality, Quantity and Intensity in Spinoza, Hegel and Deleuze.* Farnham: Ashgate, 2006.
Eagleton, Terry. *The Event of Literature.* New Haven, CT: Yale University Press, 2012.
———. *How to Read Literature.* New Haven, CT: Yale University Press, 2013.
———. *The Trouble with Strangers: A Study of Ethics.* Oxford: Wiley-Blackwell, 2009.
Eldridge, Richard. "Introduction to Eldridge," *Oxford Handbook*: 3–15.

———. *Leading a Human Life: Wittgenstein, Intentionality, and Romanticism.* Chicago: University of Chicago Press, 1997.

———, ed. *The Oxford Handbook of Literature and Philosophy.* New York: Oxford University Press, 2009.

Eldridge, Richard, and Bernard Rhie, eds. *Stanley Cavell and Literary Studies: Consequences of Skepticism.* New York: Continuum, 2011.

Elgin, Catherine Z., ed. *The Philosophy of Nelson Goodman: Nelson Goodman's Philosophy of Art.* New York: Garland, 1997.

Eliot, T. S. *Knowledge and Experience in the Philosophy of F. H. Bradley.* New York: Farrar, Straus, 1964.

Felski, Rita. *Uses of Literature.* Oxford: Blackwell, 2009.

Ferro, Marc. *Resentment in History.* Translated by Steven Rendell. Cambridge: Polity, 2010.

Finkelstein, David H. *Expression and the Inner.* Cambridge, MA: Harvard University Press, 2003.

Gibson, Andrew. *Toward a Postmodern Theory of Narrative.* Edinburgh: Edinburgh University Press, 1996.

Gibson, John. "The Question of Poetic Meaning." *Nonsite* 4 (2011). http://nonsite.org.

Goodman, Nelson. *Languages of Art.* Indianapolis: Hackett, 1976.

Graeber, David. *Toward an Anthropological Theory of Value: The False Coin of Our Own Dreams.* London: Palgrave, 2001.

Grossman, Allen. *True Love: Essays on Poetry and Valuing.* Chicago: University of Chicago Press, 2009.

Guillory, John. *Cultural Capital: The Problem of Literary Canon Formation.* Chicago: University of Chicago Press, 1993.

Hacker, P. M. S. "The Autonomy of Humanistic Understanding." In Allen and Turvey, *Wittgenstein*: 39–74.

———. "Wittgenstein and the Autonomy of Humanistic Understanding." In Allen and Turvey, *Wittgenstein*, 39–74.

Hagberg, Garry. *Describing Ourselves: Wittgenstein and Autobiographical Consciousness.* Oxford: Oxford University Press, 2008.

———. *Meaning and Interpretation: Wittgenstein, Henry James, and Literary Knowledge.* Ithaca, NY: Cornell University Press, 1994.

———. "Wittgenstein, the Human Face, and the Expressive Content of Poetry: On Bernard Rhie and Magdalena Ostas." *Nonsite* 3 (2011). http://nonsite.org/issues/issue-4/wittgenstein-the-human-face-and-the-expressive-content-of-poetry-on-bernard-rhie-and-magdalena-ostas.

Hegel, G. W. F. *Phenomenology of Spirit.* Translated by A. V. Miller. Oxford: Oxford University Press, 1976.

Heidegger, Martin. *On the Way to Language.* Translated by Peter Hertz and Joan Stambaugh. New York: Harper and Row, 1971.

———. *Poetry, Language, Thought.* Translated by Albert Hofstader. New York: Harper and Row, 1971.

Hellman, Geoffrey. "Symbol System and Artistic Styles." In Elgin, *Nelson Goodman's Philosophy of Art*, 297.

Hickman, Miranda, and John D. McIntyre, eds. *Rereading the New Criticism*. Columbus: Ohio State University Press, 2012.

Hutto, Daniel D. "Two Wittgensteins Too Many: Wittgenstein's Foundationalism." In Moyal-Sharrock, *Third Wittgenstein*, 25–41.

James, Henry. *Henry James: European Writers and the Prefaces*. Edited by Leon Edel, 1160–63. New York: Library of America, 1984.

James, William. "The Continuity of Experience." In *The Writings of William James*, edited by John J. McDermott: 292–301. Chicago: University of Chicago Press, 1977.

Jameson, Frederic. *The Political Unconscious: Narrative as a Socially Symbolic Act*. Ithaca, NY: Cornell University Press, 1981.

Kant, Immanuel. *Critique of the Power of Judgment*, Translated by Paul Guyer and Eric Matthews. Cambridge: Cambridge University Press, 2001.

Kaplan, David. "Demonstratives: An Essay on the Semantics, Logic, Metaphysics, and Epistemology of Demonstratives and Other Indexicals." In *Themes from Kaplan*, edited by Joseph Almog, John Perry, and Howard Wettstein, 481–564. New York: Oxford University Press, 1989.

Kaufman, Robert. *Negative Romanticism: Adornian Aesthetics in Keats, Shelley, and Modern Poetry*. Ithaca, NY: Cornell University Press, forthcoming.

Keenan, Thomas. *Fables of Responsibility: Aberrations and Predicaments in Ethics and Politics*. Palo Alto, CA: Stanford University Press, 1997.

Kivy, Peter. *The Corded Shell: Reflections on Musical Expression*. Princeton, NJ: Princeton University Press, 1981.

———. *Sounding Off: Eleven Essays in the Philosophy of Music*. New York: Oxford University Press, 2012.

Knapp, Steven, and Walter Benn Michaels. "Against Theory." *Critical Inquiry* 8, no. 4 (1982): 723–42.

Köhler, Wolfgang. *The Place of Value in a World of Facts*. New York: Liveright, 1976.

Kripke, Saul. *Wittgenstein on Rules and Private Language: An Elementary Exposition*. Cambridge, MA: Harvard University Press, 1982.

Landy, Joshua. *How to Do Things with Fictions*. New York: Oxford University Press, 2012.

Levinson, Marjorie. "What Is New Formalism?" *PMLA* 122, no. 2 (2007): 558–69.

———. *Wordsworth's Great Period Poems: Four Essays*. New York: Cambridge University Press, 1986.

Luscombe, Belinda. "10 Questions with William Kentridge." *Time* (December 2, 2013): 68.

Maharaj, Ayon. *The Dialectics of Aesthetic Agency: Revaluating German Aesthetics from Kant*. London: Bloomsbury, 2013.

Malevich, Kasimir. *The Non-Objective World*, In Chipp, *Theories*: 341–45.

Marinetti, F. T. "The Exhibitors to the Public" (1912). In Chipp, *Theories*, 294–98.

Matisse, Henri. "Four Self-Portraits, October 1939." In Chipp, *Theories*, 138–39.

McDowell, John. *Mind and World*. Cambridge, MA: Harvard University Press, 1996.

———. *Mind, Value, and Reality*. Cambridge, MA: Harvard University Press, 1998.

———. "Wittgenstein on Following a Rule." *Synthèse* 58 (March 1984): 325–63.

Melchiori, Giorgio. *The Whole Mystery of Art*. New York: Macmillan, 1961.

Miller, J. Hillis. "How to Be 'in Tune with the Right' in *The Golden Bowl*." In Davis and Womack, *Mapping the Ethical Turn*: 271–86.
Miller, Tyrus. *Singular Examples: Artistic Politics and the Neo-Avant-Garde*. Evanston, IL: Northwestern University Press, 2009.
Moore, Marianne. *The Poems of Marianne Moore*. Edited by Grace Schulman. New York: Penguin, 2003.
Moran, Richard. *Authority and Estrangement: An Essay on Self-Knowledge*. Princeton, NJ: Princeton University Press, 2001.
———. "Cavell on Outsiders and Others." *Revue internationale de philosophie* 256 (2011–2012): 239–54.
Moretti, Franco. *Distant Reading*. London: Verso, 2013.
Morton, Timothy. "An Object-Oriented Defense of Poetry." *New Literary History* 43 (2012): 205–24.
Moyal-Sharrock, Danièle, ed. *The Third Wittgenstein: The Post-Investigations Works*. Hampshire: Ashgate, 2004.
———. *Understanding Wittgenstein's* On Certainty. London: Palgrave Macmillan, 2004.
Ngai, Sianne. *Our Aesthetic Categories*. Cambridge, MA: Harvard University Press, 2012.
Nietzsche, Friedrich. *Beyond Good and Evil*. In *Basic Writings of Nietzsche*, translated and edited by Walter Kaufmann. New York: Modern Library, 2000: 181–438.
———. *Daybreak: Thoughts on the Prejudices of Morality*. Translated by R. J. Hollingdale. Cambridge: Cambridge University Press, 1982.
Nowell Smith, David. *Sounding/Silence: Martin Heidegger at the Limits of Poetics*. New York: Fordham University Press, 2013.
Nozick, Robert. *Anarchy, State, and Utopia*. New York: Basic Books, 1974.
Nussbaum, Martha C. "The Discernment of Perception." In Martha C. Nussbaum, *Love's Knowledge: Essays on Philosophy and Literature*: 54–105. Oxford: Oxford University Press, 1990.
———. "Exactly and Responsibly: A Defense of Ethical Criticism." In Davis and Womack, *Mapping the Ethical Turn*, 59–82.
O'Brien, Geoffrey. *People on Sunday*. New York: Wave Books, 2013.
O'Hara, Frank. *The Collected Poems of Frank O'Hara*. Edited by Donald Allen. Berkeley: University of California Press, 1995.
Ostrow, Matthew. *Wittgenstein's* Tractatus: *A Dialectical Interpretation*. Cambridge: Cambridge University Press, 2002.
Perloff, Marjorie. *Wittgenstein's Ladder: Poetic Language and the Strangeness of the Ordinary*. Chicago: University of Chicago Press, 1996.
Reed, Brian. *Phenomenal Reading: Essays on Modern and Contemporary Poetics*. Tuscaloosa: University of Alabama Press, 2012.
Rhie, Bernie. "Wittgenstein on the Face of a Work of Art." *Nonsite* 3 (2011). http://nonsite.org/issues/issue-3/wittgenstein-on-the-face-of-a-work-of-art.
Ricoeur, Paul. *Freud and Philosophy: An Essay on Interpretation*. Translated by Denis Savage. New Haven, CT: Yale University Press, 1979.
Ridley, Aaron. *Music, Value, and the Passions*. Ithaca, NY: Cornell University Press, 1995.
Robertson, Lisa. *Nilling: Prose*. Toronto: Bookthug, 2012.

Robinson, Jenefer. "Expression and Expressiveness in Art." *Postgraduate Journal of Aesthetics* 4, no. 2 (August 2007): 19–41.
Ross, Stephen. Introduction to *Modernism and Theory: A Critical Debate*, edited by Stephen Ross: 1–17. London: Routledge, 2008.
Rudd, Anthony. *Expressing the World: Skepticism, Wittgenstein, and Heidegger*. Chicago: Open Court, 2003.
Scheffler, Samuel. *Equality and Tradition: Questions of Value in Moral and Political Theory*. Oxford: Oxford University Press, 2010.
Scheler, Max. *On Feeling, Knowing, and Valuing*. Edited by Harold J. Bershady. Chicago: University of Chicago Press, 1992.
———. *Ressentiment*. Translated by William W. Holdheim. New York: Free Press, 1961.
Schiller, Friedrich. *On the Aesthetic Education of Man*. Translated by Reginald Snell. New York: Frederic Ungar, 1954.
Sellars, Wilfrid. *Empiricism and the Philosophy of Mind*. Cambridge, MA: Harvard University Press, 1997.
Shakespeare, William. *Hamlet*. Edited by Barbara A. Mowat and Paul Werstine. New York: Simon & Schuster, 2003.
———. *The Tempest*. Edited by Robert Langbaum. New York: Signet, 1990.
Sircello, Guy. *Mind & Art: An Essay on the Varieties of Expression*. Princeton, NJ: Princeton University Press, 1972.
Spivak, Gayatri. *An Aesthetic Education in the Era of Globalization* Cambridge: Harvard University Press, 2012.
Staten, Henry. *Wittgenstein and Derrida*. Lincoln: University of Nebraska Press, 1986.
———. "The Wrong Turn of Aesthetics." In *Theory after "Theory,"* edited by Jane Elliott and Derek Attridge, 223–36. London: Routledge, 2011.
Stroll, Avrum. "Wittgenstein's Foundational Metaphors." In Moyal-Sharrock, *Third Wittgenstein*, 13–24.
Taylor, Charles. *Hegel*. Cambridge: Cambridge University Press, 1977.
Tiffany, Daniel. *Toy Medium: Materialism, and Modern Lyric*. Berkeley: University of California Press, 2000.
Toomer, Jean. *The Collected Poems of Jean Toomer*. Edited by Robert B. Jones and Margot Toomer Latimer. Chapel Hill: University of North Carolina Press, 1988.
Vendler, Helen. *Our Secret Discipline: Yeats and Lyric Form*. Cambridge, MA: Harvard University Press, 2007.
Verdi, John. *Fat Wednesday: Wittgenstein on Aspects*. Philadelphia: Paul Dry Books, 2010.
Yeats, William Butler. *The Variorum Edition of the Poems of W. B. Yeats*. Edited by Peter Allt and Russell K. Alspach. New York: Macmillan, 1957.
Wiggins, David. *Needs, Values, Truth: Essays in the Philosophy of Value*. 3rd ed. Oxford: Clarendon, 1998.
Williams, Bernard. *Ethics and the Limits of Philosophy*. Cambridge, MA: Harvard University Press, 1985.
Williams, William Carlos. *Imaginations*. New York: New Directions, 1970; originally published in 1921.

Wintz, Sara. "From Cut-Up to Cunt Up: Dodie Bellamy in Conversation." *Poetry Foundation: Open Door* (November 21, 2013). http://www.poetryfoundation.org/harriet/2013/11/from-cut-up-to-cunt-up-dodie-bellamy-in-conversation.

Wittgenstein, Ludwig. *The Blue and Brown Books*. Edited by Rush Rhees. New York: Harper, 1965.

———. *Culture and Value*. Edited by Peter Winch. Chicago: University of Chicago Press, 1984.

———. *On Certainty*. Edited by G.E.M. Anscombe and G.H. von Wright. Oxford: Basil Blackwell, 1969

———. *Philosophical Investigations*. Revised Fourth Edition. Translated by G. E. M. Anscombe, P. M. S. Hacker, and J. Schulte and edited by P. M. S. Hacker and J. Schulte. London: Blackwell, 2009.

———. *Philosophical Occasions 1912–1951*. Edited by James Carl Klagge and Alfred Nordmann. Indianapolis: Hackett, 1993.

———. *Philosophy of Psychology—A Fragment*. Edited by P. M. S. Hacker and J. Schulte and translated by G. E. M. Anscombe, P. M. S. Hacker, and J. Schulte. Oxford: Wiley-Blackwell, 2009.

———. *Remarks on Colour*. Edited by G. E. M. Anscombe and translated by Linda L. McAlister and Margarete Schattle. Oxford: Wiley-Blackwell, 1991.

———. *Tractatus Logico-Philosophicus*. Translated by D.F Pears and B.J. McGuinness. London: Routledge and Kegan Paul, 1961.

———. *Zettel*. Edited by G. E. M. Anscombe and G. H. von Wright. Berkeley: University of California Press, 1970.

Wollheim, Richard. "Are the Criteria of Identity That Hold for a Work of Art in the Different Arts Aesthetically Relevant?" In Elgin, *Nelson Goodman's Philosophy of Art*, 73–92.

———. "Nelson Goodman's Languages of Art." In Elgin, *Nelson Goodman's Philosophy of Art*, 18–42.

———. *Painting as an Art*. Princeton, NJ: Princeton University Press, 1987.

Permission to reprint has been granted by the following:

Quotations from "The Instruction Manual" from *Some Trees* by John Ashbery appear with the permission of Georges Borchardt, Inc., on behalf of the author, and with the permission of Carcanet Press, Ltd. Any third party use of this material, outside of this publication, is prohibited. Interested parties must apply directly to Georges Borchardt, Inc., and to Carcanet Press, Ltd. for permission: *Some Trees* by John Ashbery, copyright 1956 by John Ashbery.

Quotations from "Chaucer," "e.e. cummings," "William Carlos Williams," and "Wordsworth" from *Cunt Norton* by Dodie Bellamy appear with the permission of Les Figues Press on behalf of the author. Any third party use of this material, outside of this publication, is prohibited. Interested parties must apply directly to Les Figues Press for permission: *Cunt Norton* by Dodie Bellamy, copyright 2012 by Dodie Bellamy.

Quotations from "Something" from *The Collected Poems of Robert Creeley, 1945–1975* by Robert Creeley appear with the permission of The University of California Press. Any third party use of this material, outside of this publication, is prohibited. Interested parties must apply directly to The University of California Press for permission: *The Collected Poems of Robert Creeley, 1945–1975* by Robert Creeley, copyright 2006 by The Regents of the University of California.

Quotations from "A Song" from *The Collected Poems of Robert Creeley, 1945–1975* by Robert Creeley appear with the permission of The Permissions Company, Inc., on behalf of the Estate of Robert Creeley. Any third party use of this material, outside of this publication, is prohibited. Interested parties must apply directly to The Permissions Company, Inc. for permission: *The Collected Poems of Robert Creeley, 1945–1975* by Robert Creeley, copyright 1962 by Robert Creeley.

Quotations from "An Egyptian Pulled Glass Bottle in the Shape of a Fish" from *The Collected Poems of Marianne Moore* by Marianne Moore appear with the permission of Scribner Publishing Group, a division of Simon & Schuster, Inc., and with the permission of Faber & Faber, Ltd. Any third party use of this material, outside of this publication, is prohibited. Interested parties must apply directly to Scribner Publishing Group and to Faber & Faber, Ltd. for permission: *The Collected Poems of Marianne Moore* by Marianne Moore, copyright 1935 by Marianne Moore, renewed 1963 by Marianne Moore and T.S. Eliot.

Quotations from "Face" from *Cane* by Jean Toomer appear with the permission of W.W. Norton and Company, Inc. Any third party use of this material, outside of this publication, is prohibited. Interested parties must apply directly to W.W. Norton Company,

Inc. for permission: *Cane* by Jean Toomer, copyright 1923 by Boni & Liveright, renewed 1951 by Jean Toomer.

Quotations from "The Red Wheel-Barrow" from *The Collected Poems: Volume I, 1909–1939* by William Carlos Williams appear with the permission of New Directions Publishing Corp. Any third party use of this material, outside of this publication, is prohibited. Interested parties must apply directly to New Directions Publishing Corp. for permission: *The Collected Poems: Volume I, 1909–1939* by William Carlos Williams, copyright 1938 by New Directions Publishing Corp.

Quotations from "Leda and the Swan" from *The Collected Works of W.B. Yeats, Volume I: The Poems, Revised* by W.B. Yeats, edited by Richard J. Finneran, appear with the permission of Scribner Publishing Group, a division of Simon & Schuster, Inc. Any third party use of this material, outside of this publication, is prohibited. Interested parties must apply directly to Scribner Publishing Group for permission: *The Collected Works of W.B. Yeats, Volume I: The Poems, Revised* by W.B. Yeats, edited by Richard J. Finneran, copyright 1928 by The Macmillan Company, renewed 1956 by Georgie Yeats.

INDEX

Adorno, Theodore, 15, 210, 221n26
Aesthetics, 2, 16–20, 24, 180, 197–213
Altieri, Charles, 235–36nn26, 27, 31, 239n18, 242n11, 243n20, 246n1
Appiah, Kwame Anthony, 241n9
Appreciation, 13–14, 30–31, 80, 87–88, 194–213
Ashbery, John, 21, 43–44, 47–55, 60, 75, 143, 225n6, 226–27nn13–14; "Instruction Manual," 21, 43, 47–54, 59–62, 131
Attridge, Derek, 15–16, 37, 162–68, 172–73, 175–77, 200
Attunement, 22, 78, 93, 176, 181, 199–200, 220, 222n29
Austen, Jane, 13, 143, 243n18
Austin, J.L., 151

Badiou, Alain, 241n8
Bellamy, Dodie, 145–50, 238n12; Chaucer, 145; E.E. Cummings, 146–47; W.C. Williams, 147, 149; Wordsworth, 146

Beckwith, Elizabeth, 236n27
Bernstein, Charles, 156
Berry, Ralph, 129
Best, Stephen, 19–20, 222nn27–28
Blake, William, 172
Blevins, Jeff, 44
Booth, Wayne, 162
Butler, Judith, 151

Cascardi, Anthony, 133
Casey, Edward, 42–46, 53, 225n5, 226n10
Cavell, Stanley, 124, 129, 159, 168, 175, 218n7, 220n7, 234–35n24, 242n11
Cézanne, Paul, 231n4
Close-reading, 1–2, 16–20, 30, 161, 179–81, 222n27
Clune, Michael, 15–17
Coleridge, Samuel Taylor, 38–39
Conant, James, 218n7
Conrad, Joseph, 81
Crary, Alice, 162, 168–77, 242–43nn13, 19

Index

Creeley, Robert, 155–58; "A Song," 155–57; "Something," 157–58
Critchley, Simon, 240n6
Croce, Bendetto, 101, 229n2
Culler, Jonathan, 224n1, 239n15
Cultural studies, 132

Dante, 4, 14, 28, 116, 207
Deconstruction, 17–18, 32–34, 68
Deleuze, Giles, 231–32n7
de Man, Paul, 40–42, 167
demonstrative speech act, 150–58
Denis, Maurice, 231n2
Derrida, Jacques, 75, 162, 218n7, 239n14
Diamond, Cora, 218n7
Dubrow, Heather, 1–2, 216n3

Eagleton, Terence, 160, 218–19n11, 241n8
Eldridge, Richard, 23, 91, 132, 133, 217n7, 233n17
Eliot, George, 79, 136
Eliot, T.S., 32, 81, 139, 143, 210, 247n8
Ethics in literary criticism, 29, 159–77, 188, 241n7–9
Exemplification, 28–29, 78, 91, 114, 129, 130–58, 176, 196, 205, 237–38nn6–7
Expression, 3, 7, 25–26, 64–65, 91–129, 196–98, 232n13, 234n22; History of the concept in the 20th century, 101–6
Expressivist theory, 4–14, 64–65, 104–7, 232n13, 234n22, 236n30

Felski, Rita, 218–19n11, 222n30, 244n22
Ferro, Mark, 247n10
Finkelstein, David, 117, 234n32
Flaubert, Gustave, 186
Formalism, 6, 215n1, 245–46n35, 246–47n3
Freud, Sigmund, 46

Gibson, Andrew, 240–41nn5, 8
Gibson, John, 139, 221n25, 223n39
Gooding, Nicholas, 97
Goodman, Nelson, 137–40, 142, 233n18, 237n31
Graeber, David, 245n26
Grossman, Allen, 240n3
Guillory, John, 229n3

Hacker, P.M.S., 91–93, 217n7
Hagberg, Gary, 230n15, 231n6, 236n27

Hegel, G.W.F., ix, 7, 21, 82, 95, 116, 211, 220n, 233n16–17; expression, 3–5, 25–26, 97–110, 217n5, 229n2, 232n13, 237n22; Substance and Subject, 95, 98–109, 118, 190–92, 233nn14, 15
Heidegger, Martin, 65, 94, 132, 229n2
Hellman, Geoffrey, 140
Hickman, Miranda, 215n1, 222n27
Homer, *Odyssey*, 207
Husserl, Edmund, 181
Hutto, Daniel, 229n9

Imagination, ix, 3, 19, 21–25, 37–62, 63–64, 194–208, 225n8, 225–26n10, 227n13; Limits of Romantic models of imagination, 38–42, 225–26n10; Phenomenology of imagination, 26, 42–47
Instrumental criticism, 12, 16–17, 22, 25, 30, 65, 93, 178, 185, 219n11, 221n23
Intentionality, 32–36, 79–80, 82–87

Jackson, Virginia, 225n7
James, Henry, 173, 186, 194
James, William, 121–22, 130
Jameson, Fred, 215n2
Joyce, James, 36, 59–60, 79, 82, 187

Kane, Daniel, 227n14
Kant, Immanuel, ix, 3–5, 64, 99, 112, 165, 216–17n6, 246–47n3; Approving vs. liking, 205–6; Determinate and Reflective Judgments, 180–81, 205–6, 216n4, 244–45n25; Imagination 19, 21, 197, 225–26n10, 229n2; Purposiveness, 8–11, 34, 79, 180, 188, 199–200
Kaplan, David, 238–39n13
Kaufman, Robert, 216–17n4
Keats, John, 26, 94, 133
Keenan, Thomas, 237n6
Kentridge, William, 46
Knapp, Stephen, 34
Köhler, Wolfgang, 181–83, 185
Kripke, Saul, 228n1

Landy, Joshua, 132, 218–19n11, 223n38
Levinas, Emmanuel, 161, 163–65, 175, 240n6, 240–41n7
Levinson, Marjorie, 216n2
Logic, 23, 65–66, 72–74, 77, 88–90

Maharaj, Ayon, 217n4, 239n17
Malevich, Kasimir, 91–94, 247n4
Marcus, Sharon, 19–20, 222n8
Marinetti, F.T., 231n5
Marx, Karl, 61
Matisse, Henry, 231n2
McDowell, John, 173, 218n9, 219n12, 228n1, 243n14
McEwan, Ian, 237n7
McIntyre, John D., 215n1, 222n7
Melchiori, Giorgio, 227–28n17
Michaels, Walter, 34
Miller, J. Hillis, 162, 239n14
Miller, Tyrus, 133, 223n38
Milton, John, 116, 186
Moore, G.E., 73–76, 230n13, 233–34n14
Moore, Marianne, 82–87, 187; "Egyptian Glass Bottle in the Shape of a Fish," 83–87
Moran, Richard, 66, 140, 229n3, 234–35n24
Moretti, Franco, 216n2
Moyal-Sharrock, Danièle, 23, 217n7, 230n9
Munch, Edward, 138

New Criticism, 1, 32, 39–41, 43, 132, 215n
New Formalism, 1–2, 215–16n2
New Historicism, 16–17
Ngai, Sianne, 244n22
Nietzsche, Friedrich, 109, 152, 159, 161, 174, 207, 210–11, 223n40
Nowell-Smith, 132, 229n2
Nozick, Robert, 245n30
Nussbaum, Martha, 46, 162, 168, 176, 242n11

O'Brien, Geoffrey, 225n4, 226n12
O'Hara, Frank, 225–26n13
Ostrom, Matthew, 89
Otherness, 162–68

Participation, 78, 100, 127, 129, 130, 144, 176, 184
Pater, Walter, 194
Perloff, Marjorie, 230n15
Porte, Rebecca, 244n22
Post-structuralism, 160–62
Pound, Ezra, 36, 80, 173
Proust, Marcel, 176

Realism, 79
Realization, 25, 93, 127, 231n4

Reed, Brian, 216n2
Resentment, 13–14, 30–31, 42, 207–13
Rhie, Bernie, 231n6
Richards, I.A., 39
Ricoeur, Paul, 215n2
Ridley, Aaron, 181, 185–86
Robertson, Lisa, 224n41
Robinson, Jenefer, 101–3, 116
Romantic Poetry, 38–40, 224n1
Ross, Anthony, 217–18n7
Ross, Stephen, 221n26
Rudd, Anthony, 232n13

Sartre, Jean Paul, 40–41
Scheffler, Samuel, 181, 184–5
Scheler, Max, 194, 206, 210–11
Schiller, Friedrich, ix, 3–7, 11–12, 14, 21
Searle, John, 7
Self-consciousness, 7, 53, 179–81, 185, 187–92, 196, 203–5
Sellars, Wilfrid, 73, 79, 218n9
Sensuousness, 5
Shakespeare, 4, 5, 9–10, 13, 14, 30, 47, 176, 200, 213; *Hamlet*, 9–10, 13, 47, 130, 133, 135, 136, 139, 143; *The Tempest*, 207–9
Sircello, Guy, 101–2
Spivak, Gayatri, 216n4
Staten, Henry, 216n3, 218n7, 230n13, 247n4
Stein, Gertrude, 82
Stroll, Avrum, 229n9
Surface Reading, 19–20
Sutherland, Keston, 245n32

Taylor, Charles, 103–5, 217n13
Tiffany, Daniel, 223n38
Tolstoy, Leo, 27–28, 59, 79, 125–26
Toomer, Jean, 95–98, 109, 111, 136, 144

Valuation, 12–13, 29–30, 161, 172, 177–93, 195, 203, 240n4, 244nn22, 24
Value, 2, 11–13, 29–38, 77–78, 115–19, 210–13, 244n23; ethical values, 29, 160–62, 244nn21
Van Gogh, Vincent, 94
Vendler, Helen, 188, 190, 245n33
Verdi, John, 71

Wiggins, David, 178–79, 242n13, 245n27
Williams, Bernard, 242n9, 243n16
Williams, W.C., 82; *Red Wheelbarrow*, 82

Index

Wittgenstein, Ludwig, ix–x, 3, 49, 63–99, 110–32, 217–18n7, 228n1, 234n19; Alice Crary's account, 170–71, 242n12; Aspect-seeing, 24, 25–27, 37, 70–72, 83, 98, 110, 126–27, 135, 184, 223n36; Avowal, 23–24, 26, 68, 70, 81, 94, 96–99, 111–12, 116, 117–18, 124, 128, 234; Confession, 118–26, 235n27; Display, 6, 23–26, 63–91, 94, 97, 120, 123, 131, 134, 140, 150, 153–54, 176, 196, 218–19n7, 228n1, 235n25; Duck-rabbit, 8, 71; Ethics, 30, 159–61, 168, 235–36n27; Example, 131, 134–42, 152, 155, 238n9; Expression, 8, 103, 110–29, 234n22, 236n30; grammar, 21; Model, 25–27, 78–79, 81, 96–98, 110, 126–28, 223n38, 229n8; Myself, 69, 119–23; *On Certainty*, 72–77, 79, 88–90, 118, 229n9, 230n11; Perspicuous representation, 134; Style, 122–24, 235n26; Tractatus Logicus Philosophicus, 65–66, 72, 74, 77, 88–90, 118–20, 164

Wollheim, Richard, 9–10, 142, 219n15, 238n9

Woolf, Virginia, 187

Wordsworth, William, 26, 47

Yeats, William Butler, 21, 44, 53–61, 187–91, 200–5, 227n17; "A Drinking Song," 201–3; "An Irish Airman Forsees His Death," 187–91; "Leda and the Swan," 53–61, 72, 135, 142; "The Magi," 202–3

Reckoning with the Imagination